ANN W. ASTELL is Assistant Professor of
English at Purdue University. She received her
B.S. and Ph.D. degrees from the University of
Wisconsin–Madison, and her M.A. from Mar-
quette University. Articles of hers have ap-
peared in *Anglo-Saxon England*, *The Chaucer
Review*, *Renascence*, *The Centennial Review*,
Journal of English and Germanic Philology,
Studies in Philology, and *Studies in English Liter-
ature*. She has also published a volume of po-
etry, *The Saints in Soliloquy: A Collection of
Dramatic Monologues* (1984).

The Song of Songs
in the Middle Ages

The Song of Songs
in the Middle Ages

Ann W. Astell

Cornell University Press

ITHACA AND LONDON

First published 1990 by Cornell University Press.

International Standard Book Number 0-8014-2347-3
Library of Congress Catalog Card Number 89-70831
Printed in the United States of America
Librarians: Library of Congress cataloging information
appears on the last page of the book.

♾ The paper used in this publication meets the minimum requirements of the American National Standard for Permanence of Paper for Printed Library Materials Z39.48–1984.

To the memory of Joseph Kentenich
(1885–1968)

"Fortis Est Ut Mors Dilectio"

Contents

Acknowledgments

As a first-semester graduate student at Marquette University, I enrolled in Judson B. Allen's seminar "The Lyric Ego and *Piers Plowman*." I felt insufficiently prepared and considered withdrawing until he quelled my fears with an (appropriately solemn) exhortation to "consider the course a retreat." The first seeds of this book were planted at that time.

This book is a "book of love" in more ways than one. Although it has gone through multiple drafts, I have never wearied of it—partly because the subject matter engages me personally; partly because my first readers, Alger N. Doane, Sherry Reames, and Fannie LeMoine, never ceased to encourage me. To them I owe a tremendous, heartfelt debt of gratitude.

I also acknowledge gratefully the institutional support of the University of Wisconsin–Madison in the form of two successive fellowships during the spring of 1986 and the academic year 1986–87. The English Department there afforded me access to the Wang Computer Laboratory, and the staff kindly supported my efforts at word processing.

The debt of gratitude extends to dear friends, teachers, and colleagues—Martin Winkler, Donald Rowe, Carol Braun Pasternack, Barbara Fowler, Jerome Taylor, Valerie Lagorio, and Dolores Frese—whose moral support has sustained me through the progress of this work. My fellow medievalists at Purdue University, Charles

Ross, Shaun F. D. Hughes, and Thomas Ohlgren, have eased the revision process with their good counsel, interest, and enthusiasm. Bernhard Kendler and the readers at Cornell University Press have given me invaluable advice and guided the work into print with generous and expert care.

Portions of this book have appeared elsewhere. I thank the editors of the *Ball State University Forum* for permission to republish a portion of Chapter 7 which appeared in that journal under the title "The Song of Songs and the Medieval Idea of Drama." In May 1987 I delivered an early version of Chapter 5 as a paper at the International Medieval Congress in Kalamazoo, Michigan. Much of Chapter 4 was given as a paper the following year at Kalamazoo and has been published subsequently in *Mystics Quarterly*. I thank Valerie Lagorio for permission to republish it.

Caroline Walker Bynum has my gratitude for allowing me to see and cite the text of her plenary address, "Bodily Miracles and the Resurrection of the Body in the High Middle Ages," given in Kalamazoo at the May 1988 International Medieval Congress. I am grateful, too, to E. Ann Matter, who kindly allowed me to read a prepublication copy of Chapter 6 of her book *"The Voice of My Beloved": The Song of Songs in Western Medieval Christianity*, forthcoming from the University of Pennsylvania Press.

I owe inexpressible thanks to the Schoenstatt Sisters of Mary, with whom I lived, worked, and prayed during the time of research and writing. Their sisterly support has made everything possible. The affection of my parents, brothers, and sisters has been similarly warm, constant, and strengthening.

The final debt of love is to Fr. Joseph Kentenich, the founder of Schoenstatt, to whom I have dedicated this work. I did not meet him during his lifetime. His writings, however, have been my daily spiritual reading for the past fifteen years, and they have shaped my thinking, living, and loving in inestimable ways. I hold myself accountable for whatever errors and infelicities this book may contain; I honor him for whatever genuine wisdom it possesses.

ANN W. ASTELL

West Lafayette, Indiana

Abbreviations

ASE   *Anglo-Saxon England*
CCCM   Corpus Christianorum Continuatio Medievalis
CCSL   Corpus Christianorum, Series Latina
EETS   Early English Text Society
ELH   *English Literary History*
JEGP   *Journal of English and Germanic Philology*
MP   *Modern Philology*
NLH   *New Literary History*
PG   Patrologiae Cursus Completus, Series Graeca. Ed. J. P.
         Migne. 162 vols., with Latin translation. Paris, 1857–66.
PL   Patrologiae Cursus Completus, Series Latina. Ed. J. P.
         Migne. 221 vols. Paris, 1844–64.
PMLA   *Publications of the Modern Language Association*
RB   *Revue Bénédictine*
SP   *Studies in Philology*

The Song of Songs
in the Middle Ages

Introduction

The Song of Songs posed two interrelated problems for the Fathers of the early church, both of which were articulated and addressed in Origen's voluminous third-century commentary. The first problem arises from what the Song leaves unstated; the second from what it actually says. Included among the sacred books from the earliest times, the Song makes no direct mention of God; instead it celebrates the passionate joys and sorrows of unnamed lovers.[1] Indeed, the literal meaning is so lushly erotic that it endangers the carnally minded reader who approaches it and is seemingly incited to fleshly lust by sacred Scripture itself: "occasione divinae Scripturae commoveri et incitari videbitur ad libidinem carnis."[2] For such a reader, as Origen observes, the Song represents no small difficulty and danger: "non parum discriminis periculique" (PG 13, c63).

1. The *Canticum* was included in the Septuagint translation, circa 200 B.C. Rabbinical authorities numbered it among the five *Megilloth* of the Bible, along with Ruth, Lamentations, Ecclesiastes, and Esther, and prescribed its annual reading during the solemn festival of the Passover. Melito, bishop of Sardis, included the Song in the earliest known Christian list of the Old Testament canon (circa 170 A.D.). Nuptial imagery elsewhere in the Bible, which explicitly identifies Yahweh or Christ with the Bridegroom, Israel or *ecclesia* with the Bride, encouraged both the Jewish Midrash and the Christian allegoresis that contextualized the *Canticum*. See, for instance, Ezechiel 16:8–13; Isaiah 62:4–5; Psalm 45; Hosea 2:8–22; John 3:25–29; Matthew 25:1–13; 1 Corinthians 11:1–3; Ephesians 5:21–33; Apocalypse 19:5–10, 21:1–4, 22:17.
2. Origen, *In Canticum Canticorum*, trans. Rufinus, PG 13, c63. Subsequent references to this work are given parenthetically.

Having isolated the double problem of the Song, Origen concerns himself at the outset with two topics: *amor* and *allegoria*, what the Song literally expresses (carnal love) and what it does not (spiritual love). Given the canonicity of the text, Origen reasons that it must refer in an oblique way to the God it does not name: "If these words are not to be spiritually understood, are they not mere tales? If they contain no hidden mystery, are they not unworthy of God?" ("Haec si spiritualiter non intelligantur, nonne fabulae sunt? Nisi aliquid habeant secreti, nonne indigna sunt Deo?")[3] Origen then applies to the Song the exegetical principles he outlines in full in *De Principiis* IV. Proceeding on the assumption that "all things visible have some invisible likeness and pattern" (p. 220), Origen insists that the literal carnality of the Song veils a spiritual meaning (*allegoria*), even as the human body houses a soul. Indeed, the overt ("in prima fronte") eroticism of the text offers a series of stumbling blocks ("offendicula"), calling the reader to search for a deeper truth ("ad inquisitionem veritatis altius") and discover a divinely appropriate meaning: "dignum Deo sensum in Scripturis."[4] The Song's hidden meaning then unfolds in a rich array of correspondences once the exegete has correctly identified the principal actors veiled behind the outward masks of the drama. As Origen explains it, the Song actually refers to the mystical union between the church and Christ or the soul and the Word ("vel de Ecclesia ad Christum . . . vel de animae cum Verbo Dei conjunctione") under the appellations of Bride and Bridegroom: "sub sponsae vel sponsi titulo" (PG 13, c83).

Origen's discussion of love (carnal and spiritual) parallels his treatment of literal and spiritual meaning. Observing that even the wise Greeks have been known to misinterpret texts dealing with love, Origen calls any attempt to write about love difficult and dangerous: "difficilem diximus et periculo proximam de amoris natura disputationem" (PG 13, c64). Part of the problem, Origen explains, is that the word "love" (*amor*) has opposite meanings. It denotes both the cupidinous love of the flesh which comes from

3. *Origenis in Canticum Canticorum*, trans. Saint Jerome, PL 23, c1121; Origen, *The Song of Songs: Commentary and Homilies*, trans. R. P. Lawson (1957), p. 270. Subsequent references to both translations are parenthetical.
4. Origen, *De Principiis* IV, trans. Rufinus, PG 11, c375–76. For a complete English translation, see Rowan A. Greer, trans., *Origen*, Classics of Western Spirituality (1979), pp. 171–216.

Satan ("amor carnalis a Satana veniens") and the love of the spirit
which originates in God ("amor spiritus a Deo exordium habens")—
the two forms of love being mutually exclusive: "nemo potest
duobus amoribus possideri" (PL 23, c1121).[5] The word *amor*, in
short, is actually a homonym—"homonymia" (PG 13, c65)—designating antonyms, the center of a dialectic.

What, then, is the relationship between the two *amores* and the
two (overt and hidden) meanings of the Song? According to Origen, no adult escapes the power of *amor*: "Omnis namque qui ad id
aetatis venerit, quam pubertatem vocant, amat aliquid" (PG 13,
c71). *Eros* is laudable ("amor probabilis"), however, only when it is
directed toward God; indeed, a passionate love for God is syn-
onymous with charity: "non ergo interest utrum amari dicatur
Deus, an diligi" (PG 13, c70). Achieving the intensity of an erotic
love for God depends, moreover, on the sublimation of every bodily
desire—even, in Origen's own case, at the cost of self-castration.
Through heroic suppression, the corporeal drives that constitute, in
part, the soul's burdensome punishment actually become its *re-
medium*, enabling its ascent back to the realm of pure spirits. The
mark of a perfect soul is precisely this power "to forsake things
bodily and visible and to hasten to those that are not of the body and
are spiritual" (p. 234) (PG 13, c181: "corporea et visibilia relinquere,
et ad incorporea et invisibilia ac spiritalia properare").

Origen's method of exegesis, then, directly parallels the process
of mystical marriage which is the Song's secret subject. Even as the
exegete moves away from the *Canticum*'s literal, carnal meaning to
its *sensus interioris*, the bridal soul, renouncing what is earthly,
reaches out for the invisible and eternal: "saeculo renuntians tendet
ad invisibilia et aeterna" (PG 13, c75). An almost violent departure
from the body itself and from literal meaning energizes the soul's
ascent. To pass beyond the literal, carnal *sensus* is to escape the
prisonhouse of the flesh. To discover the spiritual *sensus* is to fly,
angellike, toward the God who is Spirit.

The Bride receives the kisses of the Spouse, Origen says, "when
she has begun to discern for herself what was obscure, to unravel
what was tangled, to unfold what was involved, to interpret para-

5. See also Origen, *In Canticum*, PG 13, c67.

bles and riddles and the sayings of the wise along the lines of her own expert thinking" (p. 61) (PG 13, c85: "ubi vero sponte jam coeperit obscura cernere, enodare perplexa, involuta dissolvere, parabolas et aenigmata, dictaque sapientum competentibus intelligentiae lineis explicare"). For the Bride—and Origen presents himself as *sponsa*—the illumination of every obscure meaning ("uniuscujusque obscuri sensus illuminationem") is a divine kiss. In Origen's mystical experience, intellection and loving are one and the same. As Etienne Gilson puts it, his "is the mysticism of an exegete."[6]

Origen's stress on enlightenment derives from his understanding of the soul. Behind his exegesis stands his theology. Origen believed in the preexistence of rational souls who received their bodies as an outward sign of their fall away from God. The body as such is thus not integral to the human being, who is a soul temporarily placed in a body: "Homines autem nunc dico animas in corporibus positas" (PG 11, c371). Fallen and joined to the body, the rational soul (*mens* or *nous*) loses its initial fervor for the Good ("a refrigescendo") and becomes a mere *anima* or *psyche*, its spiritual power dissipated by the flesh (see PG 11, c222–24). Overcoming carnal desires ultimately enables the soul to return to its original state and become once more a *mens*: "anima quae si reparata fuerit et correcta, redit in hoc ut sit mens" (PG 11, c223). When Origen identifies the Bride of the Song with the perfected soul ("anima perfecta"), then, he actually means a *mens* withdrawn from the body and its lusts: "mentem magis quam animam Spiritui sancto conjungit et sociat" (PG 11, c221).[7]

Origen's identification of the Bride with the church or soul remained the basis for all subsequent interpretation (*allegoresis*) of the Song's veiled meaning (*allegoria*).[8] The definition of *anima* and the understanding of human nature, however, changed in time, affect-

---

6. Etienne Gilson, *The Mystical Theology of St. Bernard*, trans. A. H. C. Downes (1940, repr. 1955), p. 216, n. 7. Gilson emphasizes the "noticeable difference in spirit" between Origen's "essentially cognitive" mysticism and the "marked affectivity" of Bernard.

7. For a discussion of Origen's doctrine of the Fall, see Rowan A. Greer, "Introduction," in *Origen*, pp. 11–17.

8. Richard Frederick Littledale (*A Commentary on the Song of Songs from Ancient and Medieval Sources* [1869]) observes that all the Christian commentaries up until the Renaissance presented the Song as "wholly mystical" (p. xiv). The only two exceptions he names are the works of Theodore of Mopsuestia and Jovinian.

ing reader response to the Song and inspiring new approaches to the text. While Origen's Neoplatonic theory of fallen souls met with early ecclesiastical censure, his denigration of the body continued to haunt theological circles.[9] Saint Augustine, replying to the Manicheans, was the first to affirm the composite nature of humankind ("homo et anima constat et corpore") and to link emphatically the doctrines of the Creation, Incarnation, and Bodily Resurrection.[10] It was only in the twelfth-century renaissance, however, that theologians, drawing on the authority of Augustine, began to explore the body/soul relationship from a psychological perspective, spurred on by the new scientific interest in humankind's microcosmic relationship to the world and by attempts to systematize the *via mystica*. Treatises on the subject ("De Natura Corporis et Animae") proliferated, especially among the Cistercian and Victorine writers.

Isaac of Stella's *Epistola de Anima* stands as representative of the genre.[11] Isaac (d. 1169?) insists on the unitary nature of the soul ("una est anima"), while giving several *divisiones* of the soul's powers. The simplest scheme distinguishes between a higher (reflective) and lower (sensitive) faculty, the *ratio* and *anima*, respectively: "Anima vivit; ratio sapit" (PL 194, c1877). A second *divisio* names a trinity of powers: "anima rationalis, concupiscibilis, irascibilis." Yet a third scheme presents an elaborate, ascending scale of

9. Rufinus charged Jerome, for instance, with having taught (in his commentary on Ephesians 5:28–29) that we would receive new spiritual bodies, not our own, in the afterlife and that women would be changed into men: "uxores in viros convertantur." See Rufinus, *Apologia* I.24, PL 21, c562. Jerome defended himself by citing Origen (PL 23, c414–20). Like Origen, too, the Manicheans invoked in support of a variety of Gnostic tenets the Pauline dictum that "flesh and blood can obtain no part in the Kingdom of God" (1 Corinth. 15:50). Origen's teachings about the Resurrection and the soul were finally condemned by the Fifth General Council of 553. The twelfth-century Albigensian heresy and the Cathar cult, in particular, may be seen as a revival of Manichean dualism which provided impetus for a contemporary, orthodox reaffirmation of material goodness.

10. For an instructive discussion of Augustine's position on the body, see Henri Irénée Marrou, *The Resurrection and St. Augustine's Theology of Human Values*, trans. Mother Maria Consolata, S.H.C.J., St. Augustine Lecture Series (1966).

11. Isaac of Stella, a Cistercian abbot, wrote his *Epistola de Anima* (PL 194, c1875–90) at the request of Alcher of Clairvaux. It was used in the famous *De Spiritu et Anima* (PL 40, c779–832), once attributed erroneously to Augustine. Other works in the genre include William of St. Thierry's *De Natura Corporis et Animae* (PL 180, c695–726) and Hugh of St. Victor's *De Unione Corporis et Spiritus* (PL 177, c285–94). Subsequent references to the *Epistola* are parenthetical.

five powers: "sensus, imaginatio, ratio, intellectus, intelligentia" (PL 194, c1880), by which the soul is joined to the body (in the "imaginatio" or "phantastico animae") and linked connaturally to the macrocosm.[12] Isaac's various *divisiones* overlap in an intricate, kaleidoscopic array. All of his outlines, however, serve to establish essential linkages between the body and the soul, between the lower and higher faculties. Unlike Origen, who identifies the redeemed person with the *mens* alone, and who predicates a flight from the body and its affects ("omne corpus fugiendum") as a necessary precondition for holiness, Isaac envisions a holistic redemption of body and soul made possible through a firm identification with, and engagement of, the lower, body-linked powers—that is, the affects. There are, as Isaac observes, concupiscible and irascible drives ("motus") in the soul that express themselves in four primary affects: joy and hope, sorrow and fear. These *affectus* are the root cause ("elementa") of all vices and virtues. The cardinal virtues stem, in particular, from the affect of love ("ex amoris vario quodam affectu"), which Isaac identifies with desire: "De concupiscibilitate igitur propensio, titillatio, delectatio, dilectio" (PL 194, c1879). Perfection, according to Isaac, consists in harnessing and directing the affective faculties so that one is able "to choose the good with eager desire and abhor what is evil" (PL 194, c1878: "eligere per concupiscibilitatem bonum . . . et reprobare per irascibilitatem malum").[13]

Redeeming the *affectus* or instinctive powers of the soul—in particular, the *affectus* of love—means for Isaac and his contemporaries a reclaiming of the feminine within themselves. While the Fall perverted man's nature chiefly by warping his reason "ad curiositatem" (PL 194, c1886), it inclined woman's nature toward sensual pleasure-seeking: "ad voluptatem." The sexes, then, tend to foreground

---

12. Isaac likens the earth to the bodily senses, the water to the imagination, the air to the reason, the firmament to the intellect, and the heavenly empyrean to the *intelligentia* (PL 194, c1886). Compare Isaac's model to that presented in Hugh of St. Victor's *Didascalicon* I.i–iii. Hugh emphasizes that the soul comprehends all things connaturally because "it is composed of all of them." See *The Didascalicon of Hugh of St. Victor*, trans. Jerome Taylor (1961, repr. 1968), pp. 46–50. According to Hugh, the rational soul subsumes all the lower powers (nutrient and sensitive) and distinguishes humankind from other creatures.

13. Here and throughout the book, all unattributed translations are my own.

different consequences of the Fall which are, nevertheless, experienced in various ways by every individual. Salvation for both men and women must come through the feminine powers of the soul (the *anima* or *affectus*, as opposed to the *ratio*) because love is the beginning and end of perfection. The reversal of the Fall depends metaphorically on the action of a new Eve, the woman within each one, the Bride of God. If the higher powers of the soul (*ratio, spiritus, mens*) are to be joined to God, the process must be supported, sustained, and perfected by the *affectus*, so that in the end, as Etienne Gilson says, "God is felt in love."[14]

In a discussion of the tropology of the Song of Songs—that is, the dimension of the text that assimilates the lives of its readers—Honorius of Autun speaks of an internal marriage that takes place when the "anima," which is the lower, affective power of the soul ("vis inferior"), is coupled with the higher, rational power ("interioris hominis spiritui") as her husband ("eius vir")—a union engendering good works. He calls this internal marriage, with its psychological ramifications, the sign and seal of a second marriage mystically joining the soul ("animam Christi sponsam") to Christ.[15] The repetition of the word "anima"—first to designate the affective realm in relation to the rational, then to name the soul as a whole in relation to God—emphasizes the role of the feminine principle in the perfection of the personality. It is the bridal self that submits to both the dictates of conscience and the *Logos* of revelation and thus lovingly incarnates the Word.

Origen's definition of the bridal soul led him to stress its higher, rational powers (*mens, spiritus, logos*) at the cost of suppressing the body and its drives. Accordingly, his exegesis of the Song follows a two-part pattern—first, an examination of the literal meaning, fol-

14. Gilson, p. 209.
15. Honorius of Autun, *Expositio in Cantica Canticorum*, PL 172, c349. The entire text reads as follows: "[Tropologically considered, the marriage] by which the soul, because it is the power inferior to the spirit of the inner man, is joined to that higher spirit which is her husband through the harmony of divine law, from which union is engendered children, that is, good work" ("quo anima quod est inferior vis interioris hominis spiritui, quo est superior vir ejus per consensum divinae legis conjungitur, de quo conjugio spiritalis proles, id est bonum opus gignitur"). Traditionally associated with Autun, Honorius actually did most of his work among the Irish Benedictines at Regensburg. I use the familiar appellation.

lowed by an exposition of its *allegoria* or spiritual sense.[16] The procedure is dialectical, aimed at the discovery of truth, and characterized by unbroken ascent.[17] In contrast, the twelfth-century understanding of the soul gives prominence to its lower, affective powers, which are intimately connected with the bodily senses and the volition.[18] The soul's mystical union with God is thus experienced not primarily as intellectual enlightenment, but as a loving, personal surrender to the will of God, who is, in the words of William of St. Thierry, "amatum potius quam cogitatum, gustatum, quam intellectum."[19] Accordingly, when twelfth-century commentators approach the Song of Songs, their exegesis moves beyond an exposition of hidden meaning (*allegoria*) to tropological exhortation—that is, they apply the interpreted text to the concrete life situation of their auditors and use the affective force of the Song's literal imagery to move them to virtuous action. In the process the allegory is reliteralized, joined again to the letter from which it was derived, and ascent turns into descent. The procedure as a whole is rhetorical, not dialectical; aimed at the application, not the discovery, of truth.

It is no mere coincidence, then, that the same twelfth-century circles which produced the numerous *De Anima* treatises also wrote innovative commentaries on the Song of Songs. The voluminous Christian commentary tradition, which stems from Hippolytus and Origen in the early third century, temporarily exhausted itself in the ninth century, only to experience a new flowering during the twelfth-century renaissance. At that time, Anselm of Laon, Bruno of Segni, Bernard of Clairvaux, Rupert of Deutz, Honorius of

16. Greer notes that while Origen sometimes subdivides the deeper meaning into the "soul" and "spirit" of Scripture, his "fundamental distinction is between the letter and the spirit" (*Origen*, p. 31).

17. As Hans Urs Von Balthasar observes, Origenist spirituality tends to interpret Christian life "as an unequivocal 'ascent' " (*Origen*, trans. Greer, p. xiv), with a resultant neglect of the evangelical theme of descent.

18. A. J. Minnis notes that the twelfth-century emphasis on the *affectus* fueled the early-thirteenth-century debate on the powers of the soul, which opposed the *aspectus* to the *affectus*. The tendency to associate the *aspectus* with logic and human science, the *affectus* with rhetoric, divine science, and Scripture, contributed to the widening gap between reason and faith, science and religion. See Minnis, *Medieval Theory of Authorship*, 2d ed. (1988), pp. 119–30.

19. William of St. Thierry, *In Cantica Canticorum*, PL 180, c507; quoted by Gilson, p. 209.

Autun, Philip of Harveng, Gilbert de la Porree, William of St. Thierry, Gilbert of Hoyland, John of Ford, Thomas the Cistercian, and Alain de Lille all produced *expositiones* of the Song, the sheer bulk of writings attesting to the peculiar fascination the Song of Songs had for the medieval psyche.[20] The resurgence of interest in the Song after two centuries of virtual neglect strongly suggests that the men of the twelfth century were discovering something new in the *Canticum*—a conclusion borne out by even a cursory examination of their commentaries.

Jean Leclercq has shown that social conditions in the monasteries of that period predisposed these exegetes to read and use the Song in ways significantly different from those of their predecessors. Unlike the Black Monks, who raised the children offered to them as oblates and drew their members chiefly from that group of aspirants, the rising new orders—the Cistercians, the Augustinian canons, the Praemonstratensians, and the regular canons of St. Victor in Paris—recruited their members from among adults, all of whom had lived in secular society. Many were drawn from aristocratic circles; a high percentage had been married; most were familiar with secular love literature; some—notably the trouvère Folquet—had written secular love songs prior to their entrance. The spiritual formation of recruits such as these required (and inspired) a body of monastic love literature which is noticeably different from earlier writings on charity in its incorporation of feminine imagery and in its preferred symbolism of God's love for humankind by the love between a man and a woman—a symbolism explicitly derived from the Song of Songs.[21]

Following Leclercq, Caroline Walker Bynum has pointed to an increased feminization of religious language, beginning in the twelfth century with the rise of the Cistercian order.[22] She has argued convincingly that although this kind of imagery does not

20. For a convenient listing of the various commentaries in chronological order, together with summary comments, see Marvin Pope, ed., *The Song of Songs*, Anchor Bible Series (1977), pp. 114–24, 236–42.
21. See Jean Leclercq, "New Recruitment—New Psychology," in *Monks and Love in Twelfth-Century France* (1979), pp. 8–26. I am simply summarizing his findings here.
22. See Caroline Walker Bynum, *Jesus as Mother: Studies in the Spirituality of the High Middle Ages* (1982)

reveal much about the attitudes of celibate men toward their women contemporaries, it does reflect their conscious relationship to the contrasexual, affective powers within themselves. A long tradition in the West—exemplified in the classical myth of Psyche and Cupid, the Sapiential books of the Old Testament, the allegorical commentaries on the Fall of Adam and Eve, theological discussions of human nature as *imago Dei*, and sacramental tracts on matrimony—had, of course, associated feminine *figurae* with both the human soul and the affective side of human nature. Medieval psychology, such as it was, thus prepared the exegetes to use the *Sponsa* of the Song as a way of analogous self-knowledge and self-expression, as a means to actualize the Socratic dictum often repeated by humanists like Bernard Sylvestris, John of Salisbury, and Peter Abelard, as well as by the mystic saints of the twelfth century: "Know thyself" ("Scito teipsum").[23]

The allegory of the Song had defined the place of audience identification as the Bride, not the Bridegroom. The central consciousness of the Song *ad litteram*, moreover, is feminine, not masculine—a feature which sets the *Canticum* apart from other eastern love literature and from the courtly tradition of the West.[24] The reliteralization of the Song of Songs, beginning in the twelfth century, is thus marked by a powerful coalescence of the objective, allegorical placement with the emotive directives of the literal text. The exegetes all encourage their auditors to identify their "bridal self" with the Bride, using the feminine *figura* as a way of evoking, expressing, and directing the emotional domain within themselves. The exegetes insist that the proper human re-sponse to the divine call issued through the inspired text is that of the *Sponsa*.

Saint Bernard considers the Song to be God's wooing, his way of stimulating humankind to make a bridal self-surrender to him.[25]

23. Richard P. McKeon has observed that in the twelfth century philosophy and poetry shared a common subject matter (human nature) and a common method (rhetoric)—a coincidence that led readers to approach poetry as a vehicle of self-knowledge and ethical instruction. See "Poetry and Philosophy in the Twelfth Century: The Renaissance of Rhetoric," *MP* 43 (1945–46): 217–34.
24. See Chaim Rabin, "The Song of Songs and Tamil Poetry," *Studies in Religion* 3 (1973): 205–19. Rabin reports that fifty-six of the verses of the Song are clearly put into the woman's mouth as against thirty-six into the man's.
25. See Bernard, *Sermo* 7:II.2, in *Sermones super Cantica Canticorum*, vol. I, ed. J. Leclercq, C. H. Talbot, H. M. Rochais (1958), pp. 31–32.

His *Sermones super Cantica*, therefore, stress the distinctly feminine emotion of longing appropriate to receptive self-surrender. Richard of St. Victor calls the Song a visionary text that employs the sensuous imagery of earthly things to approximate the bliss of heaven and thus awaken in its readers the longing for God.[26] The *Summa Theologica* attributed to Alexander of Hales (1186–1245) classifies the Song of Songs as a work written in the "modus orativus" in order to move the affections from within and place them at God's service.[27] Hugh of St. Victor speaks of ardent gratefulness in response to the love tokens of God, of chaste union with him, and of virtues conceived within the soul.[28] The commentators all connect the Bride and the bridal self with the humble admission of guilt, need, frailty, and thus with the openness to receive forgiveness, grace, and transforming love. Archetypally, it is the Bride who obeys the will of God, suffers, endures, and waits. To the bridal self, too, the commentators ascribe the capacity for contemplation—that suprarational knowledge of God associated with love-longing and its fulfillment. Finally, the bridal self is manifestly the maternal self, compassionate, charitable, sheltering, and serving, engaged in works of mercy.

The role assigned by these exegetes to the *Sponsa* of the Song of Songs and to the reader, male or female, who identifies with her, bears the distinctive features Carl G. Jung has taught us to associate with the feminine: personal attachment, longing, receptive self-surrender, intuitive/contemplative insight, and maternal fruitfulness. Indeed, Jung's Latinate terminology—"anima" referring to the feminine principle that compensates the masculine consciousness, "animus" designating the masculine principle in the inverse relationship—derives from ancient and medieval sources while, at the same time, powerfully elucidating them. Even as Isaac of Stella, following Augustine, distinguishes the *anima* from the *ratio*, Jung names the *anima* and *animus* as a complementary pairing. Even as Isaac's *anima* subsumes the affective drives that must be judged by the *ratio*,

26. Richard of St. Victor, *Benjamin Minor* 24, PL 196, c16–17.
27. See A. J. Minnis, "Literary Theory in Discussions of *Formae Tractandi* by Medieval Theologians," *NLH* 11 (1979): 134–45; *Medieval Theory of Authorship*, pp. 49–52.
28. Hugh of St. Victor, *De Amore Sponsi ad Sponsam*, PL 176, c987.

Jung's *anima* archetypally contains the powers of love and life-giving, while the *animus* represents the capacity for logical analysis and detached reflection.

The Jungian understanding that both men and women are governed by the polaric interplay of complementary masculine and feminine principles within themselves finds its orthodox theological formulation in Augustine and Thomas Aquinas, both of whom insist that the male or female body, as the form of the soul, determines which of the human qualities common to both sexes will gain the ascendancy and which will be recessive.[29] In the case of a man, the abstract reason ("consilium vel rationem")—with its capacity for what Jung calls "objective interest"—dominates and seeks its necessary counterpart and creative completion in the affective domain, which is often stimulated by, and exteriorized in, the *figura* of a beloved woman.[30] In the case of a woman, the life of the emotions ("appetitum rationem")—with its "personal interest"—is foregrounded and seeks its "otherness" in the objective realm of self-discipline, duty, unchanging principle, and disinterested observation—powers within her that are awakened and strengthened by the men to whom she is attracted. As Jung puts it, feminine psychology "is founded on the principle of Eros, the great binder and loosener, whereas from ancient times the ruling principle ascribed to man is Logos."[31]

The common definition derived inductively from Jungian psychology and deductively from Christian dogma, then, affirms that the integrity of the personality depends to a large extent on the strength of the conscious interplay between the masculine and feminine principles. The unconscious or recessive principle, which is initially projected onto a person of the opposite sex, must be consciously recognized and integrated in the process of individuation. Thus the marital language of Canticles, applied in the Middle Ages to mystical and moral experience, describes a process whereby the reason, perfected through faith, can enable, sustain, and direct a full

29. Two key texts in this discussion are Augustine's *De Trinitate* XII (CCSL, vol. 50, especially pp. 358–67) and Thomas Aquinas's *Summa Theologica*, Q 90–93. The notion of the body as the form of the soul is, of course, also the basis for the ancient and medieval theory of the temperaments.

30. See Carl Gustav Jung, *Aspects of the Feminine*, trans. R. F. C. Hull, Bollingen Series (1982), pp. 65, 95, 98–99; Augustine, *De Trinitate* XII.vii, CCSL 50, p. 367.

31. Jung, p. 65.

unfolding of the emotions; conversely, *eros*, joined to God as its ultimate object, stimulates and supports the perfection of *logos* in wisdom. Honorius of Autun, for instance, speaks of the inner "conjugium" that produces good works, and Augustine uses the image of intercourse to describe the conversion of abstract recognition into practiced charity.[32]

The power to embody the Word, to carry out the dictates of conscience, is especially associated with the feminine principle as the principle of emotive love, attraction, and (therefore) motivation. The distinctly feminine readings of the *Canticum*, then, reflect the commentators' desire to evoke, engage, and direct the *anima* in the work of their own salvation, to bring into consciousness the affective soul-life and set it at the service of a personal God. Even more, the feminization of self and audience reifies psychologically the allegory that represents humankind as a woman, the soul as spouse. In the metaphysics of sexuality, every person, male and female, is more feminine than masculine in relation to God—because receptive, dependent, and small. Thus the same principle of complementarity that joins a woman to a man in the social sphere, and the emotions to the reason in the psychological order, also works in the religious dimension to effect contemplative *unitas*, the suprarational knowing of God through love.[33]

As a figural union, the marriage of the Bride and Bridegroom promotes not only the soul's oneness with God but also its own psychological *integritas* through the internal joining of complementary masculine and feminine principles. Depending on the rhetorical aim of the commentary, the exegete tends to emphasize different aspects of the feminine principle in the person of the Bride, who appears variously as: (1) the Virgin who resists conquest; (2) the Mother who nurtures; (3) the Medial Woman who makes peace and voices prophecy; and (4) the maidenly Hetaira with her power to awaken chivalry.[34] In every case the specific *anima* that is evoked

---

32. See Honorius, *Expositio*, PL 172, c349; Augustine, *De Trinitate* XII.iii, CCSL 50, pp. 357–58.

33. For an excellent presentation of the role of the feminine principle in religious experience, see Ann Belford Ulanov, *The Feminine in Jungian Psychology and in Christian Theology* (1971).

34. Ulanov names and defines these four archetypes in *The Feminine*, pp. 196–211. She draws upon Toni Wolff, *Structural Forms of the Feminine Psyche*, trans. Paul Watzlawik (1956).

through reader identification with the Bride is appropriately complemented by the masculine principle represented in the Bridegroom. His characterization by the exegetes as Priestly Father, Divine Child, Poet-Prophet, or Knightly Hero embraces a fourfold
archetypal variety correspondent to the four different images of the
Bride.

The matching is rhetorically purposeful and geared toward the
psychology of reception. The male auditor who brings the recessive
feminine principle (*anima*) within himself into consciousness
through an identification with the Bride discovers himself in a new
way as a masculine type. He sees himself, as it were, through the
feminine and configured according to it as part of a pairing. The
Bride's recessive masculinity, her *animus*, corresponds to his conscious self-image, even as his recessive femininity is personified
archetypally in her. Acknowledging the feminine within him as an
integral part of himself thus leads to total self-discovery. The psychological process, in short, parallels (and actually depends upon)
what happens in human love relationships as one partner brings out
qualities in the other.

A feminizing exegesis of the Song, then, aims at a variety of ends.
The *affectus* enabling an ardent, personal surrender to God should be
evoked. The resulting union with God should find its expression,
means, and security in an analogous marriage of the masculine and
feminine powers within the soul. That coupling, in turn, should
produce good works. The *anima*, as a principle of love, should (1)
unite the auditor to God, (2) restore him to himself, and (3) render
him fruitful in service to others. As the *Glossa* says of the Song,
"Through these words we are enriched with virtues, we are joined
to the Lord" ("Per ista locupletamur virtutibus, Domino con-
jungimur").[35]

The rhetorical engagement of the *anima* as a moving force leading
a variety of audiences to various ends helps to explain the different
twelfth-century readings of the Song. In them the Bride assumes
different faces, depending on what the auditor who identifies with
her is called to do. Indeed, the four major feminine archetypes
delineated by Jungian psychologists—Virgin, Mother, Medial

35. *Glossa Ordinaria*, PL 113, c1127–28.

Woman, and Hetaira—correspond to, and essentially characterize, the four emergent varieties of interpretation of the Song: ecclesiastical, Marian, Victorine, and Cistercian.

These four interpretive streams, moreover, cluster in complementary pairs sharing a common basis in *historia*. The Victorine and Cistercian readings of the Song make its text descriptive of the mystical life pursued and actually experienced by the auditor, whereas the ecclesiastical and Marian interpretations present the Bride as an exemplary figure whose historical existence inspires timely imitation. The mystic's relationship to the Bride is one of immediate identification (*Einschaltung*), whereas for the readers of the Marian and ecclesiastical commentaries the Bride stands as a model welcoming their configuration to her (*Gleichschaltung*).

The Exemplary Bride: *Ecclesia* and Mary

The traditional interpretation had identified the Bride with *ecclesia*. In the timely context of the investiture crisis, that identification was reified in Bruno of Segni's exposition of Canticles in order to gain bridal supporters for Christ's vicar, Gregory VII, in his struggle against the Holy Roman emperor, Henry IV. In his commentary (as we shall see), Bruno consciously imitates the inspired poetry of the Song in prose and verse to arouse an affective response in his auditors, thus combining the *logos* of allegory and the *pathos* of the letter in a single appeal. Drawing upon the military imagery in the Song, Bruno presents the Bride as the valiant Virgin whose resistance against heretics is secured by the priestly *doctores* who instruct her in truth. Brideship for the reader, then, consists in alliance or coordination with the church as Virgin-Bride.

Closely related to the ecclesiastical reading of the Song are the Marian interpretations. The twelfth century produced the first commentaries that interpret the Song entirely from the perspective of Mary's historical relationship to Jesus. In Mary, as the perfect type of the church, the exegetes find the literal Bride of the Bridegroom, the one in whom the letter and the allegory are inseparably joined under the aspect of the Mother-Bride. In the expositions of Rupert of Deutz, Honorius of Autun, and Alain de Lille, the details of Mary's historical life and her human, emotive response to Christ serve to reliteralize the Song, heighten its *pathos*, and stimulate the audience's appropriation of the maternal affections conveyed by the Bride's speeches. Mary's historicity, joined to the "historia" of the Song's literal meaning, thus invites the auditor's imitation of her as a Mother-Bride.

Taken together, the ecclesiastical and Marian interpretations evoke the *anima* under the linked forms of the Virgin and Mother, the former associated in Jungian psychology with the dynamic, the latter with the static, pole of the feminine. Similarly, the mystical commentaries take up complementary concerns—the Victorine seeress, or Medial Woman, reflecting (at the static pole) the contemplative's approach to the world, the Cistercian Hetaira embodying the feminine as a dynamic principle of personal development.

Personal Brideship: The Mystical Treatments

The new mystical interpretations—both Victorine and Cistercian—promote the reader's immediate identification with the Bride by drawing parallels between the audience's life experiences and hers. In accord with the specific asceticism of a given school, the individual is encouraged to appropriate the Bride's utterance and attitude in prayer and realize them in social action. The Victorine usage of the Song presents the Bride under the archetype of the Medial Woman. For the mystics of St. Victor, the Bride is the seeress who sees the many-in-the-One, articulates that synthesis prophetically, and enables a similar integration of experience in those who identify with her. The Bernardine sermons on the Song, on the other hand, delineate the Bride's responses according to the emotive pattern of the Hetaira, the romantic heroine and childlike handmaid, whose consciousness is complemented by the masculine principle in the double form of the Christ-Knight and Father-God. Both mystical schools draw upon the literal imagery of the Song to express inner processes in the souls of their auditors. They read the Song as "the book of our experience."[36] Indeed, the tropological (reader-

36. Bernard, Sermon 3:I.1, in *On the Song of Songs* I, trans. Kilian Walsh (1976), p. 16.

applicable) dimension is stressed at the cost of minimizing allegoresis. As Bernard says, his purpose "is not so much to explain
words as to move hearts."[37]

Origen, confronted by the problem of the Song's unstated meaning (*allegoria*), had used its *sensus litteralis* as a point of departure. He
(unlike Bernard) had felt an acute need to "explain words." In the
twelfth century, the Song's dogmatic meaning was no longer a
matter for discovery. Centuries of exegesis, resting upon Origen's
own ten-volume work, had filled in the gaps ("intercapedines"),
removed the stumbling blocks ("offendicula"), and rendered profoundly meaningful the apparent uselessness of the Song's erotic
content. The cumulative *glossa* functioned to resolve any apparent
contradictions, supplying an authoritative interpretation for the auditor so that text and commentary formed a single entity. The
vertical dimension of the text—its *allegoria*, its "higher" or "deeper"
meaning—gradually fused with the horizontal (because inherently
paratactic) dimension of literal/historical meaning so that the two
became one in a rhetorical synthesis of meanings.

For exegetes and poets alike, reliteralizing Canticles meant joining its tenor (defined by the "spiritual" allegory) to its vehicle (the
corporeal images of the Song *ad litteram*) in order to affect an audience with truth. As Michael Murrin has phrased it, when "the old
interpretation becomes the text"[38]—that is, when the literal narrative incorporates its own gloss, the poet obviates the need for the
reader to discover the philosophical/dogmatic meaning and dis-
places allegory itself as the "hidden" or "spiritual" sense. The original allegory (in the derived sense of allegoresis) becomes part of the
face value of the text; the allegorical Other becomes rhetorically
present. The *Judith* poet, for instance, calls Holofernes "se deoful-
cunda," thus eliminating any need to search for the Assyrian general's Satanic otherness while using it to evoke the reader's antipathy,
aversion, and active resistance toward him and what he represents.[39]
The unstated dimension of the text, the part awaiting discovery, is

37. Bernard, Sermon 16:I.i, in *On the Song of Songs* I, p. 114.
38. Michael Murrin, *The Allegorical Epic: Essays in Its Rise and Decline* (1980), p.
178. Murrin is referring to Alexander Pope's translation of Homer.
39. I explore this proposition in "Holofernes' Head: *Tacen* and Teaching in the Old
English *Judith*," *ASE* 18 (1989): 117–33.

then no longer *allegoria* but *tropologia*, not dogma but the concrete, ethical application of dogma to be carried out in the lives of the audience.

To be sure, the twelfth-century exegetes incorporated the traditional *allegoria* into their expositions of the Song. More than their predecessors, however, they took the allegory for granted, not as something hidden which must be discovered, but as something already known which must be applied. As part of the "scientia" of the Song, the identification of the Bridegroom with Christ was seen to be rhetorically potent in drawing the *affectus* toward God and engaging the whole person in a bridal coordination with him and his will. Rather than saying "the Bridegroom—that is, Christ," replacing the letter with its allegorical correspondent, twelfth-century exegetes were more likely to say "Jesus is our Bridegroom," combining the logical appeal (*logos*) of the allegory with the emotive appeal (*pathos*) of the literal meaning. They, in short, reliteralized the spiritual meaning of Canticles by clothing it in poetry and prose replete with the moving sensual power of the original text.

This process of reliteralization began in the late eleventh and early twelfth centuries when the commentators on the Song of Songs—Bruno of Segni, Michael Psellus, Peter Damian, and Williram of Ebersberg—began to include metrical paraphrases of the *Canticum* in their exegesis. At the same time, the Marian interpreters of the Song were using affective apostrophe and prosopopoeia in their expositions of the text, fusing the letter with its gloss; the Victorine poets were employing the images of the *Canticum* in their liturgical sequences; and Bernard was unfolding the tropology of the Song for his monks in cadenced prose eloquent with biblical imagery. The trend unfolded in the later Middle Ages in popular devotional texts—poems, plays, and meditations—in which the Christ-Bridegroom identification, derived from traditional allegoresis, became rhetorically charged through the force of the Song's love language.

Origen's dialectic, as we have seen, depends upon the opposition of the carnal and the spiritual, on the adversarial relationship between two loves: one demonic, the other divine. In the understanding of Bernard and his contemporaries, however, there is only one love, not two. That love, poured out into our hearts, comes from God ("Deus Charitas est") and urges our return to him. As creatures

of body and soul, our love (especially in its most primitive, developmental stage) is of necessity carnal; as fallen creatures, moreover,
our love for God is tainted with self-interested cupidity, frequently
misdirected and mistaken in its object. Concupiscence is thus a
blinded *charitas*, what Etienne Gilson calls "a love of God become
unaware of itself."[40] Learning to love—and that is the special curric-
ulum of the cloister as a *schola charitatis*—includes a number of stages
and frequent correction, but one and the same elemental power of
love is at work at every point, restlessly seeking its proper attachment.

Whereas Origen sought to sublimate eros by suppressing the
carnality of the Song, the twelfth-century exegetes, impressed by
the unitary nature of love, aimed at an organic transference of the
affectus by joining the literal image of the Bridegroom to its Christological tenor, thus directing the bridal love of the soul to its divine
object. The Bride, according to Bernard, is a soul thirsting for God
("anima sitiens Deum"), and his own rhetoric serves to awaken
desire in his auditors.[41] Richard of St. Victor, struck by obvious
parallels in the psychology of lovers and mystics, uses the passionate
relationship between a man and a woman to illustrate the four
degrees of violent charity—"insuperabilis, inseparabilis, singularis,
insatiabilis"—which he is experiencing as God's Bride: "Vulnerata
charitate ego sum."[42] Similarly, Hugh of St. Victor expresses the
soul's desire for the possession of her beloved ("Dilectus") as a
laudable (because God-oriented) concupiscence: "Hoc opto, hoc
desidero, hoc totis praecordis concupisco."[43]

While it must be granted that a reader's imaginative identification
with the Bridegroom would surely pose a temptation for celibate
men—and Bernard's pastoral concern recognizes it as such—a
strong rhetorical alignment with the Bride effectively avoids that
danger and provides a way for an awakened eros to be sublimated
into the love of God and neighbor. Indeed, as we shall see, the

40. Gilson, p. 45. For a classic exposition of Bernard's doctrine of love, see pp. 33–
99.
41. See Bernard, *Sermo* 7:II.2, in *Sermones super Cantica Canticorum*, vol. I, pp. 31–
32.
42. Richard of St. Victor, *De Quatuor Gradibus Violentae Charitatis*, PL 196, c1213,
1207.
43. Hugh of St. Victor, *Soliloquium de Arrha Animae*, PL 176, c970.

exegetes are bold in affirming that the divine Author employs erotic images in the Song precisely because he desires to evoke a response rooted in human sexuality with its inherent drive for complementarity. Pseudo-Richard of St. Victor echoes Gregory the Great when he describes the corporeal love language of the Song ("verba amoris") as a means ("machina") to awaken love for God: "Sic ad amorem vocat."[44] Similarly, the *Glossa* speaks of the transference of the emotional impulse ("motum animae tuae") and the fire of natural love ("naturalis amoris incendium") into one's affection for God.[45]

To be sure, the twelfth-century commentators, like the Fathers before them, warn against reading the Song merely literally, as the *Glossa* says, "lest acquaintance with it teach slippery minds so much that the composition causes them to yield to bodily lusts" ("ne tam erudiret cognitio lubricas mentes, quam textus ad concupiscentias corporales converteret").[46] Whereas Chaucer's lecherous old January in "The Merchant's Tale" reads the text in a baldly literal way, the exegetes effectively avert that kind of textual seduction (and reduction) for their readers by joining the Christological tenor again and again to its corporeal vehicle in a two-in-oneness that sacramentalizes "in Christo et Ecclesia" (Ephesians 5:32) the human marriage celebrated in the Song.[47] The reading process thus becomes safe through the repeated intersection of the literal/horizontal line of imagery with the allegorical/vertical line of interpretation, the combination of *logos* and *pathos*.

The close relationship I am delineating here between (1) the two-in-oneness of text and gloss and (2) the rhetorical interest of the twelfth-century commentaries finds its theoretical medieval formulation in the writings of Hugh of St. Victor, who departed from earlier exegetes in joining the letter to its allegory and considering the two in combination as the knowledge ("scientia") which is a necessary foundation and motivation for moral action ("tropo-

44. Pseudo-Richard, *Explicatio in Cantica Canticorum*, PL 196, c405.
45. *Glossa Ordinaria*, PL 113, c1128.
46. Ibid., c1127.
47. I have generally used biblical quotations as they appear in context in cited Latin commentaries. I have consulted the *Biblia Sacra Iuxta Vulgatam Versionem*, 2 vols., ed. Robert Weber, O.S.B. (Stuttgart: Württembergische Bibelanstalt, 1975), as well as the Douay-Challoner translation of the Vulgate.

logia").[48] According to Hugh's pairing, the "factum" that provides a basis for response includes both the historical deed recorded and the allegory that illumines it, both the letter (with its *pathos*) and the allegory (with its *logos*). Not a simple induction from the letter alone, tropology derives from the analogous relationship between the letter and the spirit and constitutes their synthesis in personal application.[49] Tropology is the reader's response to the rhetorical appeal of the text, rightly understood: the meeting point of life and letter.[50] Indeed, Hugh insists that *tropologia* is best understood not as part of the text but as an extension of the text into the world. It consists in each reader's heartfelt, personal discovery of what he or she ought to do in order to realize the moral implications of the event recorded: "Quid etiam per hoc factum, faciendum . . . inquiramus."[51]

Scholars have long recognized that the Victorine writers, arguing for the primacy of the literal meaning, were influential in opposing the spiritualist mode of exegesis associated with Origen and Gregory the Great.[52] What have not been sufficiently understood are the

48. See Hugh of St. Victor, *De Scripturis* XIII, PL 175, c20; *Didascalicon* VI, trans. Jerome Taylor (1961, repr. 1968), p. 127.

49. See G. E. R. Lloyd, *Polarity and Analogy: Two Types of Argumentation in Early Greek Thought* (1966), pp. 400–402, for the importance of analogies in ethical persuasion.

50. Judson Boyce Allen discusses tropology from a rhetorical point of view in "The *Grand Chant Courtois* and the Wholeness of the Poem: The Medieval *Assimilatio* of Text, Audience, and Commentary," *L'Esprit Créateur* 18 (1978): 5–17. See also Ann W. Astell, "*Sir Gawain and the Green Knight*: A Study in the Rhetoric of Romance," *JEGP* 84 (1985): 188–202. Medieval *artes praedicandi* are emphatic in assimilating rhetoric and tropology. Indeed, the rhetoric proper to a sermon may be regarded as an amplification of scriptural *tropologia*. Alain de Lille defines preaching by the same twofold purpose Hugh of St. Victor ascribes to scripture as a whole, "morum et fidei instructio," underscoring the importance of moral instruction (PL 210, c112; PL 175, c20). Guibert de Nogent, commenting on the biblical senses available to the preacher, singles out *tropologia* as the most useful: "magis commoda ac intelligibilis in tractando moralitas esse videtur" (PL 156, c26).

51. Hugh of St. Victor, *De Scripturis*, PL 175, c12. See also *Didascalicon* VI.v, PL 176, c805: "By contemplating what God has done we realize what we ourselves ought to do" ("Contemplando quid fecerit Deus quid nobis faciendum sit agnoscimus"). Hugh stresses that tropology concerns the meaning of things more than the meaning of words ("ad eam magis rerum quam vocum significatio pertinere videtur") because positive justice ("disciplina morum nostrorum") finds its base in natural justice; the order of acting follows the order of being.

52. See Beryl Smalley, *The Study of the Bible in the Middle Ages*, 2d ed. (1952), p. 89, for a discussion of the importance of Hugh's differentiation in terms of the increased dignity of the historical sense.

rhetorical implications of that reliteralization. As we shall see, the more "historical" the letter of the text is perceived to be—with respect to actual events and literal reference—the more immediately applicable it becomes to the lives of its auditors. The Christological allegory, by its participation in "the fullness of time," only serves to bridge the gap between the two histories, making one the prophetic type and one the timely fulfillment of the other.

Origen, to be sure, conceded a historical reference for the Song— Solomon's marriage to Pharaoh's daughter (see PG 13, c61–62)— but he treated the epithalamium as an allegory based on *verba*, not *res*—that is, as a kind of verbal code intended to convey a significa- tion other than the obvious one. The exegetes of the twelfth century were more ready than Origen had been to consider the letter of the text as historically true—that is, prophetic in the sense of typology. As we shall see, reliteralizing the historical nuptials celebrated in the Song supports the exegetes' call for temporal application ("facien- dum"). Bruno of Segni's ecclesiastical commentary reifies the mar- riage covenant between the Pope and the church, between the clergy ("doctores") and *ecclesia*. The Marian commentaries center on the fact of Mary's espousal by God as a basis for imitating her. The mystical expositions link the Song to each one's personal experience of union with God, both in the present and in the life to come. The historicity of Solomon's marriage, in short, makes it imitable in the form of other marriages and therefore rhetorically potent.

Origen, as we have noted, values the Song primarily as an *alle- goria* whose hidden meaning, once it has been discovered, has a didactic benefit that compensates for its potentially dangerous literal modality. He loves the Song for what it does not say, rather than for what it does. The twelfth-century exegetes, on the other hand, tend to value the Song for the affects it awakens, the example it sets, the images it provides for the communication of personal and commu- nal experiences.[53] Their commentaries prepared the way for, and actually initiated, the literary imitation of the Song by the Christian poets of the later Middle Ages. Indeed, from the twelfth century on,

53. Cf. Wesley Trimpi's comment on the characteristic difference between dialec- ticians and rhetoricians in "The Ancient Hypothesis of Fiction," *Traditio* 27 (1971): 64. See also Michael Murrin, *The Veil of Allegory: Some Notes toward a Theory of Allegorical Rhetoric in the English Renaissance* (1969).

the *Canticum* stands as the most notable example of a biblical poem that exerted an incontestable formal and inspirational influence on contemporary literary composition, both profane and devotional.[54]

In this study I examine several Middle English devotional works—*Pearl*, the writings of Richard Rolle, the religious lyrics, and the York cycle plays—to demonstrate the influence of the Song on a variety of literary genres. Taken together, these interpretive and imitative texts provide evidence of a holistic, emotive-and-rational medieval response to the Song of Songs which rests upon a recognition of, and cooperation with, its markedly rhetorical *modus agendi*.

Only after centuries of exegetical enterprise had sufficiently exposed and formulated the allegory embedded in the letter of the Song could commentators and practicing poets alike reverse the process, descending along the line of ascent, clothing the "spirit" of the *Canticum* anew in its corporeal imagery, joining what allegoresis had separated.[55] In doing so, Christian writers found their proper identity as imitators of the divine Poet who had authored the Song originally, presenting spiritual love, as William of St. Thierry says,

---

54. Among the recent studies of the influence exerted by the Song in the composition of poetry, see R. E. Kaske, "The *Canticum Canticorum* in The Miller's Tale," *SP* 59 (1962): 479–500; Peter Dronke, *Medieval Latin and the Rise of European Love-Lyric*, vols. I and II (1965–66); J. I. Wimsatt, "Chaucer and the Canticle of Canticles," in *Chaucer the Love Poet*, ed. Jerome Mitchell and William Provost (1973); Theresa Anne Moritz, "Married Love and Incarnational Imagery: Bernard of Clairvaux's *Sermones super Cantica Canticorum* within Medieval Spirituality as a Model for Love Allegory in Chaucer's *Canterbury Tales*" (diss., University of Toronto, 1981); E. Ann Matter, "*The Voice of My Beloved*": *The Song of Songs in Western Medieval Christianity* (1990); Mark Infusino, "The Virgin Mary and the Song of Songs in Medieval English Literature" (diss., University of California–Los Angeles, 1988).

55. As Jon Whitman has demonstrated recently, there are two inverse allegorical traditions. Allegoresis, beginning with the Stoic interpretation of Homer and systematized as a method of scriptural exegesis by Philo and Origen, predicates a movement away from the literal meaning to its derived philosophical or dogmatic *sententia*. Compositional allegory, on the other hand, characteristically (but not always) "personifies abstract concepts and fashions a narrative around them," moving from truths to fictions, from philosophy to poetry. See *Allegory: The Dynamics of an Ancient and Medieval Technique* (1987), pp. 1–5. Whitman's categories recall the similar allegoresis/allegory distinction made by Maureen Quilligan in *The Language of Allegory* (1979). Both Whitman and Quilligan join with Carolynn Van Dyke (*The Fiction of Truth: Structures of Meaning in Narrative and Dramatic Allegory* [1985]) and others in a redefinition of allegory that militates against the old Romantic symbol/allegory opposition. My book continues that enterprise by exploring the rhetorical presence of the Other in medieval interpretations and imitations of the Song of Songs.

"in images borrowed from the love of the flesh."[56] By joining tenor and vehicle, gloss and letter, poets could create a new, incarnational art form imitative not only of the biblical Word but of the Word-Made-Flesh. At the same time they could share in God's own rhetorical aim: the wooing of humankind, the eliciting of the *affectus*, the fructifying of the bridal self in its various forms.

56. William of St. Thierry, *Exposition on the Song of Songs*, trans. Mother Columba Hart (1970), p. 18.

I

The Song of Songs
Ad Litteram

I have suggested that the emotive force of the Song's literal meaning became an essential part of the rhetoric of a new, fourfold
wave of affective interpretation in the twelfth century. Before turning (in the next two chapters) to the practical criticism of those
readings, however, we need to consider how the theoretical understanding of the Song's *sensus litteralis* first laid the basis for, and then
accommodated descriptively, the innovative praxis of the exegetes.

The problem of the Song *ad litteram* is twofold. First of all, there is
the issue of authorial intent. Did Solomon intend the Song to be read
literally (in which case, he simply composed an erotic poem), or did
he write the Song as an allegory, intending its words to be understood "aliter quam scripta sunt"? Is the Song the libidinous outpour-
ing of the old Solomon, a king given over to womanizing and
idolatry? Or is it the prophetic utterance of the young Solomon, the
lover of wisdom?[1]

The *accessus* that introduce the various commentaries on the Song

---

1. According to the account in 3 Kings (1 Kings) 11:1–8, Solomon had seven
hundred wives and three hundred concubines. Augustine comments on the scriptural
censure of Solomon in *De Doctrina Christiana* III.xxi.31. Solomon's early career,
however, testifies to his great wisdom (see 3 Kings [1 Kings] 3–10), and Dante
includes him among the saints in the sphere of the sun in *Paradiso* X. The issue of
authorial intent in the case of the Song parallels the problem the Stoics faced in their
interpretation of Homer. See J. Tate's discussion of historic vs. intrinsic interpretation
in "On the History of Allegorism," *Classical Quarterly* 28 (1934): 105–14.

partially circumvent the question by stressing divine inspiration over human intent.[2] At the same time, however, the exegetes call attention to Solomon's surpassing wisdom. Honorius of Autun, for instance, writes: "Auctor libri hujus est Spiritus Sanctus, loquens per vas sapientiae, Salomonem, hujus libri scriptorem, qui fuit rex sapientissimus et propheta praecipuus."[3] After distinguishing between the Holy Spirit as author ("auctor") and Solomon as scribe ("scriptor"), Honorius goes on to classify Solomon's three books (Proverbs, Ecclesiastes, and the Song of Songs) according to the three divisions of philosophy, indicating that Solomon wrote the Song after he had advanced through a knowledge of creatures (ethics and physics, shown in Proverbs and Ecclesiastes, respectively) to the knowledge of God himself (logic or theology) in the Song.[4] The implication, of course, is that Solomon, as an outstanding prophet and the wisest of kings, had at least a glimmer of the Song's true subject and wrote his epithalamium (as Isidore of Seville says) "in laudem Ecclesiae et Christi."[5]

The history of Solomon's reign, moreover, invested him with typological authority so that he, in the *persona* of the Bridegroom, could appropriately prefigure Christ. As the *Glossa* indicates, Solomon resembles the great Prince of Peace "quia in regno ejus pax per quam futura pax Ecclesiae figurabatur."[6] Indeed, *Pacificus* (the Peace-

2. See A. J. Minnis, *Medieval Theory of Authorship*, 2d ed. (1988), pp. 47–48. For a discussion of the *accessus* to the Song as a school for symbolic thinking, see Jean Leclercq, *Monks and Love in Twelfth-Century France* (1979), pp. 40–44.

3. Honorius of Autun, *Expositio in Cantica Canticorum*, PL 172, c347. Subsequent references to this work are given parenthetically.

4. Honorius connects Canticles with logic because of Solomon's intent to teach the rational soul how to be joined to God through love. He cites as proof the verse "Fortis est ut mors dilectio" (Cant. 8:6). Later, in the second prologue to the *Expositio*, he repeats the ethics/Proverbs, physics/Ecclesiastes formulation, but substitutes "theology" for "logic" as the teaching of Solomon in the Song (PL 172, c356). Origen uses both logic and enoptics to characterize the Song. He associates logic with the use of reason required to discover "the meanings and proper significances" of language, especially when "one thing is openly said, and another is inwardly meant." He uses enoptics or inspection to characterize the process "by which we go beyond things seen and contemplate somewhat of things divine." See *The Song of Songs: Commentary and Homilies*, trans. R. P. Lawson (1957), pp. 40–46.

5. Isidore of Seville, *Etymologiarum* I, PL 82, c120. See Augustine's discussion of the spiritually minded men of the Old Testament in *De Doctrina Christiana* III.ix.13. He observes that, lacking the fullness of revelation, they nevertheless understood that their ritual observances and sacred texts were signs pointing beyond themselves.

6. *Glossa Ordinaria*, PL 113, c1127. Subsequent references are parenthetical.

ful One) is one of Solomon's three names, the title under which he penned the *Canticum*.[7]

The same bifurcation—lecher or prophet—that informs the question of authorial intent also characterizes the problem of reader response. In part the exegetes attempt to avert the danger of a too literal reading by limiting the Song's audience to spiritually minded men. Rabanus Maurus, Isidore of Seville, Saint Jerome, and others follow the Jewish tradition in restricting its audience to those who were at least thirty years old and who had previously studied the other books of the biblical canon.[8] The *Glossa* indicates that only a man of perfect knowledge and oaken faith ("perfectae scientiae et roboratae fidei") should read the *Canticum*, lest anyone be stirred to merely fleshly desires ("ad concupiscentias corporales") by its carnal images (see PL 113, c1127).

Such warnings, however, clearly do not prevent the possibility of abuse. The lecherous old January in Chaucer's "Merchant's Tale," for instance, gives the Song a definitively literal reading when he paraphrases it for May as an invitation to marital sex that is, in intent and practice, no more than legally sanctioned fornication: "Rys up, my wyf, my love, my lady free!"[9] The exegetes recognized (as Chaucer did) that a merely literal reading would, in fact, reduce the biblical text to "olde lewed wordes."[10] Old January is a clear example of the carnally minded reader who mistakes a figurative text for a literal one. To him, and to others like him, the oft-quoted verse applies: "Littera occidit, spiritus autem vivificat" (2 Corinth. 3:6).

Even the spiritually minded reader, however, is likely to have his difficulties with the Song *ad litteram*. As Pseudo-Richard of St. Victor, following Gregory the Great, observes,

ex sermonibus hujus amoris discimus, hujus amoris qua virtute in Divinitatis amore ferveamus. Hoc autem nobis solerter intuendum est, ne cum verba exterioris amoris audimus, ad exteriora sen-

7. See Hugh of St. Victor, *Didascalicon* IV.8, trans. Jerome Taylor (1961, repr. 1968), p. 109. Origen includes a similar discussion of Solomon's names in the prologue to his commentary.

8. See Jerome, *Prologus in Hiezechielem*, CCSL 75, pp. 3–4.

9. Geoffrey Chaucer, "The Merchant's Tale," in *The Riverside Chaucer*, ed. Larry D. Benson, 3d ed. (1987), IV.2138.

10. Ibid., l. 2149.

tienda remaneamus, et machina quae ponitur ut levet ipsa magis
opprimat ne levemur. Debemus ergo in verbis istis corporeis, in
verbis exterioribus, quidquid interius est quaerere, et loquentes de
corpore, quasi extra corpus fieri.[11]

[We learn from the words of this love; by the power of this love we
burn in the love of the Divinity. We must consider this repeatedly,
however, lest when we hear the words of outward love, we remain
with the superficial understanding, and that apparatus which is set
in place to elevate us itself weighs us down the more lest we be
raised up. We ought, therefore, to seek some inner reality in these
corporeal words, in these outer words, and come to be, as it were,
beyond the body while speaking about it.]

The letter clearly must be read. We learn from it ("discimus") and it
serves to kindle our love for God. The difficulty consists, as Hugh of
St. Victor suggests, in reading the letter without reading according
to the letter ("litteram legimus, sed non secundum litteram"); in
remembering the divine reference; in joining the letter and the spirit
in an integral reading experience.[12]

What is the difference between reading the letter ("litteram legimus") and reading according to the letter ("secundum litteram")? To
read the letter, the "historia" of a text, Hugh indicates, is to understand the words at face value ("primo loco ex significatione ver-
borum");[13] to be able to recount the story they tell ("rerum ges-
tarum narratio, quae in prima significatione litterae continetur")
with reference to who, what, when, and where: "persona, negotium, tempus, et locus."[14] Reading the letter becomes reading "secundum litteram" if one stops there. The letter should be the basis
for interpretation (the recognition of *allegoria*) and application (*tropologia*).

11. Pseudo-Richard of St. Victor, *Explicatio in Cantica Canticorum*, PL 196, c405.
Subsequent references are parenthetical.
12. I am adapting for the purposes of this discussion the wordplay of Hugh of St.
Victor in *De Scripturis et Scriptoribus Sacris* (PL 175, c13). He charges his opponents
with reading the letter according to the allegory, instead of basing their interpretation
solidly on literal meaning.
13. Ibid., c12.
14. Hugh of St. Victor, *De Sacramentis*, PL 176, c185; *Didascalicon* VI.iii, PL 176,
c799. Subsequent references to these works are parenthetical.

As Hugh of St. Victor expresses it in *De Sacramentis*, the various levels of meaning are interrelated as "factum," as history. The literal happening should call to mind an analogous historical event: "allegoria est cum per id quod factum dicitur aliquid aliud factum sive in praeterito sive in praesenti sive in futuro." Through the parallel between the literal and the allegorical "factum," readers should learn what they need to do: "tropologia est cum per id quod factum dicitur, aliquid faciendum esse significatur" (PL 176, c1185).

Hugh's historical understanding of the various levels of meaning is, in part, a twelfth-century reaction against the primarily spiritualistic mode of exegesis associated with Origen and his followers. Hugh holds that "historia" always means *something more* than what it says (as a temporal foreshadowing, factual allegory, type, or *figura*).[15] For Origen, on the other hand, the text generally means *something else*. As we have seen, Origen's answer to the problem of literal meaning was to discover in the words of the Song homonyms ("homonymias") and thus derive an allegory based on *verba*, not *res*. He considered the text primarily as an instance of figurative speech that portends many things, as Tertullian says, "per aenigmata et allegorias et parabolas, aliter intelligenda quam scripta sunt."[16] The literal Song is for Origen a kind of code requiring decipherment, not a prefiguration of other nuptials.

Origen, however, laid the basis for a figural reading of the Song simply by affirming that the Song was originally composed by King Solomon as an epithalamium: "Epithalamium libellus hic, id est nuptiale carmen, dramatis in modum mihi videtur a Salomone conscriptus."[17] Albeit brief and ambiguous about the actual occasion of composition, Origen's comment led twelfth-century exegetes to

15. For treatments of biblical typology, see A. C. Charity, *Events and Their Afterlife: The Dialectics of Christian Typology in the Bible and Dante* (1966); Holly Wallace Boucher, "Metonymy in Typology and Allegory, with a Consideration of Dante's *Comedy*," in *Allegory, Myth, and Symbol*, ed. Morton W. Bloomfield, Harvard English Studies 9 (1981), pp. 129–45; Erich Auerbach, "Figura," trans. Ralph Manheim, in *Scenes from the Drama of European Literature: Six Essays* (1959, repr. 1973), pp. 11–76.
16. Tertullian, *Adversus Marcionem*, PL 2, c326. Philip Rollinson observes that the Christian understanding of allegory always tended toward one of two poles, *res* or *verba*, with *res* (and its typological implications) dominating. Cf. *Classical Theories of Allegory and Christian Culture* (1981), p. ix.
17. Origen, *In Canticum Canticorum*, trans. Rufinus, PG 13, c61–62.

affirm that Solomon drew inspiration for the Song from his historical marriage to Pharoah's daughter (see 3 Kings [1 Kings] 3:1).
William of St. Thierry, for example, gives an imaginative summary
of the *sensus litteralis*:

> Propositi vero dramatis historialis, fabulae seu parabolae, hoc pot-
> est esse argumentum: Rex Salomon filiam Pharaonis aegyptii duxit
> uxorem. Cui primo sponsalis et amoris et osculi aliquantam grat-
> iam indulsit, deinde vero post ostensas ei ex parte divitias et partem
> gloriae suae, et a mutua conjunctione et ab osculi gratia eam
> amovit, donec aegyptia nigredine deposita, barbarae nationis exuta
> consuetudine, digna fierit, quae ad thalamum regium admittere-
> tur.[18]

> [Now the argument of the historical drama, fable, or parable
> proposed, may be stated as follows: King Solomon took to wife
> the daughter of the Pharoah of Egypt. At first he granted her
> certain favors of the bridal bed and of love and of the kiss. Then,
> after having shown her part of his riches and part of his glory, he
> cast her forth from their mutual union and the favor of the kiss
> until, by riddance of her Egyptian blackness and rejection of the
> customs of a barbarous nation, she might become worthy of access
> to the royal bedchamber.][19]

When William articulates the literal love story ("dramatis histo-
rialis argumentum"), he affords it figural importance. As a historical
"factum," Solomon's marriage resembles, antedates, and finds its
proper meaning in relation to other marriages included in the spiritual *sensus*. In William's commentary, in particular, Solomon's story
reifies as a romance the allegory of the soul's response to prevenient
grace and subsequent trial and purification; at the same time, the
allegorical marriage sacramentalizes the union of Solomon and the
swarthy princess.

As a foreshadowing of the marriage between Christ and *ecclesia*,
sexual union in the Song of Songs was understood to have the same
typological function as the union foretold in Genesis 2:24: "Erunt

18. Guillaume de St. Thierry, *Commentaire sur le Cantique des Cantiques*, ed. and
trans. P. Robert Thomas, O.C.S.O., Collection Pain de Citeaux (1961), pp. 36–38.
19. Cited and translated by Minnis, p. 48.

duo in carne una"—the Old Testament text cited by Saint Paul in Ephesians 5 in the context of a pastoral address to married couples. Thus contemporary theological writings about Christian marriage—notably Hugh of St. Victor's *De Sacramentis*—draw upon the long allegorical tradition associated with the Song to unfold the sacramental understanding of conjugal love as a great sign ("sacramentum hoc magnum") of Christ's espousal of the church.[20] Rupert of Deutz, for instance, identifies the bridal party at Cana with the *dramatis personae* of Solomon's Song,[21] and Pope Innocent III's treatise on matrimony includes a fourfold *distinctio* of marriages that corresponds to the listing in the *accessus* to Honorius of Autun's exposition of Canticles.[22]

In the first prologue to his *Expositio*, Honorius dwells at length on the typological character of the Song's subject matter, stating that the work deals with the nuptials that take place ("agit de nuptiis quae fiunt") at each of the four levels of application: historical, allegorical, tropological, and anagogical. Historical marriages, he says, include those of espousal only ("sola desponsatione"), like that of Mary and Joseph, and those physically consummated "as, for instance, that of Solomon and Pharaoh's daughter, whom he coupled to himself by right of matrimony, and whose home he built, adorned with gold and gems" (PL 172, c349: "ut Salomonis et filiae Pharaonis, quam sibi jure copulavit matrimonii, cujus domum auro gemmisque decoratam aedificavit"). He goes on to show how this literal/historical marriage can assimilate all the other marriages related to it by way of analogy: the allegorical marriages (by which the Son joins himself to a human body in the Incarnation, and to his mystical body, the church); the tropological (by which the higher powers of the soul couple with the lower); and the anagogical (by which Christ's

20. See Johan Chydenius, "Medieval Institutions and the Old Testament," in *Commentationes Humanarum Litterarum* 37 (1965): 13, 99–101, 119–21. Chydenius observes that the symbolic interpretation of Old Testament marriage presented by Hugh of St. Victor is identical with the view presented in the Canticles commentaries. He argues that the typological interest in Old Testament figures and ritual actions during the twelfth century promoted a shift in the tone and character of the contemporary expositions of the Song of Songs—a shift that influenced, in turn, the developing theology of marriage as a sacrament.

21. Rupert of Deutz, *Commentum in Joan* II, PL 169, c285.

22. Compare Innocent III, *De Quadripartita Specie Nuptiarum*, PL 217, c923–68, with Honorius, *Expositio*, PL 172, c349.

glorified body is raised to heaven and the church enters into the *visio beata*: "quo adhuc post resurrectionem totam Ecclesiam in visione deitatis suae gloriae copulavit"). Finally Honorius reaffirms his initial observation that Solomon's *Canticum Canticorum* is actually about *all* of these marriages, that is, that the other meanings are included in the literal one: "De his nuptiis materia hujus libri contexitur" (PL 172, c349–50).

The second prologue to Honorius' *Expositio* provides an imaginative application of this kind of typological understanding of the Song. In it he retells all of biblical history as a love story in which a woman, betrothed to the Prince of Heaven, offends him by giving away his love token, the jewel of obedience, to a jealous rival. Expelled from paradise, she wanders through the world and through the ages, hoping to regain the lost ornament, and with it, the favor of her Prince. The woman takes on in succession the forms of Sarah, Rebecca, Leah, Israel, and *ecclesia*. The Prince, in turn, manifests his abiding love for her in the human forms of the individual patriarchs and prophets—among them, Abraham, Isaac, Jacob, and Solomon—coming in the end to win the jewel back for her himself and adorning her with it. Honorius's prologue displays a distinct tendency to use real, historical couples—Abraham and Sarah, Jacob and Rachel, Solomon and Pharaoh's daughter—as embodiments of the divine/human relationship finally sealed in Christ's love for the church. The Old Testament *figurae* of divine love foreshadow the great Christological Incarnation and the final, celestial consummation of divine/human love. Honorius concludes with a reference to the *Canticum* which superimposes upon it the whole of the Bible: "about these actions, about these ages, about these times, and of such a bride, the book of this Scripture is composed" (PL 172, c358: "De his actibus, de his aetatibus, de his temporibus, talis sponsae contextitur liber hujus Scripturae").

The perceived power of the *Canticum* to convey the whole of salvation history, culminating in the supratemporal Wedding Feast, leads both Honorius and Hugh of St. Victor to classify the Song as one of the holy books ("agiographia") of the Bible dealing with eternal things. Inspired by the variant listings traditional among the Jews, Honorius lists seven "agiographia"—Job, David, Proverbs, Ecclesiastes, Canticles, Wisdom, and Sirach—corresponding to the seven gifts of the Holy Spirit: wisdom, understanding, counsel, fortitude, knowledge, piety, and fear. As the book of knowledge, the *Canticum* contains the knowledge of the whole Scripture ("scientia totius Scripturae Canticis includitur"), its subject being the twofold *dilectio* of God and neighbor which fulfills the law and the prophets (PL 172, c350–51).

Honorius then proceeds to relate the *Canticum*'s position as the fifth hagiograph to the five stages in sexual love: (1) seeing the beloved (analogous to God's Covenant with Abraham); (2) speaking with her (analogous to God's conversation with his people through Moses and the prophets); (3) touching her (analogous to Christ's Incarnation and historical life); (4) kissing her (analogous to the gift of peace given the disciples by the risen Lord); and (5) having intercourse with her (analogous to the perfect union enjoyed in heaven). The temporal reference of the five stages, as given by Honorius, suggests that the present-tense lyric utterance of the *Canticum* has the quality of an eternal present, assimilating not only the past events of the Old and New Testaments and the contemporary lives of Christians, but also the celestial, divine, and human consummation of love in the afterlife.

With reference to the latter, the Song of Songs is literally anagogy, a preview of heaven like Saint John's apocalyptic vision of the Bride and the Lamb. Indeed, there seems to have been a traditional association of the *Canticum* with the "new song" sung by the saints in the heavenly Jerusalem. Rupert of Deutz, for instance, relates that he was urged to undertake his own exposition by a certain holy brother who had seen our Lord Jesus himself, sitting above the altar on a throne, surrounded by the saints, and holding Solomon's book ("tenentem Cantica Canticorum") as an outward sign of the celestial music of love.[23]

In *Benjamin Minor*, Richard of St. Victor also cites the Song of Songs as a visionary book. In his interpretation of Jacob's oracular blessing of his sons Nephtalim and Dan (Genesis 49:16–17, 21), Richard explains that Nephtalim is chosen to strengthen the vir-

23. Rupert of Deutz, *Commentaria in Cantica Canticorum*, PL 168, c837–38. See Patrick S. Diehl, *The Medieval European Religious Lyric: An Ars Poetica* (1985), p. 192, for a comment on the apocalyptic "new song" as an inspiring ideal for Christian poetic in the Middle Ages.

tuous through representations of heavenly bliss (such as we find in the *Canticum*), whereas Dan is selected for the work of countering temptations in the weak through depictions of hellish torment.[24]

Richard's treatment of the Song reflects and augments the general twelfth-century tendency to read the Song typologically, to re-historicize and reliteralize it. As a blissful experience, Solomon's marriage to Pharoah's daughter foreshadows the happiness to be enjoyed in heaven in union with God and reifies it—so much so that the Song becomes a kind of enticing promise; its rhetoric, a rhetoric of anticipated rewards. Indeed, Richard insists that the union of physical imagery with a spiritual tenor in the Song is perfectly fitted to the human nature of its auditors, who are destined to share in the bliss of heaven with body and soul and who respond naturally to sensory pleasure:

Fortassis hoc per exempla evidentius ostendemus, persuadebimus plenius. Vultis audire eloquia pulchritudinis, eloquia suavitatis, plena decore, plena dulcedine, qualia Nephtalim formare con- suevit, vel qualia eum formare convenit: *Osculetur me*, inquit, *osculo oris sui* (Cant. I). *Fulcite me floribus, stipate me malis, quia amore langueo* (Cant. II). *Favus distillans labia tua, mel et lac sub lingua tua, et odor vestimentorum tuorum sicut odor thuris* (Cant. IV). Quid, quaeso, dulcius hujusmodi eloquiis, quid jucundius invenitur? Quid talibus eloquiis libentius, quid avidius auditur? Ista verba carnale aliquid sonare videntur, et tamen spiritualia sunt quae per ipsa describun- tur. Sic novit Nephtalim carnalia cum spiritualibus permiscere, et per corporalia incorporea describere, ut utraque hominis natura in ejus dictis inveniat unde se mirabiliter reficiat qui ex corporea et incorporea natura constat. (PL 196, c16–17)

[Perhaps if we show this more clearly through examples, we will persuade you more completely. You want to hear expressions of beauty, speeches of sweetness, completely decorous and delight- ful, such as Nephtalim was wont to form, or that it suited him to compose: *Let him kiss me*, she says, *with the kiss of his mouth* (Cant. I). *Sustain me with flowers, brace me with apples, because I languish for love* (Cant. II). *Your lips are distilling honeycomb, honey and milk are*

24. Richard of St. Victor, *Benjamin Minor* 24, PL 196, c16–17. Subsequent refer- ences are parenthetical.

under your tongue, and the scent of your garments is like the fragrance of incense (Cant. IV). What, I ask, is found to be sweeter, what more pleasing, than eloquence of this kind? What is heard more willingly, more eagerly, than such speeches? These words seem to say something carnal—and yet they are spiritual things which are described through these very words. Thus Nephtalim knew how to intermingle carnal things with spiritual things, and how to describe incorporeal realities through corporeal ones, so that the nature of man might find a twofold source whence he wondrously refreshes himself—he who by nature consists of body and soul.]

This passage from Richard is notable for the stress it places on the rhetorical force of the *Canticum*'s images that awaken longings in one's body and soul for the bliss of heaven, which far surpasses the comparable happiness ("totum per similitudinem") known on earth. In the context of Richard's whole discussion of the rational imagination directed by Nephtalim as the prophet of paradise, the lovemaking of the *Canticum* is similar to the vision of the bejewelled Jerusalem, and the description of the Promised Land, flowing with milk and honey, full of flowers and musical with bird song, in its arousal of human concupiscence: "For they describe invisible things through the forms of visible things, and imprint the memory of them on our minds through the beauty of their desirable appearances" (PL 196, c10–11: "Res enim invisibiles, per rerum visibilium formas describunt, et earum memoriam per quarumdam concupiscibilium specierum pulchritudinem mentibus nostris imprimunt").

Similarly, the *Brevis Commentatio*, attributed to William of St. Thierry, insists that the human mind comes to understand the quality of divine love and the nature of invisible things through the words and visible signs of human sexual love:

In omni enim carnali affectione nihil dulcius, nihil solet esse desiderabilius conjunctione sponsae ad sponsum; in spirituali vero, creati spiritus ad increatum. Ibi enim de duabus una caro; hic autem de duobus unus spiritus efficitur. Unde ducta similitudine de carnalibus ad spiritualia, de humanis ad divina, describitur hic sponsus et sponsa, Christus et Ecclesia, vel quaelibet sancta anima . . . jam anhelat ad tertium.[25]

25. *Brevis Commentatio*, PL 184, c411.

[For in the total affection of the flesh there is wont to be nothing more desirable, nothing sweeter, than the union of the bride with the bridegroom; in the spiritual sense, truly there is nothing sweeter than the joining of the created spirit with the Uncreated. For there one body is made from two; here, moreover, one spirit is brought about from two. Hence, led by similitude from carnal realities to spiritual ones, from the human to the divine, from the bridegroom and bride described here to Christ and the church or, if you will, a holy soul . . . she now pants for the third [degree of love].]

Pseudo-Richard of St. Victor echoes Gregory the Great when he describes the Song as a "machina" that leads the reader from a lower to a higher love through the words of love ("per verba amoris") which evoke natural sexual desire:

In hoc libro qui Canticum Canticorum conscriptus est, amoris quasi corporei verba ponuntur ut a corpore suo anima per ser-mones suae consuetudinis refricata, recalescat, et per verba amoris qui infra est, excitetur ad amorem qui supra est. Nominantur enim in hoc libro oscula, nominantur ubera, nominantur genae, nomi-nantur femora. In quibus verbis non irridenda est sacra Scriptura, sed amplior Dei misericordia consideranda est; quia dum membra corporis nominat, sic ad amorem vocat. (PL 196, c405)

[In this book entitled the Song of Songs, words of carnal love are placed so that from its own body the soul, renewed, regains its heat through speeches of its own customary usage, and is stirred to a love that is above through the words of a love that is below. For in this book kisses are named, breasts are named, cheeks are named, thighs are named—in which words the sacred Scriptures are not to be mocked, but the mercy of God is all the more to be considered, because while he names the members of the body, he thus calls the soul to love.]

The language of passages like these stresses affection, sweetness, desire, heat, and passion; admits the rhetorical impact of carnal imagery; and affirms a strong similarity between sexual oneness with a human spouse and spiritual oneness with God. Indeed,

Pseudo-Richard of St. Victor describes the *Canticum* as the wooing of God:

> In hoc ergo libro Dominus et Ecclesia, non Dominus et ancilla, sed sponsus nominatur, et sponsa, ut non solum timori, non solum reverentiae, sed etiam amori deserviatur et in his verbis exterioribus incitetur affectus interior. (PL 196, c408)

> [In this book the Lord and the church are named, not as Lord and handmaid but as Bridegroom and Bride, so that he might become the object not only of fear, not only of reverence, but also of love, and in these outer words an inner affect [of love] is aroused.]

Saint Bernard, too, stresses that God names himself a Bridegroom in the *Canticum*—rather than Father, Teacher, or Master—because he desires the soul to respond to his call with the appropriate emotion, the *affectus* of a Bride.[26]

Aiming to win the affectionate love of his creatures, longing to complete and perfect them by drawing them close to himself in a spiritual marriage, the divine Author draws attention to the bodily forms that, by their sexual nature, mirror and express the metaphysical need for complementarity. At the same time he renders those images transparent by illuminating them from behind, as it were, in the words of the gloss that names their tenor. The emotive response stimulated by corporeal imagery thus passes over into the auditor's relationship with God as a laudable desire for him ("laudabilis concupiscentia") and for the bliss of heaven. The divine Object of love, who surpasses all merely earthly objects of attachment, in this way confirms the sensual images in both their similarity and dissimilarity to him, while using them to bring about an organic emotional transference of the *affectus*.

Responding to God's wooing means responding to the Song *ad litteram* without losing sight of the divine Object of love. Thus the *Glossa* addresses the reader as "tu" with the imperative: "Learn to carry the emotional impulse of your soul and the fire of natural love across to better things" (PL 113, c1128: "Disce motum animae tuae

26. See Etienne Gilson, *The Mystical Theology of St. Bernard*, trans. A. H. C. Downes (1940, repr. 1955), p. 101.

et naturalis amoris incendium ad meliora transferre"). Pseudo-Richard of St. Victor points to the same sublimation in a play of words: "We ought to pass over to impassible virtue through these words of passion" ("Debemus per haec verba passionis transire ad virtutem impassibilitatis").[27] He goes on to liken the successful reader of the *Canticum* to the "nova creatura in Christo," the fully redeemed personality: "because in our resurrection the body is so joined to the spirit that everything that had been of passion is taken up into the virtue of the spirit" (PL 196, c407: "quia in resurrectione nostra, ita corpus spiritui adnectitur, ut omne quod fuerat passionis in virtute spiritus assumatur").

An integral response to the Song, such as Pseudo-Richard envisions, presupposes a specific method of reading. The lower, affective powers of the soul should be joined to the higher so that the *affectus* of love for God, grown strong, loses all the transitoriness of mere passion and becomes invulnerable, impassible, enduring, stronger than death. In order to assist that inward coupling, the reader needs to join together in his or her perception the body and soul of the text, its carnal and spiritual senses.

The play of mind which moves back and forth, verse by verse, from the text to its allegorical exposition, joining image to gloss, prevents the reader from forgetting the ultimate context in which the Song is to be understood and in which marriage becomes a sacrament. It provides the necessary ongoing reminders ("hoc autem solerter intuendum est") that the end of all our loves is the ardent love of God. The reading process thus becomes safe, for the possibility of remaining with the literal, carnal meaning alone ("ad exteriora sentienda") is averted. The reader is forced to interpret and read at the same time, moving slowly along the literal surface while the gaze is repeatedly directed upward. Thus the reading process, like the progress into the world, into *carnalia*, involves making successive connections from below to above. Joining the letter of the

27. Pseudo-Richard of St. Victor, *Explicatio*, PL 196, c406. Caroline Walker Bynum has pointed out (in a keynote address at the May 1988 International Medieval Congress at Kalamazoo, Mich.) that "impassibility" is one of the four qualities of the resurrected human body, and that the term is used regularly in medieval theological discussions to designate freedom from suffering in the glorified state. See also Bynum, "The Female Body and Religious Practice in the Later Middle Ages," in *Zone 3: Fragments for a History of the Human Body* 1, ed. Michel Feher, Ramona Naddaff, and Nadia Tazi (1989), pp. 160–219.

Song to its allegory, its verbalized otherness, insures that the central image of sexual union will remain a *figura*, a dissimilar similitude, a prophecy of paradise.

The two-in-oneness of the Song's letter and gloss enables it to communicate the affective quality of the relationship between Christ and his Bride. Indeed, far from sensing any disparity between the Song's literal meaning (carnal love) and its allegorical *sensus* (the love of God), Giles of Rome insists that the Song exemplifies a perfect oneness of form and content, both of them characterized by the same sensible quality of sweetness:

> Unde et glossa tenet quod modus huius libri est ostensivus quali desiderio membra capiti adhaereant, et ei placere contendant, et quali affectione sponsus ecclesiam diligat. Unde modus agendi huius libri convenienter notatur per huiusmodi dulcedinem, cum dicit, (Vox tua dulcis.) quia complacentia, affectio, et desiderium, quandam dulcedinem amoris important. Et hoc etiam potest haberi forma tractatus, quae talis debet esse, quale requirit modus agendi, immo quia ipse ordo capitulorum adinvicem bene intellectus animam demulcet et delectat, non inconvenienter forma tractatus per dulcedinem intelligitur.

> [Thus the glossa says that the mode of this book is to show with what desire the members cling to the head, and contend to please Him, and with what affection the husband loves the Church. Therefore the mode of doing of this book can be conveniently defined in terms of this sweetness, when he says, 'Your voice is sweet,' because pleasure, affection, and desire imply a certain sweetness of love. From this is also found the form of the treatise, which must be what the mode of doing requires, because the very order of the chapters one after the other, when well understood, soothes and delights the soul. So it is fitting that the form of the treatise be understood as the effect of sweetness.][28]

The exact fit ("convenienter") of the language to the message of the Song leads the expositors to treat the *Canticum* as a contempla-

28. Giles of Rome, *In Librum Solomonis Qui Cantica Canticorum Inscribitur Commentaria* (1555), f 2v, quoted by Judson Boyce Allen, *The Ethical Poetic of the Later Middle Ages: A Decorum of Convenient Distinction* (1982), pp. 91–92. The translation is his.

tive book through which one gains access to a personal encounter with God himself. Pseudo-Richard of St. Victor, for instance, plays upon the verbal analogy that likens the "Cantica Canticorum" to the "Sancta Sanctorum" (Holy of Holies) when he compares the biblical poetry to a tent or sanctuary with a hidden recess: "The Song of Songs is a secret, containing a certain holy mystery, which secret is penetrated through veiled understandings" (PL196, c407: "Ista Cantica Canticorum secretum, et quoddam solemne interius est, quod secretum in occultis intelligentiis penetratur"). He goes on to liken the three books of Solomon—Proverbs, Ecclesiastes, and the Canticle of Canticles—to the three-rung ladder of Jacob, at the top of which one is able to behold God himself: "ad extremum etiam Dei intima conspiciantur" (PL 196, c409). Using yet another image, he compares the poem as a whole to the liturgical season of Advent, the latter providing a temporal atmosphere, the former a linguistic space or context for the reader's private, contemplative vision of God: "so too the individual soul in a special way awaits the coming of God into his own soul, even as it looks for the Bridegroom's entry into the bedchamber" ("ut etiam specialiter unaquaeque anima ingressum Dei ad cor suum, tanquam aditum sponsi in thalamum conspiciat").

A prophetic text of this kind, which assimilates realities superseding its own power of expression, is never an isolated artifact. It requires completion; awaits its own fulfillment; draws God and humans alike into its space that they may occupy it and enter into the kind of mutual relationship proportioned by its amatory images. The *prima facie* meaning of the text is thus never something to be left behind. It remains the nexus that holds the other meanings in association with each other, the enclosing matrix that forms relationships of similitude and secures the union of things so related, the point of contact that provides the reader admission into a universe ordered analogically.[29] Its prophecy, in short, is fulfilled in—not solved by—the reader.

Thus Honorius of Autun, commenting on the equivocal nature of

---

29. For insightful discussions of the relationship between the horizontal and vertical dimensions of the text, see William F. Lynch, S.J., *Christ and Apollo: The Dimensions of the Literary Imagination* (1960), esp. pp. 133–60, 187–98; Stephen G. Nichols, Jr., *Romanesque Signs: Early Medieval Narrative and Iconography* (1983).

the word "canticum," observes that the poetic text of the Song is actually a verbal approximation of the essential quality of lives lived in union with God:

> Est autem canticum jucunditas mentis de aeternis, et intelligitur bona vita, per quam acquiritur jucunditas aeternae exsultationis. Et sciendum quod haec verba: "Osculetur me" (Cant. 1:1) non sunt canticum, sed de cantico agunt, quia bonam vitam justorum, quae in dilectione constat, canunt. Canticum quippe est vita justorum. Canticum canticorum est vita perfectorum. (PL 172, c350)

> [The canticle, moreover, is the joy of the mind concerning things eternal, and is understood to be the good life through which the sweetness of eternal exultation is acquired. And it must be observed that the words: "Let him kiss me" (Cant. 1:1) are not the canticle but treat of the canticle, because they sing the good life of the just which consists in loving. The life of the just is indeed a song; the life of perfect ones, the song of songs.]

Honorius's equation shows to what extent the *accessus* encourage the audience to appropriate the experience of love conveyed by the Song. That experience is rendered accessible to readers by the typology of the Bride-Bridegroom relationship, with its historical admission of new couplings, both in time and in the *anagogia* of eternity. The language of the Song itself, with its erotic images figuring forth the *amor Dei*, appeals directly to the human sense-nature in its sexual dimension. The reader's desire for ardent complementarity, with its ultimate trajectory toward metaphysical union with God, is immediately directed to the divine by the fusion of letter and gloss, text and interpretation, vehicle and tenor, in the reading process. The more contemplative that reading process, the more centered on the one Object of love, the more intoxicating and incantatory the words themselves become in their repetitive singularity of reference until the Song becomes, in rhetorical effect as well as in literary kind, a marriage song. Fusing together form and content, body and soul, letter and spirit, the *accessus* aim at uniting the auditor of the Song with its divine *Auctor* in a union of love—the "causa finalis" of the whole work.

2

The Exemplary Bride:
Ecclesia and Mary

As I have noted, Hugh of St. Victor conceived of allegory as a "factum" analogous to the "factum" of literal meaning. The two stories-in-parallel then become the basis for imitation ("faciendum") in the life of the auditor. This theoretical understanding helps to elucidate the practice in two twelfth-century streams of interpretation in which the Bride of the Song functions as *exemplum*. In the ecclesiastical commentaries, the situation of the contemporary church ("aliud factum in praesenti") parallels the "gesta" of Solomon's dramatized epithalamium, and the two, taken together, exert an appeal for historical involvement on the auditor's part. In the Marian expositions, the "historia" of Solomon's Bride recalls the biography of Mary ("aliud factum in praeterito"), and the two histories, fused into one through a kind of rhetorical superimposition, seek their continuance in the action of the audience. In both the ecclesiastical and the Marian treatments, then, the historicized allegory of the Bride serves as a bridge, putting the Song's emotive letter in direct contact with people's lives as a moving moral force, engaging the *affectus*. As we shall see, depending on the Bride's allegorical background—political or evangelical—her portrait varies, and she appears in archetypal fashion as either Virgin or Mother to prefigure and invite our bridal response.

Bruno of Segni's late-eleventh-century commentary on the Song of Songs gives a new answer to the question: "Who is the Bride?" For Bruno (d. 1123) and his contemporaries John of Mantua and

Robert of Tumbalenia, the Bride is not merely the church; she is the contemporary church embroiled in the investiture controversy, the faithful Virgin-Bride whose loyalty to Christ and his vicar, Gregory VII, exposes her to the persecution of Henry IV.[1] Bruno is not as politically explicit as John of Mantua, who likens the Countess Matilda of Tuscany to the Bride;[2] nor does he denounce heretics in the vitriolic terms used by Robert of Tumbalenia (d. 1090);[3] nevertheless his work shares what Jean Leclercq calls the "underlying preoccupation"[4] with ecclesiastical politics evident in their polemical expositions. Bruno does not simply historicize the Song by urging its contemporary relevance, however; he valorizes the Song *ad litteram* by imitating its poetry in metrical verse and using its images in direct tropological appeals.[5]

The Marian exegetes also historicize the Bride's identity. Although, as Friedrich Ohly notes, earlier exegetes had laid the ground for a Marian interpretation of the *Canticum*,[6] no one prior to the twelfth century had ever interpreted the Song from the single viewpoint of Mary's historical relationship to Christ. Rupert of Deutz (d. 1129) was the first Christian exegete to do so, and his commentary, innovative in treatment and tone, marks a clear break with the past.[7]

---

1. See Geoffrey Barraclough, "The Investiture Contest and the German Constitution," in *The Origins of Modern Germany* (1946, repr. 1963), pp. 101–34, for a good treatment of the historical context.

2. John of Mantua dedicated his commentary on the Song (c. 1081–83) to the Countess Matilda, Rome's great patroness. In it he urges her to be like the Bride in her continued allegiance to the true Solomon, Christ's vicar Gregory. See Jean Leclercq, *Monks and Love in Twelfth-Century France* (1979), pp. 47–48.

3. Friedrich Ohly compares Bruno's work with the "anklagenden und aufrufenden Schrift des Robert von Tumbalenia" and attributes its relative mildness to the early date (c. 1078) of composition. See *Hohelied-Studien: Grundzüge einer Geschichte der Hoheliedauslegung des Abendlandes bis um 1200* (1958), p. 104. For a treatment of Robert's commentary, see Ohly, pp. 95–98.

4. Leclercq, p. 48. Cf. Ohly, pp. 96, 98, 105, 108. A staunch supporter of Gregory VII's program of reform, Bruno was imprisoned by Henry IV in 1082. Gregory's three successors—Victor III, Urban II, and Pascal II—all relied on Bruno's counsel. For biographical information, see the *New Catholic Encyclopedia*.

5. Ohly points to Bruno's work as proof of an awakening Western interest in the Song as a poetic model. See p. 105.

6. Ibid, p. 126. Ohly lists Ambrose, Jerome, Justus von Urgel, and Bede; two Carolingian writers, Paul the Deacon and Paschasius Radbertus; and Peter Damian, whose eleventh-century sermons delivered on Marian feasts took up the exegesis of the Songs.

7. For a fascinating study of Rupert's life and work, see John Van Engen, *Rupert of Deutz* (1983).

Shortly after Rupert completed his work, Honorius of Autun (d.
1156?) wrote his short Marian exposition of Canticles, *Sigillum
Beatae Mariae*.[8] In the second half of the century, Alain de Lille (d.
1202) dedicated his extended elucidation to Mary ("ad laudem De-
iparae Virginis Mariae"). Although Bernard of Clairvaux did not
write a specifically Marian commentary, he contributed greatly to
the popularity of the Marian understanding of the Song through his
sermons; and, as Penny Schine Gold observes, the "new, totally
Marian"[9] interpretation of the *Canticum* became common in the later
twelfth century.[10]

The identification of Mary with the Bride provided for a fusion of
letter and allegory in the reader's perception, because of the historicity of both. Using an architectural metaphor, Rupert of Deutz calls
the primary reference to Mary the foundation ("historiae sive rei
gestae . . . fundamentum") for the other levels of meaning, thus
joining it inseparably to the *fundamentum* of literal meaning.[11]
Mary's historical relationship to Christ establishes a narrative context in which the Song of Songs becomes literally true. As Alain de
Lille puts it, "It must be known that everything in this canticle
which is said about blessed Mary refers to her corporal or spiritual

8. Eva Matthews Sanford lists the *Sigillum* as Honorius's second work, postdat-
ing his widely circulated *Elucidarium*. See "Honorius, *Presbyter* and *Scholasticus*,"
Speculum 23 (1948): 407. Sanford considers the *Sigillum* a key text in the corpus of his
writings, briefly introducing themes that he expanded in his voluminous later treatises. Valerie Flint also considers the *Sigillum* a very early work. She opposes Ohly,
arguing that Honorius "did not follow Rupert, and did not imitate him." See Flint,
"The Chronology of the Works of Honorius Augustodunensis," *RB* 82 (1972): 215–
42; "The Commentaries of Honorius Augustodunensis on the Song of Songs," *RB* 84
(1974): 196–211. The general scholarly consensus is that the Marian commentaries of
Rupert and Honorius were probably written "at about the same time" but that
Rupert's holds place of precedence for its boldness, originality, and subsequent
influence. See Brian E. Daley, "The 'Closed Garden' and 'Sealed Fountain': Song of
Songs 4:12 in the Late Medieval Iconography of Mary," in *Medieval Gardens* (1986),
esp. pp. 263–67.

9. Penny Schine Gold, *The Lady and the Virgin: Image, Attitude, and Experience in
Twelfth-Century France* (1985), p. 57.

10. E. Ann Matter shows how the use of verses from the Song of Songs in the
Marian liturgies antedates, prepares the way for, and generically qualifies the Marian
expositions. See "The Woman Who Is the All: The Virgin Mary and the Song of
Songs," in "*The Voice of My Beloved*": *The Song of Songs in Western Medieval Chris-
tianity* (1990). For another instructive comment on the liturgical background, see Jean
Leclercq, *Monks and Love*, pp. 38–40.

11. Rupert of Deutz, *Commentaria in Cantica Canticorum*, PL 168, c839–40; CCCM
26, p. 8.

acts" ("Sciendum est quod quidquid in hoc cantico de beata Maria dicitur, ad corporales vel spirituales ejus actus refertur").[12]

In the Marian expositions, the fusion of two histories—the evangelical biography of Mary and the Song's literal meaning ("historia")—emphasizes the typological implications of the text as a prefigurement not only of Christ's life, but also of every Christian's life. The actions described in the *Canticum*, the emotions expressed, find their fulfillment in the "historia" of Jesus and Mary—an exegetical pattern that encourages the discovery of further parallels in the actual lives of their auditors. Indeed, contextualizing the words of the Song within episodes from the Gospel narrative stimulates the audience's imaginative, emotional participation in Mary's experience and helps them to become her extended self.

Similarly, in Bruno's ecclesiastical commentary, the allegory effects a close relationship between the text *ad litteram* and the lives of his auditors. Through his mediation the *historia* of Canticles, fused with its allegory in a two-in-oneness, addresses an emotive and logical appeal to his auditors for their practical response to the demands of the times, *historia* calling to *historia* in a moving dialogue of word and world. With startling naiveté, Bruno asks his listener, "Do you want to become a garden?" ("Vis hortus fieri?")[13] At another point he offers counsel to the person who wishes he were a mountain: "Sed si tu, o homo, mons fieris cupis, erige mentem" (c1247). The more Bruno literalizes the allegory, the more immediate and pressing its tropological implications become.

Indeed, Bruno considers his reading to be "literal," rather than "allegorical," whenever the poetic image seems particularly pertinent to ecclesiastical history, past and present. For instance, in his exposition of the "lily among thorns," Bruno comments: "But the church is also afflicted, oppressed, and pierced by her daughters—namely, by the heretics and schismatics she bore in the baptismal font. This, moreover, according to the letter" (c1243: "Sed et Ecclesia a filiabus, scilicet ad haereticis et schismaticis, quos in fonte baptismatio genuit, multoties affligitur, opprimitur, et pungitur.

12. Alain de Lille, *Elucidatio in Cantica Canticorum*, PL 210, c58. Subsequent references are parenthetical.
13. Bruno of Segni, *Expositio in Cantica Canticorum*, PL 164, c1270. Hereafter all quotations from the *Expositio* and its prologue, *De Muliere Forte*, are taken from this edition and cited parenthetically by column number.

Hoc autem ad litteram"). As such a pronouncement makes abundantly clear, Bruno's understanding identifies "historia" with an allegory made literal (*ad litteram*).

In both the ecclesiastical commentaries and the Marian expositions, there is a definite gravitation toward the point of intersection between the vertical axis of the text (its *allegoria*, its upward referent) and the horizontal axis (its *littera*, its successive images with their sensory appeal)—a point of intersection localized in the tropological/rhetorical dimension that combines the two. In poetry and rhymed prose, Bruno draws on the emotive force of the Song's lush imagery in order to make its allegory a matter of practical consequence in the lives of his auditors, whom he exhorts to serve and obey the church ("servite ei, obedite ei") as represented by the hierarchy: "qui caeteros regunt et docent" (c1234).

Bruno's innovative lyricism finds its counterpart in the passionate prosopopoeia of the Marian commentaries, where Mary's voice becomes the exemplary utterance of the devout. Naming Mary as the Bride gives her, in effect, a figural primacy over the church whose allegory she particularizes and for whom she assumes a model character. As a result, recurrent images in the Song traditionally applied to the church—in particular, the king's palace and his pleasure garden—are redirected to Mary as an inclusive *figura*, a corporate personality, an embodiment of the church in its various members. Alain de Lille, for instance, identifies the houses of the king with church buildings, all of which are Mary's home ("domus Mariae") by reason of education: "ratione informationis" (PL 210, c64). Her body is the pattern for their construction as the womblike home of Christ ("domus Christi"). Even more, she is the maternal "informatio," the guiding idea, the pattern for the church, the *genetrix* whose features appear in all the children of God, even as they do in Jesus, her firstborn. Honorius develops the idea of the "hortus conclusus" in a similar way, noting that if Mary is the singular Garden of God, blossoming with virtues, bearing Jesus as the fruit of her womb, then the church too is a Marian garden to the extent that it imitates her: "Emissiones tuae, id est, imitatores tui sunt ut paradisus diversarum arborum."[14]

14. Honorius of Autun, *Sigillum Beatae Mariae*, PL 172, c508.

The notion of *imitatio* finds its deepest expression in the parallels the exegetes draw between their own experiences and Mary's, going so far as to introduce autobiographical accounts into their interpretation of the text. As Mary's true children, as *alterae Mariae*, they share in her maternal/bridal relationship to the Word. Even as she gives the *Verbum Divinum* a human body, they attend to God's Word, clothing the Scripture with its gloss and moral directive. Their ethical exhortations, in particular, aim at making the Word take flesh again in the lives of their auditors—and they do not hesitate to use the emotional valence of the literal text to that end.

Bruno, too, conforms his teaching to the model of instruction found in the Song of Songs. The lips of the church, he says, are distilling honeycomb, that is, sweet and moving words: "Favum distillant labia Ecclesiae, id est, dulcia et suavia verba" (c1259). In keeping with this insight, the poetic language Bruno employs, both in the prose sections of the exposition and in the seventeen interspersed *versus*, tends to demonstrate a formal affinity with the biblical *Canticum* it interprets.[15] Bruno's use of anaphora, balanced clauses, rhymed prose, and sensory images derived directly from the Song gives a moving power to the allegory itself which encourages tropological assimilation—that is, the reader's assent to the moral implications of the Song of Songs, rightly understood. According to Bruno's understanding, the emotional valence of the *Canticum*'s literal meaning is ultimately directed toward this end, and he uses it in his own *versus* accordingly.

The fusion of letter and allegory within the *versus* themselves—indeed, the combination of poetry and prose throughout Bruno's exposition—attests to his rhetorical reading of the Song as a text meant to teach, delight, and move its auditors. In the particular historical context of the investiture controversy, the military imag-

---

15. Ignorant of parallelism as the inner principle of Hebraic *poesis*, Isidore of Seville, Rabanus Maurus, and others bowed to the authority of Josephus and Jerome and accepted the thesis that Solomon, like the great classical poets, used hexameter and pentameter. See Isidore, *Etymologiarum* VI, PL 82, c231; Rabanus, *De Universo* V, PL 111, c108; Hugh of St. Victor, *Didascalicon* IV.8, PL 176, c782; trans. Jerome Taylor (1961, repr. 1968), p. 109. As James Kugel observes, "the metrical thesis helped to guarantee poetry a place in the Christian world; indeed, attributing meters to the Bible made metrics, like rhetoric, an essential field of study." See *The Idea of Biblical Poetry: Parallelism and Its History* (1981), p. 167.

ery of the Song naturally comes to the fore and tends to color Bruno's whole portrayal of the Bride. When Bruno encourages his audience to identify with her, he invites them to appropriate her valiant, virginal resistance to the false Bridegroom—the philosophers, heretics, and tyrants who are the true Bridegroom's deceitful "sodales." Feminization thus takes an almost Amazonian form that is tempered by the Bride's inner and outer dependency on the strong support of priestly fathers ("doctores") who instruct her and represent to her the true Bridegroom. Their teaching opposes the lying rhetoric of the Antichrist with a combination of truth and sweetness. Bruno's own poetry, which embeds the *sententia* of the Song in its literal imagery, provides a model for that kind of holistic instruction.

In Bruno's representation, the bridal church bears the distinctive features of a woman structured according to the Virgin archetype. She tends to develop, as Ann Belford Ulanov says, "a personality which is self-contained and independent," eager for self-determination—even as Bruno's *ecclesia* yearns for freedom from monarchical control. In the arena of the world, the Virgin stands side by side with the male, to whom she relates positively "as to a comrade, a colleague, or a competitor, devoted to the same conscious ideals as he is." Her *animus* (the recessive, masculine side of herself) is a father figure, personified positively as the "spiritual guide, counselor, and even priest" who assists her original development as a person; personified negatively as "a tyrannous old king."[16] Similarly, Bruno's *ecclesia* finds herself wedded either to the Gregorian clergy who instruct her in truth or to the Holy Roman emperor and his adherents who dominate and misdirect her.

Whereas the rhetoric of Bruno's ecclesiastical interpretation of the Song urges the reader to identify with the Bride as the valiant Virgin whose proper masculine complement is the Priestly Father and teacher (*doctor*), the Marian commentaries present the Bride under the specific form of the Mother-Bride who nourishes, instructs, and empathizes with her Child, vicariously sharing in his destiny. Mary's Bridegroom in these texts assumes the striking form of an

---

16. Ann Belford Ulanov, *The Feminine in Jungian Psychology and in Christian Theology* (1971), pp. 205–7.

Infant Boy nursing at the breast, while the exegetes exhort their auditors to learn from Mary in a childlike way, depend on her maternal intercession, and imitate her example.

Once again, the characterization of the Bride reflects the psychological structure of a particular type of woman—in this case, a woman whose personality, as Ulanov describes it, "is primarily maternal in its orientation." Mary as Bride exhibits "maternal cherishing and concern" for both the Christ Child and the church entrusted to her intercession. The containing functions of her womb, breast, and arms correspond to the "brooding quality" of her "feminine thought and memory" as she reflects on past and future events. Even as a woman structured as a Mother tends to see the male "primarily as the father of her children or as a paternal influence over her charges," Mary consciously leads her children to the Father God, encouraging their filial love and obedience. The Mother's own masculine otherness (*animus*), moreover, projects itself archetypally as the *puer aeternus*, a creative son "likely to evince talent, ideas, skill."[17] Thus the exegetes evoke and affirm a powerful psychological pairing when they wed Mary (in the marital imagery of the Song) to her divine Son.

The feminine principle in the Marian and ecclesiastical commentaries is thus manifested in strikingly different but complementary ways. In Bruno's reading of the Song, the Virgin-Bride embodies the feminine as a developmental principle, formed through repeated testings, changing in time, influenced by the true teaching of the Bridegroom, seduced by the lies of heretics and philosophers, sometimes guided, sometimes tyrannized, alternately respondent and resistant. In the Marian expositions, on the other hand, the Mother-Bride upholds the static pole of the feminine as teacher and nurturer, while the developmental line is taken up by the Child-Bridegroom in whom her hopes, fears, and expectations are realized.[18]

Bruno of Segni urges his auditors to join themselves to the Bride as her orthodox teachers and defenders. At the side of the church they participate in the projected masculine principle that is embodied in the pope as *vir ecclesiae*; as part of the church, they represent the

17. Ibid., pp. 198–202.
18. For a treatment of the static and dynamic manifestations of the feminine, see Ulanov, pp. 195–96.

masculine principle that is her own inward strength. Through their identification with her, the church becomes militant, vibrant, virginal, and strong. The Marian expositors, on the other hand, pursue a rhetorical strategy that encourages their auditors to attach themselves to Mary as her learners and dependents. Their identification with the Mother-Bride causes the Bride to assume a correspondent tenderness and compassion. At Mary's side, they enhance her maternal wisdom by receiving her instruction; drawn into Mary, they coexperience her own childlike openness to the Source of all sapience. The Child, in short, is the Mother-Bride's "other half," her secret self, while the Priestly Father informs the identity of the Virgin-Bride.

These two images of the Bride—Virgin and Mother—emerge from ecclesiastical and Marian readings of the Song responsive to particular rhetorical situations, employing different means to achieve different ends. Bruno historicizes the Bride to make her exemplary for his auditors chiefly by absorbing the emotive letter of Canticles into his own explication and exposition. The Marian exegetes, on the other hand, historicize the Bride by making the Song itself a lyrical component in the Gospel narrative, placing its words on Mary's lips in dramatic situations. All the exegetes model bridal assimilation for their readers—Bruno by teaching; Alain, Honorius, and Rupert by learning and longing. In the pages that follow I examine in detail the historical grounding and rhetorical thrust of these related ecclesiastical and Marian streams of interpretation.

Ecclesia as the Bride

Bruno's ecclesiastical interpretation of Canticles reflects the dominant, bridal self-image of the contemporary church. Jurists such as Huguccio of Pisa (d. 1210) were using civil marriage law as a model for canon law to address the issues raised by the investiture contest. They argued that if the church is Christ's Bride (as the authority of Ephesians 5:21–33 affirms), then the church is also husbanded by Christ's special representatives—the pope ("vir ecclesiae"), the bishops, and priests. The analogy advanced by the jurists dictated procedural guidelines for the election of bishops, protected the inalienability of church property (as a bridal dowry), and eventually led to an obligatory celibacy for priests.[19] The jurists, in short, were reifying in legal, marital terms the allegory of Christ's marriage to *ecclesia*.

In the *Expositio in Cantica*, Bruno, addressing the community of canons with whom he resided in Siena before his appointment as Bishop of Segni in 1079,[20] urges them to support the church ("Mulier Fortis") as she struggles to maintain her virginal independence in the face of the emperor's direct attack and heretical bid for power over her. Bruno prefaces his exposition of Canticles in an innovative way with a discussion of Proverbs 31:10–31 entitled *De Muliere Forte*, applying the Sapiential praise of the strong woman to Christ's Bride, the church.[21] In the *expositio* that follows, Bruno consistently depicts the Bride as the valiant Virgin, who is resistant to the seduction of false teachers and tyrants and whose active progress through the wilderness of this world depends on the energetic preaching of reliable guides. She journeys toward the Lord through the desert and trials of this age, fearing neither the ambushes of brigands, nor the swords of tyrants, nor the teeth of lions, nor the sophistries of Jews and heretics: "non latronum insidias, non tyrannorum gladios, non leonum dentes; non Judaeorum et haereticorum sophismata timens" (PL 164, c1252).

Consciously imitating the inspired poetry of the Song in order to woo his audience into a firm allegiance to the virginal church represented by the reform party, Bruno offers his own exposition to his auditors as a model of true and persuasive teaching. He insists that false doctrine be opposed by true teaching and good example.

19. See Ernst H. Kantorowicz, *The King's Two Bodies: A Study in Medieval Political Theology* (1957), pp. 212–13, 215, 217.

20. Bruno's marked emphasis in the commentary on teaching and learning as ways of opposing heresies provides an indirect commentary on the nature of his canonical audience. Caroline Walker Bynum has concluded from her comparative study of monastic and canonical treatises that "what distinguishes regular canons from monks is the canon's sense of a responsibility to edify his fellow men both by what he says and by what he does." See "The Spirituality of Regular Canons in the Twelfth Century" in *Jesus as Mother: Studies in the Spirituality of the High Middle Ages* (1982), p. 36.

21. See Ohly, p. 104. Ohly calls the use of Proverbs "Brunos Neuerung" and finds no direct counterpart in Bruno's main source, the ninth-century commentary of Haimo of Auxerre. The passage from Proverbs praises a wife, not a virgin, but that in no way nullifies the church's archetypal representation as a Virgin-Bride.

Throughout the commentary, the exegetical exaltation of "docti" and "doctores" balances rhetorically the condemnation of mute bishops, heretics, and philosophers and encourages loyalty in Bruno's auditors to the teaching magisterium of the church consolidated in the papal authority.

He denounces those bishops who, like mute dogs not strong enough to bark ("canes muti non latrare valentes"), permit God's flock to starve (c1239). In another passage he declares that many bishops and monks whose personal conduct does not coincide with their public preaching will be damned: "qui ex labiis oreque bona defluentes, interius vitia reservantes, damnabuntur" (c1273). On the other hand, in his interpretation of the Bride as a "castrorum acies ordinata," he depicts the bishops defending their flocks, and every Christian in his or her place—whether celibate or married— fighting with the arms of virtue to destroy vice and supplant evil spirits: "Docti sunt in proelio, vitia destruunt, et malignos spiritus supplantant" (c1271). The "docti" wage war, and they do so in large part by teaching ("docendo")—Bruno's own task as exegete, and the mission of those instructed by him.

The church's teaching, voiced by her *doctores* and ultimately directed toward moral application, should be both attractive and true, an organic oneness of form and content, a perfect fit of image and interpretation. As Bruno insists, the church finds the ultimate model for its inspired writing and successful preaching in the sacred Scriptures, which combine several levels of meaning in a mixture of sweetness and sapience. Inspired by the rhetorical strategies he perceives in the Song of Songs, Bruno's own exposition is remarkable for its lyricism. The seventeen poems interspersed throughout the commentary tend to imitate the Song in a way that incorporates its *allegoria* into the very letter of the poem. The *versus* show a great variety in meter, rhyme scheme, and stanzaic form; they all, however, recapitulate in one way or another the main points of the immediately preceding prose commentary, fusing the Song's letter (and the *pathos* it engenders) with its interpretation (*logos*).

Bruno's rhetorical consciousness leads him, moreover, to imitate the dialogical structure of the *Canticum* itself in the forms of his poetry. *Prayer* creates a poetic "ego" for the auditor and supplies him with a bridal utterance he can appropriate, whereas *prosopopoeia* allows Christ himself to speak as the Bridegroom. One poem, "Quis est hic qui pulsat," combines the two—prayer and prosopo-poeia—in the form of a *dialogue* in which the soul speaks in response to Christ's call. I will give examples of each kind, preparing the way for the discussion of Middle English lyrics in Chapter 6 by an examination of Bruno's basic poetic forms: prayer, prosopopoeia, and dialogue.

Prayer

The first *versus* in Bruno's *expositio* is a prayer of petition. After presenting the allegorical interpretation of the vineyard's "custo-des," Bruno encourages his auditors to pray for divine guidance in the current ecclesiastical situation: "Therefore let us ask our Lord that he show the sheepfold to us, and gather us in his mercy in the place of pasture" (c1239: "Rogemus igitur Dominum nostrum, ut et nobis ovile indicet, et in loco pascuae nos sua misericordia col-locet"). The hexameter *versus*, which follows immediately as a re-sponse to the call for prayer ("rogemus"), allows the Bride to express the auditors' own longing ("rogo te") to hear the Bride-groom's voice:

> Quid mihi tot legas, o regie sponse, prophetas?
> Cessent legati tantum dare verba parati.
> Te volo, te credo, te solum videre quaero.
> Iam miserere mei, jam te patiare videri.
> Oscula jamque tuae sponsae dare sit tibi curae,
> Auribus et nostris dulcis modulamina vocis.
> Jam resonet, rogo te, si quis tuus est amor in me.
>
> (c1239)

[Why, o royal spouse, do you dispatch so many prophets to me? Let the readied messengers cease to give so many words! I want you, I believe you, I seek to see you alone. Pity me now; permit yourself now to be seen. Let it be your concern to give kisses now to your bride, and the modulation of your sweet voice to our ears. Now, I beg you, let it resound, if you have any love for me!]

The impassioned language of the *versus* inspires a genuine longing to hear Christ's voice, even as it assimilates the words of the exegete to the "dulcis modulamina vocis" of the Bridegroom himself. It does so in the first chapter of the exposition, thus disposing the audience to be attentive to the teaching that follows. Echoing key elements in the opening lines of the biblical poem—the Bride's desire to be kissed, to hear her lover's voice—the poem captures the essential emotional quality of the literal text and applies it to an analogous situation defined by the allegory. The single word "prophetas" incorporates the allegory into the literal meaning of the *versus*, which possesses all the sensuous sweetness of a secular love lyric. Although it cannot be called a paraphrase of the Song, it nevertheless evokes a similar longing for the beloved and transfers that emotion into a specifically pious and devotional context by casting it into a prayer form.

"Quid mihi tot legas" allows the auditor to express his bridal self in oral prayer; the lyric "En lectulum Salomonis," on the other hand, invites the prayer of meditation:

> En lectulum Salomonis ambiunt fortissimi
> Omnes gladios tenentes in bello doctissimi.
> Propter timores nocturnos sunt accincti gladiis,
> Quibus suis sunt tutamen, et timor extraneis.
> Ferculum rex Salomon fecit de lignis Libani,
> Cujus utique columnae vos estis apostoli.
> Reclinatorium ibi fabricavit aureum
> Sanguine proprio fecit ascensum purpureum.
> Filiae Sion, quid statis, foras egredimini?
> Regem vestrum coronatum spinis intuemini.
> Tu tamen, Virgo Maria, coronasti Filium;
> Quia carnem de te sumens ponitur in medium.
> Quem chorus apostolorum, confessorum, virginum,
> Sic circumdat, ut corona prudentium militum.
>
> (c1255)

[The bravest ones surround the couch of Solomon, all holding swords, all very well trained in war. Because of threats by night they are girded with swords, which are a means of protection for them and a terror for strangers. From the woods of Lebanon, King Solomon made a litter for himself, whose pillars you surely are, Apostles! There he fashioned a golden recliner; he made the ascending stairway purple with his own blood. Daughters of Sion, why do you stand, why do you go out of doors? Behold your King crowned with thorns! You, nevertheless, Virgin Mary, have crowned the Son, because, assuming flesh from you, he is placed in our midst—he whom the choir of apostles, confessors, and virgins thus encircles like a living crown of wise soldiers.]

"En lectulum" first creates a dramatic setting for the poetic "ego" by describing the wondrous litter of Solomon, its ascending stairway purple with Christ's blood. Then it draws the reader into a meditation on the scene through a triple second-person address. The "vos" directed to the apostles, the question posed to the daughters of Sion, and the "tu" addressed to the Virgin Mary all imply an "ego" that is dramatically present.

The framing device employed in the poem enables the literalization of allegory. The *versus* begins with the image of well-trained soldiers surrounding the king's bier, and it ends with the vision of the saints surrounding Christ. The crown of thorns and the centralizing impact of the Incarnation develop the image of the circle throughout the middle section. The last words, "prudentium militum," recall the opening military image, and the poem itself becomes a circle or crown offered to the King—an offering in which the reader can share.

The penetration of the gloss back into the letter from which it was derived creates startling effects in the poem when Solomon suddenly assumes the bloody features of the crucified Christ, becomes the King he had prefigured. Through a strange imposition of allegory upon imagery, the opening scene is recast in the final one, its unchanged silhouette the reflection of different figures, the saints who have silently taken the places of the soldiers. The two-in-oneness of the images enforces the militancy of the church, the valor of the Virgin-Bride.

Like the above *versus*, "Omnia qui fecit" invites prayerful reflection. The exegete introduces the lyric, a meditation on Christ's suffering, with a tropological observation: "Happy that soul, exceedingly happy, between whose breasts Christ lingers, in whose heart he lies down, and who is never forgetful of him" (c1242: "Felix illa anima, nimiumque felix, cujus inter ubera Christus commoratur, cujus in corde jacet, et quae ipsius nunquam obliviscitur"). The poem that follows impresses on the bridal soul the memory of Christ's suffering:

> Omnia qui fecit, sumere carnem dignatus Dominus,
> Morte redemit humani generis sponte ruinam:
> In cruce suspensus, cum pateretur, fasciculum myrrhae.
> Crede. Fuisse. Tristis enim dixit morte.
> Insuper et Petrus flevit amare; postea vero dedit
> Nardus odorem cum coelos petit veste cruenta.
>
> (c1242)

[The Lord who created all things deigned to assume flesh. By his death he freely redeemed the ruin of the human race. When he suffered, suspended on the cross, he was a bundle of myrrh. Believe me! He was! For he said he was sad unto death. And besides, Peter wept bitterly; afterward, in truth, nard gave off fragrance when he sought the skies, his vesture bloody.]

Once again the Incarnation of the Word, celebrated in the opening lines, provides a paradigm for the infusion of allegory into the Song's letter. The body of Christ crucified becomes a bundle of myrrh hung on the cross, his Ascension a release of perfume. The effect is so startling that the poet, speaking in the *persona* of the Bride, breaks in with an appeal for faith: "crede." The weeping of Peter in response to Christ's own sorrow models the compunction the auditor is expected to feel in a specifically tropological imitation/ incarnation of the poetic word.

In the lyric "Saliens in montes" (c1248), the Bride speaks, inviting the auditor to coexperience with her the call of the Bridegroom ("Nonne vocem audis?"):

> Saliens in montes, transiliens colles, venit ecce meus
> Et Sponsus, et Deus, quam paries carnis oculis humanis
> Celat, ut Judaeus dicat: Non est Deus. Nonne vocem audis?
> Quae intima cordis penetravit mei. Surge, veni, veni.
> Hiems enim transiit, imber omnis abiit, aestas aperitur.
> Et turtur auditur, ficus dedit grossos, dabit ista botros,
> Vineaeque florent, praestant et odorem.
>
> (c1248)

[Leaping unto the mountains, crossing the hills, behold, he comes! My Bridegroom and my God, whom the wall of flesh hides from human eyes, so that the Jew says: He is not God. Don't you hear his voice? It has penetrated the innermost parts of my heart. Rise up, come, come. For the winter has passed, all the rain has gone, the summer is begun, and the turtle-dove is heard. The fig tree has given forth figs; it will give bunches of grapes—and the vines blossom and give off fragrance.]

The last three lines of the short *versus* merely paraphrase the Song, but the first section of the poem fuses allegory and imagery in a dramatic fashion that assimilates the reader into the church's ardent reception of the God-Man. The Bridegroom is God incarnate; the wall that conceals his divinity is his own body. The exegetical gloss thus becomes the tenor of a moving metaphor. The Incarnation of the Word, his leaping into flesh, is paralleled in the second half of the poem in the image of his voice penetrating the heart—a penetration that turns into pregnancy in the final images of blossoming and fruitfulness.

Prosopopoeia

In "Saliens in montes," the Bride repeats the call she has heard from the Bridegroom: "Surge, Veni" (c1248). In "Flos ego sum campi," Christ himself speaks to the soul ("dico tibi"):

> Flos ego sum campi, decus et laus ordinis almi;
> Angelicus coetus mihi subditur;
> Omnia complectur, coelum trans maris aequor:
> Cunctorum Dominus, Pater et Deus.
> Quis nisi solus ego? Nemo, dico tibi, nemo.
>
> (c1244)

[I am the flower of the field, the ornament and praise of the mothering order. The angelic host is submitted to me. I embrace all things, the sky across the surface of the sea. I, the Lord of all, Father and God! Who, if not I alone? No one, I tell you, no one.]

Only the first phrase of the *versus* uses Canticles imagery. The rest elaborates its allegory as a continuation of the Bridegroom's literal boast. The question and answer in the last line invite the soul to bow before the majestic greatness of Christ exalted over the universe. In the final image the Bridegroom is a father and conqueror, insisting on his power as the unique "flos campi."

In "Surge, amica mea," Christ the Bridegroom speaks tenderly to his Bride, inviting her response:

> Surge, amica mea; veni, columba mea,
> Vulneribus in meis, tam sana delecteris.
> Tu pulchra videaris, tu sapiens loquaris.
> Nam vox tua canora, et facies decora.
> Jam vulpes capiantur, vitia destruantur
> Ne vinearum flores pereant, et odores.
>
> (c1249)

[Arise, my love! Come, my dove! that you, completely healed, may be delighted in my wounds; that you may be seen to be beautiful and wise as you speak (for your voice is melodious and your face lovely); that the foxes may be captured and vices destroyed, lest the flowers of the vineyard perish, and their perfumes.]

The reference to Christ's wounds incorporates the allegory into the eros of the Bridegroom's call, making it rhetorically present. Christ's pierced body becomes part of the Song's carnality; his dogma, part of its literal appeal. Thus the *versus* models the kind of melodious and wise speaking it seeks to inspire in others. The Bridegroom calls to the Bride that she in turn will utter the "dulcia et suavia verba" (c1249) of truth which overcome all heresies, answering his voice with hers.

Dialogue

The lyric "Quis est hic qui pulsat" (c1266) achieves a powerful fusing of image and allegory within the context of a dialogue between divine and human lovers:

> Quis est hic, qui pulsat ad ostium,
> Noctis rumpens somnum?
> Me vocat: O virginum pulcherrima,
> Soror, conjux, gemma splendidissima

Cito surgens aperi, dulcissima:
Ego sum summi Regis Filius,
Primus, et novissimus,
Qui de coelo in has veni tenebras,
Passus mortem et multas injurias,
Liberare captivorum animas.
Mox ego dereliqui ad pessulum,
Ut dilecto domus mea pateat,
Et mens mea plenissime videat
Quem videre maxime desiderat:
At ille jam inde transierat,
Ostium reliquerat.
Quid ergo, quid miserrima facerem?
Lacrymando sum secuta juvenem
Cujus manus plasmaverunt hominem.
Vigiles urbis invenerunt me,
Exspoliaverunt me,
Abstulerunt et dederunt pallium,
Cantaverunt mihi novum canticum
Quo in regis inducar palatium.

(c1266)[22]

[Who is he who knocks at the door, disturbing the sleep of night? He calls to me: "O most beautiful of virgins, Sister, Bride, most splendid jewel! Sweetest, rising quickly, open (to me). I am the Son of the highest King, the First and the Last, who have come from Heaven into these shadows, suffered death and many injuries, to liberate the souls of captives." I quickly left my bed, ran to the bolt, that my home might open to the Beloved, and my mind very fully see him whom it had greatly desired to behold. But he had already passed by, away from there, had left the entrance. What, then, what was I—most miserable—to do? Weeping, I ran after the young Man, whose hands formed and shaped man. The guards of the city found me, stripped me; they took away, and gave me back, a cloak. They sang to me a new song by which I will be led into the King's palace.]

22. This poem, which appears in Bruno's *Expositio*, also appears in Migne's edition of the *Carmina et Preces* of Saint Peter Damian (PL 145, c939) and is most probably of his original authorship. See Chapter 6 for a treatment of this poem in relation to the Middle English lyric "Undo þi Dore."

Christ speaks (*prosopopoeia*) and the Bride responds (*prayer*). The Bridegroom knocking at the door of the bedchamber is literally Christ, bearing the marks of his Passion and appealing to be admitted into the heart of his spiritual Bride. As the prose commentary indicates to the reader, "It is wrong not to open to him, not to receive such a Spouse into the wedding chamber of the heart" (c1263: "Injustum est . . . huic non aperire, et in cordis thalamum tantum sponsum non accipere"). The Bride, speaking in her own person—an "ego" to be occupied by the "I" of the auditor—gives expression to her emotions of desire and disappointment and longing.

Like "Saliens in montes," the lyric employs successive entrances to convey the full implications of incarnation. At the beginning of the poem Christ seeks entrance into her heart; in the middle section she seeks him in the city; at the end she is admitted into the heavenly palace of the King—the three places marking the dramatic movements of the poem and the fluctuations in emotion from joyful longing to tearful searching to blissful reunion. The reference to the "novum canticum," within the *Canticum*'s allegorical context, suggests the Apocalyptic perfection and continuation of a spiritual love song begun on earth.

The Bridegroom's search is answered by the Bride's, his descent into the shadows by her running into the city at night, his Ascension by her final procession into the New Jerusalem. In the end she is recreated by her union with the Word "whose hands fashioned man" ("cujus manus plasmaverunt hominem"). The sentries, like the soldiers guarding Solomon's *ferculum*, perform the fatherly/priestly function of purification, preaching, and protection. As exponents of the masculine principle, they join her to the Bridegroom. The two-fold gift of cloak and song, with its Apocalyptic anticipation, symbolizes the Word-Made-Flesh in her through a conformity to the pattern of Christ's *historia*.

Mary as the Bride

Like Bruno, who emphasizes the emotive force of the Song by incorporating it into his own lyrics, the Marian commentators affirm and preserve the lyricism of the Song *ad litteram* by providing a historical context for its vocalization. That evangelical and legendary *narratio* frames and directs the expression of emotion, setting Mary before the reader as an exemplary figure who actualizes the prophecy contained in the Song in her own life and teaches us to do the same.

The exegetes generally use the Gospel narrative with its unbroken action to provide a connective between the verses of the Song explaining the changes in mood from speech to speech. Rupert, noting the thrice-repeated verse "Adjuro vos" which divides the Song into four periochae, assumes that Mary's whole life, as chronicled by the evangelists, is retold four times in four different ways. He himself begins his exegesis with the Annunciation hour and continues by incorporating the versicles of the *Canticum* into an orderly account of the Visitation, the Finding in the Temple, the Wedding Feast at Cana, the Calvary Sacrifice, and the Ascension— the latter event renewing Mary's initial longing for Christ in an echoic repetition of the lyric mood animating the Annunciation scene. Rupert's attempt to maintain a strict chronology is only partially successful in Book I (where he actually skips over the Nativity), and he virtually abandons the effort after the second book. Throughout Rupert's commentary, however, the different scenes of Mary's *vita* continue to provide a narrative connective for definite groupings of verses.

This fragmentary, scene-by-scene correlation of plot with poetry especially characterizes the work of Alain de Lille. Like Rupert, Alain contextualizes the opening verse of the *Canticum* with the Annunciation, starting his exposition *in medias res*:

Gloriosa igitur Virgo sponsi optans praesentiam, desiderans gloriosam conceptionem ad angelo nuntiatam, affectans divinam Incarnationem, ait sic: "Osculetur me osculo oris sui." (PL 210, c53)

[The glorious Virgin, therefore, hoping for the presence of the Bridegroom, desiring the glorious conception announced by the angel, eagerly wishing for the divine Incarnation, speaks thus: "Let him kiss me with the kiss of his mouth."]

Alain's introduction explains the motive behind the Bride's request for a kiss and her expression of longing. The historical fact of Mary's pregnancy through the descent of the Holy Spirit justifies using the language of lovers. By definition, the union between Mary and God was a real marriage consummated not only spiritually ("per unionem spirituum") but also physically in a union of the divine and human natures ("per unionem naturarum").

While the exegetes stress that God's special love for Mary preserved her from sexual arousal at the time of Christ's conception,[23] they nevertheless dwell at length on her emotional experience of the divine Presence in intimacy with her. She felt, Alain says, an inexpressible joy ("inenarrabile gaudium"). Rupert writes that Mary's encounter with the divine Lover was characterized not by carnal desire but by something sweeter, stronger, and more vehement, "the voluptuous ardor of God" ("voluptas sive amor Dei").[24] Indeed, in his description of the Annunciation hour, Rupert breaks into a direct address to the Virgin which clearly uses sexual union and its attendant emotions as a symbol for the eternal union with God consummated in eternity:

> O beata Maria, inundatio gaudii, vis amoris, torrens voluptatis, totam te operuit totamque obtinuit, penitusque inebriavit, et sensisti quod oculus non vidit, et auris non audivit, et in cor hominis non ascendit.[25]

> [O blessed Mary, the floodwaters of joy, the force of love, the torrent of pleasure, filled you totally, possessed you totally, intoxicated you completely, and you sensed what eye has not seen, nor ear heard, and what has not entered into the heart of man.]

The implication that Mary's purity intensifies, rather than diminishes, the strength of her emotional responses allows her to have a

---

23. Alain de Lille, for instance, writes that the overshadowing Holy Spirit was a protecting tent ("tabernaculum vel umbraculum") against the arousal of concupiscence ("contra concupiscentiae incentivum"). See PL 210, c65. Similarly, Rupert of Deutz insists that Mary knew nothing of the wine of carnal pleasure ("vinum voluptatis carnalis"), without which no other woman has conceived: "sine cujus ebrietate nulla unquam mulier praeter te concipere potuit" (PL 168, c841; CCCM 26, p. 12).

24. Rupert of Deutz, *In Cantica Canticorum*, PL 168, c841; CCCM 26, p. 12.

25. Ibid., c839; CCCM 26, p. 10.

"sexual" experience of God—that is, a surpassing sense of personal completion by him in body and soul—without the mediation of a man arousing those feelings first on a lower, directly physical level. Mary's virginity, then, involves both her renunciation of sexual complementarity at the human level and her entering into a marriage with God which fulfills her personally (and therefore also sexually) at a higher level.[26] The emotions she experiences in union with God are similar and dissimilar to those of a woman coupled with a man—similar in kind, dissimilar in their unmixed purity and intensity. Using the *Canticum* as a vehicle to communicate the quality of Mary's bridal experience thus affirms the figural value of human marriage as the "sacramentum magnum" of the spiritual marriage with God into which each soul is called—a union realized imperfectly on earth, perfectly only in heaven.

The fusing of plot and poetry, action and affect, which marks the treatment of the Annunciation scene also characterizes the presentation of other episodes in Mary's life. Alain inserts the Bride's words ("Nolite me considerare quod fusca sim, quia decoloravit me sol") into a dramatic dialogue between the pregnant Mary and her betrothed, Joseph (see PL 210, c57). He likens the Bride's midnight search for her beloved to the emotional quality of Mary's wait at the tomb of Christ and pictures Mary speaking there in the poetry of the Song "to express the extreme affection of the virginal mind" (PL 210, c72: "ad exprimendum nimium virgineae mentis affectum"). Later, when Mary walks through the streets of Jerusalem after Christ's Ascension, venerating with touch and kiss the places where Jesus had dined, walked, preached, and suffered, her bridal relationship to Christ is defined not so much by her unique physical closeness to him ("cum proxima est ei corpore") as by her heartfelt, inward attachment: "for she clings to him even in his absence" (PL 210, c63: "etsi contingat ei absentem esse").

Rupert, like Alain, uses the *Canticum* to express the emotions Mary must have felt; but Rupert lets the Virgin herself speak, using a series of rhetorical questions that invite the audience to participate imaginatively in her experience, supplementing what remains unspoken and inexpressible. Recalling her visit to Jesus's tomb, Mary says:

26. See Ulanov, *The Feminine*, pp. 318–21 *et passim*, for insightful comments on the contrasexual integration achieved in Mary through her openness to God.

Sepultus est, clausum et signatum fuit monumentum. Et ego quali mente quaerebam eum? Quali desiderio desiderabam eum, sciens eum esse a mortuis resurrecturum?[27]

[He was buried, and the tomb was closed and sealed. And I—in what state of mind was I seeking him? With what kind of desire was I desiring him, knowing he was going to rise up from the dead?]

In another remarkable passage, Rupert identifies the breasts of the Bride with the breasts of the nursing Madonna who, with a prophetic insight, anticipates the sufferings destined for her infant Son as she holds him to her bosom:

Prophetissa namque eram et ex quo mater ejus facta sum, scivi eum ista passurum. Cum igitur carne mea taliter progenitum, talem filium sino meo foverem, ulnis gestarem, uberibus lactarem, et talem ejus futuram mortem semper prae oculis haberem, et prophetica, imo plusquam prophetica mente praeviderem, qualem, quantam, quam prolixam me putatis materni doloris pertulisse passionem? Hoc est quod dico: "Fasciculus myrrhae dilectus meus mihi, inter ubera mea commorabitur." O commoratio, dulcis quidem, sed plena gemitibus inenarrabilibus![28]

[For I was a prophetess, and because I was his mother, I knew he was going to suffer these things. When, therefore, I fondled such a Son, born of my flesh, at my bosom, carried him in my arms, nursed him at my breasts, and had always before my eyes such a death as was destined for him, and foresaw everything with a prophetic—nay, more than prophetic—mind, what kind of passion of maternal grief, how much and how extensive, do you imagine me to have endured? This is what I mean when I say: "My Beloved is for me a bundle of myrrh; he will dwell between my breasts." O sojourn, sweet indeed, but filled with inutterable groanings!]

27. Rupert of Deutz, *In Cantica Canticorum*, PL 168, c875; CCCM 26, p. 58.
28. Ibid., c856; CCCM 26, p. 32.

Marian prosopopoeia, here and elsewhere in the commentaries, involves the Mother's appropriation of the Song. She uses its text not only to express her emotions for Christ but also to understand her life as a fulfillment of Solomon's prophecy. The Song glosses her biography even as her "historia" explains the Song. When Mary speaks, she thus becomes an imaginative *alter ego* for the exegete who is interpreting Canticles from the historical perspective of her life. The commentators, moreover, consciously cast themselves as *alterae Mariae* in the expositions by drawing parallels between their reading experience of the Song and hers. When, for instance, Alain interprets one set of verses in the context of the Resurrection and the Ascension and then finds that the succeeding verse matches the state of Mary's soul prior to the Annunciation, he makes this comment:

> Mos enim prophetarum est, ut cum modo loquuntur de praesentibus et futuris, statim revertantur ad praeterita, prout Spiritus sanctus tangebat eorum corda. Indicitur ergo Virgo loquens secundum statum ante incarnationem, in quo vacans contemplationi exuerat omnem curam saecularem. (PL 210, c85)

> [For it is the custom of prophets that just when they are speaking about present and future things, they suddenly revert to past things, even as the Holy Spirit was touching their hearts. Therefore the Virgin is indicated to be speaking according to her state before the Incarnation, in which, lost in contemplation, she had left behind every transitory concern.]

Even as Mary (in prosopopoeia) applies the various verses of the Song to the episodes of her "historia" in an order that disrupts their normal chronology, so too the exegete accommodates his voice to the Word of God, bridging the perceived gaps with an upward reference to God himself, whose divine vision of things nullifies the usual distinction between "before" and "after" and "now." The same Bridegroom who teaches Mary how everything written in the Old Testament ("in lege, prophetis, et psalmis") applies to his Person (PL 210, c104) also inspires the exegete to interpret the Song in terms of Mary's *vita*.

This general parallel between Mary's interpretive activity and the exegete's becomes a rationale for the incorporation of personal accounts of mystical experience into the commentaries. In his prologue Rupert indicates that he had a vision of the blessed Trinity and was commissioned by God himself to write about the *Canticum*. In the opening paragraphs of the commentary, he tells how Mary encountered the triune God in the Annunciation hour and was commissioned by him to conceive the *Verbum Divinum*. The bold parallel between the two visionaries, Mary and Rupert, makes Rupert's elucidation authoritative on the basis of personal revelation rather than time-honored tradition.[29]

In the writings of both Rupert and Alain, the Virgin's knowledge of God is frequently described in the language of prophetic seizure. Rupert speaks of the descent of the Holy Spirit as an *afflatus*. Alain uses the whole vocabulary of ecstatic transport:

> Per cellam vinariam intelligitur mentis excessus, qui et extasis dicitur, quo Virgo ad coelestium contemplationem rapiebatur, quae et apotheosis, id est deificatio vel theophania divina apparitio nuncupatur, in hanc Virgo ab amore terrenorum suspensa rapiebatur. (PL 210, c66)

> [Through the wine cellar is understood the flight of the mind, which is also called "ecstasy," by which the Virgin was taken up to celestial contemplation, which is also termed "apotheosis"—that is, a deification or theophany, a divine apparition—into which the Virgin, lifted up, was carried away from the love of earthly things.]

The striking thing about this image of Mary in ecstasy is that it is, to a large degree, an image of the exegete's own self, his own soul rapt in contemplation. The *Canticum* is, after all, understood to be a contemplative work, and no one knowledgeable in the Scriptures aspires to read it without, at the same time, reaching out for the closest intimacy with God. To make his personal identification with

29. Ohly links Rupert with the beginning of German mysticism and the growing conviction that religious knowledge must be experiential. A series of visions in Rupert's adolescence convinced him that he had been granted full understanding of the Scriptures. See p. 129.

Mary unmistakable, Rupert interrupts his exposition with an extended account of one of his own visionary experiences. The text that he applies to both Mary and himself is Canticles 5:4: "My Beloved sent his hand through the opening, and my belly trembled at his touch."

> Memorabat etiam eadem adolescentula, scilicet anima nuptiis istis dedita, canticisque nuptialibus intenta, quoniam dilectus in visu noctis conspicuus, manum suam miro modo pectori ejus, quasi per foramen, injecit, et cor ejus intrinsecus apprehendit, tenuitque aliquandiu suavissime stringens, et gaudebat ineffabili gaudio cor illud intra manum illam subsiliens atque tripudians.[30]

> [The young girl—namely, the soul devoted to these nuptials and earnest in these wedding songs—was also recalling the same things, since the Beloved, seen in a vision of the night, in a wondrous fashion thrust his hand into her chest—through an opening, as it were—and grasped her heart within, and held it for some time, binding it very sweetly; and that heart, leaping up and dancing inside that hand, was rejoicing with unspeakable joy.]

After describing Mary's experience, Rupert goes on to tell how, in one of his night vigils, he was praying before a crucifix when the figure of Christ suddenly came to life before him. In a dreamlike state, his own body merged with that of the living image "so that mouth seemed moved to mouth, the whole body to his body" ("ut os quoque ori, totumque corpus admotum videretur ejus corpori").[31] Reflecting on the sweet power of the encounter, Rupert concludes in wonderment that Mary's experience of the divine must have been inestimably more tender than his, given her status as one uniquely beloved by God ("dilecta dilecti singularis").

The use of sexual imagery to describe Mary's (and Rupert's) intimate love relationship with God has its literal basis in her virginal consecration to him. Alain hints at an inner relationship between the heroic practice of virtue and the sublimation of the sex drive

---

30. Rupert of Deutz, *In Cantica Canticorum*, PL 168, c914; CCCM 26, p. 110.
31. Ibid., c915; CCCM 26, p. 111.

when he explains Mary's early decision for virginity in terms of her bridal attachment to Christ:

> Ita dilectio qua Virgo Christum dilexit totam Virginem huic mundo mortificavit, et insensibilem reddidit, soli Christo viventem, et mundo mortuam. (PL 210, c106)

> [Thus the love with which the Virgin loved Christ mortified the Virgin in her whole being to this world, and rendered her insensible to its attractions, living for Christ alone, and dead to the world.]

In another passage Alain discusses the umbilicus of the Bride as the seat of sexual desire and identifies it with the power of knowing and loving ("vis intelligendi," "vis diligendi") with which Mary loved God (see PL 210, c98). The vocabulary of Alain's explanation, which begins with "concupiscentia" and ends with "charitas," minimizes the distinction between the two in the context of Mary's "historia." Sinless, Mary the New Eve was free from any disorder in her sexual nature which could set her natural need to be loved and complemented in opposition to her self-surrender to God, his will, and his work; in her, no such disorder could invert the God-willed supremacy of spirit over matter. Her inner life was a paradise state. In her, everything was in harmony, and every power of love merged with *charitas* in a powerful continuity that fallen human beings struggle with the help of grace to regain.

Mary's perpetual virginity suits her to be Christ's Bride as well as his Mother and sets her apart as a unique type of, and model for, longing for God. The exegetes therefore associate the mood of longing which sounds repeatedly throughout the *Canticum* with various times when Mary experienced historically the absence of Christ: (1) before his Incarnation, (2) during the three days when he was lost (and later found) in the temple, (3) at his death and entombment, and (4) after his Ascension into heaven. Left behind on earth for the specific purpose of instructing the disciples in virtue, she longs for heaven, where she will enter into a bridal union with Christ which exceeds every earthly experience of closeness to him.

The "historia" of Mary, then, provides a narrative context in which the lyrical description of the Bridegroom's manly beauty can be preserved *in toto* as a symbol for the soul's *desiderium* and appropriated by the reader as such. At one point Rupert comments reflexively on the experience of reading the Song as anagogy—that is, as an alluring preview of the heavenly *visio*. He likens the person who reads the Song to the biblical whore Ooliba, who sees Chaldean warriors depicted on a mural, feels attracted to them, and chooses them in real life for her lovers:

> Et ego vobis dico: sicut illa, videlicet non Hierusalem sed Ooliba, exhibuit oculos suos videre viros depictos in pariete, videre imagines Chaldaeorum expressas coloribus, videre balteos eorum, tiaras eorum, et formam eorum, ita nunc exhibete oculos vestros, oculos interiores, videre dilectum hunc, videre aureum caput ejus, nitentes oculos ejus, reverendas genas ejus, candida et gloriosa labia ejus, tornatiles et aureas manus ejus, eburneum et sapphiris distinctum ventrem ejus, rectissima crura ejus, et tangite suavissimum guttur ejus, juxta illud: "Gustate et videte, quoniam suavis est Dominus" (Ps. 33).[32]

> [And I say to you: even as that woman—not Hierusalem but Ooliba—opened her eyes to see men depicted on a wall, to see the images of the Chaldeans expressed in painted colors, to see their belts, their crowns, and their bodily beauty, so now you—open your eyes, your interior eyes, to see this Beloved, to see his golden head, his brilliant eyes, his awe-inspiring cheeks, his radiant and glorious lips, his smooth and golden hands, his ivory stomach set with sapphires, his upright legs. And touch his throat, surpassingly sweet, in accord with the words: "Taste and see how sweet the Lord is" (Ps. 33).]

Origen in his third-century commentary also briefly compares the *Canticum* as a composition to Ooliba's mural—only to dismiss any superficial resemblance as misleading. The *Canticum*, he says, is surely about an altogether different kind of love. To prove his point,

---

32. Ibid., c929–30; CCCM 26, p. 130. The Scripture reference is to Ezechiel 23, where Ooliba figures in an allegorical history of Jerusalem and Samaria in their infidelity to Yahweh.

Origen calls upon the scriptural tradition that honors Solomon's Song and just as unequivocally censures the harlot's voyeurism.[33] Rupert, however, actually encourages the reader to imitate Ooliba, suggesting that the same *affectus* which led that woman into sin can lead the soul to sanctity, if directed toward the proper object ("hunc dilectum") in the way intended by God. Mary herself proves the possibility.

The Marian reader of the Song of Songs, then, approaches it as a prophetic text typologically related to "historia," echoing the images of personal visionary experience, and anticipatory of celestial joy. Affective response, reinforced and directed in part by the logic of allegory which confirms the appropriateness of one's feeling, is a constant factor in the reading process. Indeed, it is essential to the right reading of the *Canticum* as poetry and love lyric, crucial to the discovery of its prophetic meaning, and necessary for any tropological application of the text.

The Marian exegetes insist that the divinely inspired lyricism of the Song indicates that the God-willed response to it is, and must be, emotive. Rupert, like Bruno of Segni, responds to the poetry of the Song with poetry, hexameter verses that reflect on the sensible sweetness of the prophetic text:

> Tale tuum nobis carmen, divina prophetes,
> Quale sopor fessis in gramine, quale per aestum
> Dulcis aquae saliente sitim restinguere rivo.[34]

[Your song, divine prophets, is for us like a slumber for weary ones in the grass, like quenching one's thirst on a hot day from a flowing stream of sweet water.]

He immediately concludes that the Song of Songs may be recognized as genuine poetry ("legitimum carmen") by the sort of response it engenders: "The [Bridegroom's] friends would hear nothing more willingly, the maidens would receive nothing with greater delight, and likewise, whoever has ears for hearing, and a responsive

---

33. Origen, *In Canticum Canticorum*, trans. Rufinus, PG 13, c67–68.
34. Rupert of Deutz, *In Cantica Canticorum*, PL 168, c920; CCCM 26, p. 118.

sensibility" ("Nihil amici libentius audierint, nihil adolescentulae delectabilius acceperint, quaecunque habent aures audiendi sensumque promptum").[35]

As prophetic poetry, the Song of Songs begins on earth the "new song" sung in heaven. As Rupert puts it, "The end of the canticle repeats the beginning" ("Finis cantici idem sonat quod principium").[36] Rupert finds formal proof of the celestial echo of the Song of Songs in its repetitive structure—not only four periochae marked by the thrice-repeated verse "Adjuro vos," but also a verse octave that begins and ends with the words "terribilis ut castrorum acies ordinata."[37] The chord once sounded in diapason within the Song itself extends in a series of overtones reverberating through heaven itself—attesting to a structural anagogy that preserves the Song *ad litteram* as poetry to be sung forever in praise of Jesus and Mary.

Equally sensitive to the Song's artistry and moving power, Alain declares his wish to write a commentary on the text commensurate with its beauty. Lacking the eloquence of Cicero, he nevertheless attempts an exposition, being driven on by the same divine power which elicits the Mother's praise from every signifying creature and gives every Scripture reference to her: "et in omni scriptura matris dignitas praedicitur" (PL 210, c53). As the *genetrix* of the Word, Mary deserves to receive a return of words, the imitation of the faithful, the praise of poets, and Alain's own filial *elucidatio*.

The Marian commentators use the letter of the Song in combination with its historicized allegory—the story of Mary's life—to bring about the auditor's tropological realization of the text, his moral transformation into another Mary (*altera Maria*). When Mary's voice is heard in prosopopoeia, using the language of the Song to respond to her own life's circumstances, she provides a successful model for her listeners, who are called to appropriate the Song *ad litteram* as an expression of their their own love and longing for God. The *affectus* within them, constellated as Mother-love, will

35. Ibid.
36. Ibid., c937; CCCM 26, p. 140.
37. Ibid., c932; CCCM 26, p. 133. Medieval number symbolism regarded the octave as a perfect number, reducible to one, and therefore a symbol of the divine consonance.

then manifest itself especially in compassion for the weak and suffering, self-forgetful service, solicitude, patience, longing, and invincible faith. In the auditors' lives, as well as in Mary's, the Song should find its fulfillment.

Similarly, as we have seen, Bruno of Segni encourages his auditors to become the Bride by following her in her concrete historical realization, the *ecclesia* that is loyal to Gregory VII and respondent to true teaching. As *exemplum* the church prefigures a response of virginal love which shows itself in courageous acting and suffering, in the single-hearted adherence to high ideals, in the quest for justice, and in striving for integrity. In order to evoke that *affectus*, Bruno imitates the rhetoric of God, joining the letter and the interpretation of the Song together in a single rhetorical appeal in both his prose and poetry. He moves and teaches his auditors that they, in turn, may be *doctores*.

When the interpreted Song becomes, through Bruno's mediation, a vehicle for speaking to God (*prayer*), hearing Christ's voice (*prosopopoeia*), and entering into a *dialogue* with the divine Lover, he anticipates not only the Song-inspired poetry of the later Middle Ages but also the tropological immediacy the Song acquired in Victorine and Cistercian circles as a vehicle for personal mystical experience. No longer merely an imitable "alter ego," the Bride becomes, in the mystical treatments of the Song, the auditor's very "I."

3

Personal Brideship:
The Mystical Treatments

Behind the "factum" of the Song's literal meaning, the ecclesiastical and Marian commentators see the "factum" of contemporary and evangelical history. The corporate Bride, the reformed church, and the figural Bride, Mary, set an example for the auditor to follow. In the mystical treatments, on the other hand, the "factum" lightly veiled by the Song's letter is the rule of the community to which the auditor belongs, the ascetical program to which he has committed himself, the general life-style he has adopted as his own. The Song is, as Saint Bernard tells his monks, "the book of our experience."[1] The individual still has to discover a personal, ethical application of the text, depending on his immediate spiritual condition, but the distance between the allegorical history and his own is minimized. The mode of exegesis directs him to understand the Song as referring to his own love relationship with God, to himself as Bride.

The Bride thus emerges from these mystical texts in various archetypal forms, depending on the particular asceticism they reflect and express, the "I" they evoke. The Victorine Bride bears the distinctive features of the seeress or Medial Woman, described by Ann Belford Ulanov as a spiritual channel who "relates to the

1. Bernard, Sermon 3: I.1 in *On the Song of Songs* I, trans. Kilian Walsh (1976), p. 16.

nonpersonal objective psyche upon which consciousness rests."
Deeply intuitive, the Medium "is immersed in the psychic atmosphere of her environment and the spirit of her period, but above all
in the collective (impersonal) unconscious." With prophetic insight
she "gives shape to what is beneath the surface," preparing the way
for cultural expression and the articulation of communal ideals. Her
whole personality is defined by her function to create bonds, to
draw disparate elements into one, to be a connecting link.[2]

Like a woman constellated as a Medium, the Victorine mystic
concentrates his spiritual vision on the many-in-the-One and the
One-in-the-many, focusing the world in God. He activates within
himself the *intelligentia*, the cognitive faculty to which Richard of St.
Victor ascribes the power "of coordinating many objects of points
of view, of seeing the likeness in many different objects of thought,
or the principle underlying them."[3] According to Richard, the *intelligentia* operates at the third level of contemplative apprehension,
where intelligible (that is, invisible but conceivable) things are
known in the reason according to the imagination.[4] At that level the
intelligentia, in the process of reading, "converts" or "translates" the
earthly images present to the imagination by seeing them in relation
to their Source, as transparencies illumined from behind by the
radiant light of the One. The ability of the reader to make that kind
of connection between *res* and *signa*, vehicle and tenor, allows him to
participate in the Pauline reconciliation of heaven and earth which
redeems creation itself, making it new and diaphanous.

The Victorine emphasis (in both cognitive theory and poetic
practice) on symbolism, on the created order as a dissimilar similitude of the Creator, underscores the medial nature of their contemplation. Under the spell of the pseudo-Dionysian *Hierarchia
Caelestia*, the Victorine writers read the images of the Song of Songs
and incorporate them into their own writings in much the same

2. See Ann Belford Ulanov, *The Feminine in Jungian Psychology and in Christian
Theology* (1971), pp. 207–10.
3. Clare Kirchberger, "Introduction," in *Richard of St. Victor: Selected Writings on
Contemplation* (1957), p. 40.
4. See *Benjamin Major* I.vi for a definition of the six types of contemplative
apprehension. See *Benjamin Minor* XVIII for a discussion of the rational imagination
in particular. The Bibliography cites convenient English translations of these works
by Kirchberger and Yankowski.

symbolic way they contemplate the world.[5] In the words of Patrick S. Diehl, the Victorine approach to nature and God represents a mentality "fundamentally analogous to the poetic habit of mind"[6] with its propensity toward metaphoric expression. Unlike the figures of poetry presented in medieval treatises and *artes poetriae*, however, the images used by the Victorine writers are not decorative circumlocutions, epithets, or paraphrases used to embellish a given tenor.[7] The relationship between the juxtaposed terms is not horizontal but vertical, the creaturely reality being named and called into the reader's consciousness as "an avenue toward knowledge of the mystery of things divine and human."[8] As Charles Sears Baldwin puts it, the images stand as "immediate lyrical approaches"[9] to divine realities that cannot be known except through their sense-perceptible reflections.

Whereas the mystics of St. Victor evoke the feminine within themselves and others primarily in terms of the static, objective *anima* that enables a symbolic relation to things, Saint Bernard uses the Bride of the Song to bring into consciousness the subjective *anima* with its personal interest. As a dynamic principle of change and growth within the individual, the feminine emerges in Bernard's writings in the archetypal form of the Hetaira, the priestly handmaid, dedicated to the service of love, who (in Ulanov's words) "inspires men to prodigious feats."[10]

The healthy psychological development of a woman structured as

5. Strictly speaking, there is no twelfth-century Victorine commentary on the Song of Songs. C. Ottaviano and Friedrich Ohly have demonstrated that Richard could not have written the commentary attributed to him by J. P. Migne, Beryl Smalley, and Clare Kirchberger. See Ohly, *Hohelied-Studien: Grundzüge einer Geschichte der Hoheliedauslegung des Abendlandes bis um 1200* (1958), pp. 223–28. The Song is, nevertheless, an important supporting text in the writings of Hugh and his students, Richard and Adam—so much so that the Victorine contribution to the exegetical tradition eventually gained summary expression in the three thirteenth-century commentaries (dated 1224, 1237, and 1244) of Thomas Gallus.

6. Patrick S. Diehl, *The Medieval European Religious Lyric: An Ars Poetica* (1985), p. 135.

7. Cf. Marcia L. Colish, *The Mirror of Language: A Study in the Medieval Theory of Knowledge*, rev. ed. (1983), p. 162.

8. M.-D. Chenu, *Nature, Man, and Society in the Twelfth Century*, ed. and trans. Jerome Taylor and Lester K. Little (1968, repr. 1983), p. 113.

9. Charles Sears Baldwin, *Medieval Rhetoric and Poetic to 1400* (1928), p. 203.

10. Ulanov, p. 203.

a Hetaira bears a striking resemblance to the Cistercian process of spiritual formation. The Hetaira type identifies so closely at the subconscious level with her father's *anima* (that is, his latent feminine "otherness") that her whole conscious life is marked by childlike service and loving obedience, even to the point of total self-sacrifice. When this dominant vertical relationship to the great Father is complemented and balanced by the integration of the Hero-*animus*, the "puella aeterna" achieves her identity as a woman. Usually a love relationship with a man who exteriorizes the subconscious masculine side of herself ("animus") in the form of a strong masculine equal assists the process of self-possession. A prince, as it were, appears at her door and she, Cinderella-like, becomes a princess. The integrated presence of the heroic Other in her life, according to Ulanov, arouses "the individual, subjective, psychic life in herself and others" and enables a nearly "total realization of personality."[11]

Similarly, the person on the Cistercian *via ad Deum* first relates to God primarily as a servant and child. The relationship includes awe and fear, a deep yearning to please, and an enormous sense of vertical distance and "unlikeness." When the practice of charity has sufficiently conformed the whole person to God's will, God discovers and loves his own likeness in the human soul, which is then allowed to perceive and love the likeness of God, the Christ-Word within the self. The Bride suddenly finds herself in his nearness. This discovery precipitates a new self-confidence and a heady, fearless "fiducia" of love in the human partner who now dares to long for mystical marriage with the Word. Union with the Word, like the integration of the Hero-*animus*, preserves and confirms the original relationship to the Father by enhancing its depth, richness, and freedom. To this stage applies the scriptural word: "Perfect love casts out fear" (1 John 4:18).[12]

By evoking the *anima* within his monks in the form of the Hetaira-Bride, Bernard helps them to come to a deep self-knowledge; promotes a natural psychological development congruent to the working of grace; and assists the inner feminine complementarity that supports and inspires their own conscious striving for heroic

11. Ibid.

12. For a classical study of Cistercian asceticism, see Etienne Gilson, *The Mystical Theology of St. Bernard*, trans. A. H. C. Downes (1940, repr. 1955).

sanctity. At the same time, the developmental processes involved in the spiritual life (mirrored in the Song of Songs) tend to constellate in a narrative line that allows every auditor to discover his personal myth and retell his own life story as a romance of rescue and ravishment, heroic labors and longing, seeking and finding.

The relationship Bernard fosters between his auditors and the Hetaira-Bride thus serves to make the Song of Songs an eminently occupiable text. Because of Bernard's example and instruction, medieval readers and writers could freely appropriate the bridal "ego" and use the words of Canticles to express their emotions, inner attitudes, and aspirations. Indeed, Bernard's widely circulated *Sermones super Cantica Canticorum* taught them to read the Song as "the book of our own experience" and provided a successful model for its reliteralization in courtly and devotional works alike.[13]

In the pages that follow, I trace the narrative of the reading process recorded for us in the mystical treatments of the Song. In attempting to answer the question: "How did Bernard, how did the mystics of St. Victor, read the Song?" I am, of course, also addressing their reading of the world, of personal experience. The intimate tropology of the text renders inseparable the readings of the Song and of the self.

The Victorine Writings and the Medial Bride

Hugh of St. Victor indicates that the *Canticum* is to be read in the purely contemplative frame of mind, which is associated with sentiments of inner joy ("totam in gaudium") and sweetness ("dulcedo") and focused on God himself.[14] He further defines contemplation by distinguishing between it and meditation:

---

13. See Bernard, Sermon 3: I. 1 in *On the Song of Songs* I, trans. Walsh, p. 16. Before Bernard's canonization in 1174, the *Sermones* had already been translated into French. In that language and in Latin, they influenced Chretien de Troyes, the tales of the Grail cycle, Wolfram von Eschenbach, the anonymous author of "Jesu Dulcis Memoria," and others. Jean Leclercq offers a bibliography and other information in *Monks and Love in Twelfth-Century France* (1979), pp. 8–26, 86–108.

14. Hugh of St. Victor, *In Salomonis Ecclesiasten*, PL 175, c118. Subsequent references are parenthetical.

Meditatio est assidua et sagax retractatio cogitationis, aliquid, vel involutum explicare nitens, vel scrutans penetrare occultum. Contemplatio est perspicax, et liber animi contuitus in res perspiciendas usquequaque diffusus. Inter meditationem et contemplationem hoc interesse videtur. Quod meditatio semper est de rebus ab intelligentia nostra occultis. Contemplatio vero de rebus, vel secundum suam naturam, vel secundum capacitatem nostram manifestis. (PL 175, c116–17)

[Meditation is an assiduous and shrewd drawing back of the thought, either laboring to explicate something complicated or seeking to penetrate a mystery. Contemplation is a sharp and free observation of the mind expanding everywhere to look into things. Between meditation and contemplation there is this difference: meditation is always about things hidden from our understanding, whereas contemplation deals with things manifest in accordance either with their own nature or with our capacity to comprehend them.]

According to Hugh's definition, then, the twelfth-century reader of the *Canticum* did not approach the Song in a meditative way—that is, with a mind "laboring to explicate something complicated (*involutum*) or occult" through the discovery of allegorical correspondences. Rather, he took the traditional allegorical interpretation for granted and accepted the object of contemplation as something clearly visible ("manifesta") from the start. Whereas *meditatio* is occupied with one thing at a time ("semper circa unum") in a discursive mode of reasoning suited to seriatim allegorical analysis, *contemplatio* has a broad, expansive, all-embracing ("ad multa, ad universa") field of vision suited to the symbolic synthesis of image and tenor, letter and signification. For the contemplative, the Bridegroom is transparently revelatory of Christ.

The link Hugh establishes between contemplation as the proper way of reading the *Canticum* and contemplation as the direct vision of God enjoyed by the soul in eternity has a threefold importance for our discussion of the Song *qua poetica*. First of all, it places a primary emphasis on the anagogical dimension of the text's meaning—that is, its ability to communicate through its literal meaning essential, desirable qualities of the afterlife: love, beauty, and ecstatic joy.

Secondly, the nature of the contemplative act that, directed *ad multa*, finds God in every creaturely image, suggests a rationale for a new realism. As Richard emphasizes, visible goods have the power to assist us in our investigation of invisible realities ("ad invisibilium investigationem . . . nos adjuvare valerent") because of an essential likeness between the sensible and intelligible realms: "visibilia ad invisibilia similitudinem haberent."[15] At the same time, knowing creatures in their fallenness, transitoriness, and insufficiency ("caduca, transitoria, et insufficientia") leads us to a contrastive apprehension of the future plenitude reserved for us in heaven. In either case—whether likeness or difference is foregrounded in our awareness—the things of this world in their concrete reality have an essential place in the plan of salvation. They are, as Marcia Colish says, "the means by which God chooses to descend to man, in and through the conditions of human life . . . . not merely the rungs of a ladder by means of which man can transcend the world to get to God."[16]

Thirdly, the notion that the *Canticum*, as a contemplative work, requires a contemplative reading focused on God himself, suggests that the successful medieval reader of the Song found a single tenor behind each of the poetic images, a single, summary Word behind all the words, a transcendent Signified. The perceived aesthetic unity of the Song of Songs, then, depends on a common, vertical point of reference, not on logical or narrative connections uniting image to image on the horizontal plane. Indeed, as Diehl has brilliantly observed, "the principle of vertical coherence militates against horizontal connections among elements."[17] The need for a "continuity of vehicle" is virtually eliminated by the guarantee of a "continuity of tenor." Hugh of St. Victor gives expression to this very principle when he comments on the song of the turtledove which sounds within the *Canticum* as an embedded self-image of the Song. Hugh notes that the dove never varies her voice, never changes her song ("nunquam canticum suum mutat"). Her canticle is constant because she has one, unchanging beloved ("singularem dilectionem") to whom she directs her song—whether she sings of joy in his

15. Richard of St. Victor, *Benjamin Major* II.xvi, PL 196, c95.
16. Colish, p. 192.
17. Diehl, p. 124.

presence or expresses longing for him in his absence ("vel praesenti gaudium, vel absenti affectum").[18]

By classifying the Song as a work to be read contemplatively and defining that activity within the scheme of a systematic mystical theology (the first to be formulated in the West), the Victorines actually make it possible for us to name essential mental and emotional processes included in the medieval psychology of reading, processes that certainly operated in the reading and writing of other texts related to the *Canticum* such as gloss poems or *imitationes*. Their definition of the contemplative soul as a medial figure who sees the many in the One, the One in the many (Hugh's "omnia in omnibus"),[19] led them to read the Song "in modus contemplativus" as a fusion of letter and gloss, image and allegory. Their reading, in turn, influenced their writing. As a biblical model of poetry, the Song inspired Victorine writers to compose poems, meditations, and sermons marked by a joining together of disparate images (on the horizontal axis) through the pronounced power of a single, subsuming referent (on the vertical axis). To accomplish that coupling they employed four tropes particularly expressive of their medial vision of things: parataxis, paradox, *comparatio*, and *conversio*.

Paratactic Enumeration

The contemplative vision *ad multa* tends to perceive both world and text as a thesaurus of *signa*, each with its own separate, atomistic relationship to God as *auctor* and Creator. The ability of each sign to function independently and point ultimately to the same divine reality helps to account, as Diehl has suggested, for the marked parataxis in medieval religious poetry. Images can appear in almost any order, whole stanzas can be omitted or rearranged "without materially injuring the coherence and meaning of the text,"[20] because the tenor of every term remains constant.

The disjunctive structure of the literal *Canticum* as a collection of lyrics, as a drama without clearly assigned speeches or narrative

---

18. Hugh of St. Victor, *De Assumptione Beatae Mariae*, PL 177, c1221–22. Subsequent references are given parenthetically.
19. See Hugh of St. Victor, *In Salomonis Ecclesiasten*, PL 175, c118.
20. Diehl, p. 15.

connectives,[21] as a set of present-tense utterances registering a full range of emotions, is manifestly apparent. Commentaries oriented toward either spiritual or historical allegoresis had reduced that disjuncture for their readers by filling in the gaps, supplying logical and/or narrative bridges between the verses, glossing every image, and grouping clusters of details. Paradoxically, the density of the interpreted text, maximized by the cumulative *glossa*, led in the twelfth century to a new dispersion of its images in the Victorine treatments of the *Canticum*, in which the centrality of the divine person as the transcendent Signified of the Song secures its aesthetic unity to such a degree that its individual images become separable from one another and the order dictated by the source context. They become independent elements able to be inserted into spiritual treatises, homilies, and liturgical sequences in new orders and arrangements, without losing the allegorical *sensus* that remains theirs as *signa* of the Beloved.[22]

Hugh's *De Arca Noe Morali*, for instance, defines the soul as the site of God's in-dwelling "as a Bridegroom in a wedding chamber" ("ut sponsus in thalamo").[23] This microcosmic ark of the world is the place where the soul encounters God in special intimacy ("per dilectionem") through a multiplicity of *signa*. Those creaturely signs of God's presence are then enumerated by Hugh in his description of Noah's ark as a macrocosmic symbol of the whole created order redeemed through the Incarnation. Hugh lists fifty-two terms— from stars to trumpets to vineyards—paratactically, identifying each of them with a single tenor: "All this is one, is the house of God" (PL 176, c622: "totum hoc unum est, domus Dei est"). Thirty-five of the vehicles listed by Hugh are also found in the Song of Songs—among them, the pastoral images ("grex, pastor, columba, ovis, pascua"), the images of gardens ("paradisus, palma, ager, hor-

21. The exegetes, following Origen, commonly recognize four *personae*—the Bride, the Bridegroom, and the double chorus of their attendants—but the grammar of an individual line frequently allows its assignment to more than one *persona*. Who is speaking and why are then subject to interpretation. See Chapter 7 for a full treatment of the Song as drama.

22. For an excellent recent study of disjuncture as a symbolic mode, see Carol Braun Pasternack, "Stylistic Disjunctions in *The Dream of the Rood*," *ASE* 13 (1984): 167–86.

23. Hugh of St. Victor, *De Arca Noe Morali* I.i, PL 176, c621.

tus, rosa, lilia, fons, fluvius"), the military images ("turris, castra, acies"), the signs of kingship ("regnum, corona, thronus"), and the names of the Bride ("filia, soror"). The coincidence of terms underscores the *thalamus*/ark, microcosmic/macrocosmic, word/world analogy. Hugh concludes by saying that every Scripture ("omnis Scriptura") and the world itself ("mundus") have been created "propter hanc"—that is, for the sake of God's in-dwelling, for the divinization of *res* and *verba*. Everything bears reference to the One.

Perhaps the best example of the Victorine tendency to use the images of the *Canticum* in an enumerative, paratactic fashion is found in the Marian sequences of Adam of St. Victor.[24] Legend has it that the Virgin herself appeared to Adam as he was in the process of composing "Salve mater salvatoris" to be used on the feast of her Assumption.[25] That sequence, held to be one of Adam's most beautiful poems, praises Mary (in words echoing the Song) as a flower without thorns, a fountain of the gardens, a storehouse of fragrant unguents and pigments ("Cinnamomi, calamum, / Myrrham, thus et balsamum"), a sweet-smelling nard, a flower of the field, the singular lily of the valleys, a celestial paradise, the throne of Solomon, ivory and gold, a spreading palm tree, a woman brighter than the moon and stars, one whose love never dies ("Ardor indeficiens / Immortalis charitas").[26] Another of Adam's sequences, "Lux advenit veneranda," praises Mary as the sealed fountain, the enclosed garden, the bridal chamber of God (S XIX, PL 196, c1481–84).

No particular order governs the listing of symbols. Indeed, the apparent lack of order calls attention to the poem itself as a compendium, a thesaurus of images not unlike the world itself. The sheer length of the enumeration—like Hugh's catalogue of creatures on the universal ark—encourages the reader to contemplate the summary term on the vertical axis, the one name that subsumes all the

---

24. Adam (c. 1110–1180) is credited with perfecting the sequence poetry initiated by Notker Balbulus. According to F. J. E. Raby, Adam employs all the Old Testament images traditionally held to be prefigurations of Mary. See Raby, *A History of Christian-Latin Poetry from the Beginnings to the Close of the Middle Ages*, 2d ed. (1953), pp. 363–75.

25. Ibid., pp. 348–49.

26. Adam of St. Victor, *Sequentiae* XXV, PL 196, c1502. Subsequent references are given parenthetically by sequence and column number.

others—in this case, Mary. Hugh calls attention to the need for this kind of completion by the reader in the passage from *De Arca* cited above when he repeats "est" over and over again, leaving it up to his auditors to fill in the unstated predicate nominative: "domus Dei." *Contemplatio* sees the many ("ad multa") in terms of the One.

Paradox

F. J. E. Raby, Walter Ong, and other scholars of Victorine poetry note that the speculative theology that gave rise to Adam's liturgical writings often manifests itself in paradoxical wordplay and witty conceit.[27] The delight in paradox, as a mode of expression and cognition, naturally results from the Victorine practice of contemplation which is oriented toward a single transcendent Signified and, at the same time, looks *ad multa*, seeing every image in its distinct particularity as a unique manifestation of the One. Paradox is, after all, the yoking of two *signa* in a paratactic way that refuses to subordinate one reality to the other or deny the truth value of either. The seeming contradiction between the implications of the *signa* leads the mind from the horizontal to the vertical axis, upward to the divine (or divinized) reality to which both refer—a reality that subsumes and substantiates them both.

Hugh begins his sermon on the Assumption, in which he explicates the verses of the *Canticum* included in that feast's Office, with an extended consideration of a complex of paradoxes, among them, Mary's virginal motherhood, Christ's espousal of his mother, and the exaltation of Mary's humility. The letter of the *Canticum* signifies the relation of lovers, whereas the allegory brings the virginal mother-child relationship to the fore. Paradox results from collapsing the hypotaxis that subordinates *littera* to *allegoria* and considering the two *signa* paratactically: "Ipsa est genetrix tua, ipsa amica tua" (PL 177, c1210). The paradox of a mother/lover is resolved through a single, miraculous Signified ("Ipsa") on the vertical axis which is identified with each term separately. Hugh goes on to explain the truth value of each of the designations in a one-after-the-other man-

---

27. Cf. Walter F. Ong, S.J., "Wit and Mystery: A Revaluation in Medieval Latin Hymnody," *Speculum* 22 (1947): 310–41; Raby, p. 354.

ner that preserves the parataxis, while heightening the sense of a
religious mystery:

> Certe amica est tua, et genetrix tua. Amica tua quod intacta, gen-
> etrix tua quod fecunda. Tu siquidem integritatis filius, et fecun-
> ditatis amicus, matrem habens virginem, et amicam prole lae-
> tantem. (PL 177, c1211)

> [Surely she is your beloved, and your mother—your sweetheart
> because intact, your genetrix because fertile. You are indeed the
> child of integrity and the lover of fecundity, having a virgin-
> mother and a darling rejoicing in a child.]

Hugh's awareness of the rhetorical power of paradox to awaken
sentiments of wonder and awe is clearly indicated by his use of
apostrophe ("O res mira! O admirabilis amator!") and rhetorical
questions: "O humble virginity and virginal humility! How have
you come together into one?" (PL 177, c1211–12: "O virginitas
humilis et humilitas virginalis! Quomodo in unum convenistis?").
Because every paradox actually leads the reader to ask the same
question—the "how" behind the yoking of terms (usually) mutually exclusive—it is a composite *signum* that points to the divine
reality with peculiar force, while urging a reconsideration of the
individual elements joined together.

Adam of St. Victor's Assumption sequence, replete with borrowings from the *Canticum*, introduces the Marian paradox of an un-
plowed field ("terra non arabilis") which bears fruit. In the same
poem he greets the Virgin:

> Salve, Verbi sacra parens,
> Flos de spinis, spina carens,
> Flos, spineti gloria.
>   (S XXV, PL 196, c1502)

> [Hail, holy bearer of the Word,
> Flower from thorns, lacking thorns,
> Flower, the glory of the thorn hedge.]

The second line of the strophe enunciates the paradox of Mary as the
sinless offspring of a sinful race, a lily among thorns. The third line

points to a resolution on the vertical axis, the *gloria*, the apotheosis of the Virgin as one specially graced. Mary bears the word in a twofold sense within the lovely wordplay of the poem, not only by giving birth to Christ, but by being herself a paradoxical *mysterium* explicable only in terms of the divine. As such she generates poetry (at least as the Victorines understood it), for one cannot name her without contemplating the One in the many.

Comparison and Conversion

In the allegorical treatment of Jacob's song in *Benjamin Minor*, Richard of St. Victor assigns to Dan the duty of overcoming temptations in the weak through graphic depictions of the hellish punishments incurred by sinners in the afterlife; Nephtalim, on the other hand, strengthens the virtuous soul in fortitude, patience, and laudable desires through imagistic representations of the joys of heaven: "Dan gives warning, Nephtalim coaxes."[28] Richard illustrates the kind of sweet and winning language appropriate to Nephtalim, as the poet of paradise, with passages from the *Canticum*,[29] adding a rhetorical analysis of the tropes proper to anagogic expression:

> Ad Nephtalim pertinet per considerationem praemiorum inflammare desideria bona. Mirabiliter enim animum nostrum Nephtalim ad eorum desiderium accendit, quoties aeternorum bonorum imaginem ante mentis oculos adducit quod tamen duobis modis facere consuevit. Utitur namque aliquando translatione, aliquando autem comparatione. (PL 196, c15)

> [It pertains to Nephtalim to inflame good desires through the consideration of rewards. For Nephtalim wondrously enkindles our soul with desire for them as often as he brings the image of eternal goods before the eyes of the mind—something he is, moreover, wont to accomplish in two ways. For he sometimes employs translation, sometimes comparison.]

28. Richard of St. Victor, *Benjamin Minor* XXXIII, trans. S. V. Yankowski (1960), p. 45.

29. See Richard of St. Victor, *Benjamin Minor* XXIV, PL 196, c16–17. I quote and translate the passage in full in Chapter 1. Subsequent references are given parenthetically by column number.

A little later Richard actually identifies Nephtalim with this twofold use of *signa*, using "conversio" (a term, usually translated as "metaphor," found in the rhetorical handbooks) as a synonym for "translatio": "Nephtalim namque comparatio vel conversio interpretatur" (PL 196, c16).

Every sensory image—as a dissimilar similitude of God—communicates something of God's essence and thus is inherently anagogic: "Through the quality of visible things, Nephtalim rises to the knowledge of invisible realities" (PL 196, c15: "Nephtalim per rerum visibilium qualitatem surgit ad rerum invisibilium cognitionem"). In anagogic literature such as the *Canticum*, the use of tropes corresponds to the use of things. Metaphoric translation and comparison thus stand as two distinct methods of imagistic communication, the first grounded in similitude, the second in a lack of likeness.

In the Victorine writings inspired by the Song of Songs, comparison, as a technique leading to the imaginative apprehension of eternal goods, takes two forms. The first involves a simple use of the comparative degree and *a fortiori* exhortation. In Adam's Marian sequences, for instance, he asserts that even as the sun is brighter ("lucidior") than the moon, and the moon brighter than the stars, so too Mary is exalted above all creatures: "dignior creaturis omnibus" (S XXV, PL 196, c1503). In another poem he describes the Virgin's attributes by comparing them to the earthly goods they excel:

> Super vinum sapida,
> Super nivem candida,
> Super rosam rosida,
> Super lunam lucida,
>   veri solis lumine.
>   (S XIX, PL 196, c1483)

> [More than wine, sweet to taste.
> More than snow, shining white.
> More than the rose, blushing red.
> More than the moon, reflecting bright
>   the light of the true Sun.]

The second form the *comparatio* takes in relation to the Song involves a more sophisticated reading process. Not only are readers expected to take the text in its literal meaning and reflect that heaven is even more beautiful, sweet, and pleasant than the lovers' spring-time described there. They are sometimes called upon to read the literal text in an adversative, antithetical way that takes the negative terms to be symbols of this world, while interpreting the positive terms in a figurative sense as *signa* of the world to come.

A case in point is Hugh's commentary in *De Assumptione* on Canticles 2:11–12: "For now the winter has passed, the rains are over and gone; flowers have appeared in our land" (PL 177, c1214). The qualitative change from winter to spring in the temporal order (which is, by definition, paratactic) becomes a *comparatio* expressive of the hierarchical difference between this world and the next:

> Adversa quoque commemorantur, ut ardentis desiderium ad ef-fectum festinet, et properet inde exire, ubi tristitia sedet, ubi luctus commoratur, et miseria regnat. Hoc totum exsilium est. Deinde patriam suam laudat, et dicit quae gaudia, quae deliciae, quantae jucunditates et amoenitates ibi sunt. (PL 177, c1214)

> [And opposite things are called to mind, so that eager desire has-tens to act, and hurries to go out from that place where sadness has its seat, where mourning dwells, and misery reigns. This is all an exile. Then he praises his own Fatherland and says what joys, what delights, how many sweet and pleasant things are there.]

The difficulty of such a comparison, of course, is that it uses the vernal beauty and bliss of this world to prefigure the next while, at the same time, depicting this world in a constant winter of sorrow. The imagery of blossoms and bird song cannot be heard without an emotional response grounded in our sensory enjoyment of this present existence:

> Nihil hic est quod animum non subeat, quod cor non penetret, et quod affectum non transtigat. In ipso auditu inardescit mens, fla-grat desiderium, et concupiscentias suas animus ipse non capit. Neque enim sine delectatione audiri potest quod tanta dulcedine plenum est. (PL 177, c1214–15)

> [There is nothing here which does not steal into the mind, which fails to penetrate the heart, which does not pass into the affection.

For in the very hearing (of these words) the mind catches fire, longing bursts into flame, and the mind itself cannot contain its own desires. For anything filled with such sweetness cannot be heard without delight.]

Hugh thus formulates the perennial problem of the Song *ad litteram*, conceding that the imagery of the passage can either increase our attachment to this world or fix our hearts on the world to come, depending on whether or not we are willing to accept the text (and the earthly goods to which it refers) as a coaxing invitation to elsewhere. As Hugh says, there are many who love the goods of this world for the sake of possessing them ("ad habendum"), not for following them ("ad sequendum") back to their Source. And yet God and his poet-prophet call the Bride in this way that she might come closer to him, "for whoever does not come, does not arrive" (PL 177, c1215: "quoniam qui non venit, non pervenit").

The rhetorical power of pleasurable sense-images to provide such an anagogic summons explains the use of the trope that Richard calls the "conversio" or "translatio." It presents the images of the human body and the symbols of flowers, song, and scent—tangible things known through the senses—not for the sake of the things to which they literally refer, but because of the likeness they bear to unseen realities: "they are set forward by reason of similitude so that man might surmise from them what he does not know" (PL 177, c1215: "ipsae ad similitudinem proponuntur, ut ex eis cogitet homo quae non novit").

The rational imagination, active in the right reading of the Song of Songs, thus leads the reader into a medial condition, into a world that is both heaven and earth: "Et coelum et terra est terra ista" (PL 177, c1220). Sensory experience nourishes and brings forth ("nutrit et portat") its elements through the imagination, while faith and reason protect and illumine ("protegit et illuminat") them as *signa* of a higher reality. Accordingly, the vineyard of Canticles, the land of an eternal spring, is, as Hugh insists, in us ("in nobis") and contains the whole world ("continet totum mundum") through the contemplative exercise of the *intelligentia* which combines the sensible and intelligible realities.

The person who reads the Song (and the world) in this way is a medium like Jacob's son Issachar, whom Richard describes as living constantly on the borderline between heaven and earth (see *Benjamin Minor*, chapters 36–39). Even as the "conversio" combines an earthly vehicle and a divine tenor, and contemplation looks *ad multa* to see the One, so too the conversion of the reader/beholder involves detachment and attachment, self-denial and the sublimation of desires, based on the recognition of a dissimilar similitude between creatures and their Creator. At the same time, "conversio" of the poem strengthens him in virtue by giving him a foretaste of the world to come which engages him emotionally.

The earthly vehicle with a celestial tenor thus bridges the boundary between the sensible and intelligible realms for the reader with a contemplative approach to the text and enables his own bridal union with God; as Hugh declares, "toto in ignem amoris converso."[30] For the Bride whose *anima* constellates as a Medial Woman, the personal, contemplative coupling with God presupposes the visionary joining of earth and heaven and expresses itself in anagogic tropes— paratactic enumeration, paradox, comparison, and, above all, *conversio*—which link the many to the One, the One to the many.

Bernard's *Sermones* and the Hetaira-Bride

Even as the Victorine uses of the Song reflect and promote the symbolic asceticism of that school, Saint Bernard's *Sermones super Cantica Canticorum* are best understood in terms of their intended audience. Jean Leclercq has shown that Bernard's eighty-six sermons on the Song are not, as scholars long believed, transcriptions of the spoken word, but rather, carefully written and revised compositions prepared for a reading audience.[31] Using the generic form of talks delivered in chapter, Bernard fictionalizes himself and his auditors within the *Sermones*, thus preserving at once the intimacy of oral presentation and the stylistic precision needed to elucidate diffi-

---

30. Hugh, *In Salomonis Ecclesiasten*, PL 175, c118.

31. See Jean Leclercq, "Were the Sermons on the Song of Songs Delivered in Chapter," in Bernard, *On the Song of Songs* II, trans. Kilian Walsh (1976), pp. vii–xxx; also Leclercq, "The Making of a Masterpiece," in *On the Song of Songs* IV, trans. Irene Edmonds (1980), pp. ix–xxiv.

cult doctrinal discussions. The small Cistercian audience, whose fictional responses are recorded within the text, serves as *causa exemplaris* to assimilate the larger, intended reading audience and model the appropriate response to Bernard's exegesis. Preliminary versions of the *Sermones* were probably addressed to the monks at Clairvaux, but the sermon series as a whole was clearly intended for all of Bernard's spiritual sons as a *summa* of Cistercian asceticism.

As I have noted earlier, Leclercq's research into Bernard's historical audience reveals that the Cistercian communities (like the other new orders) were composed of men who had entered religious life as adults. Many of them had been married or had had sexual experiences. A high percentage were *nobiles* who had come from court circles and from the armies. Their ranks included former troubadors, and evidence suggests that the Cistercian recruits were familiar with the popular songs of secular love literature.[32] Internal evidence from the *Sermones* suggests a high-minded, striving community whose members were struggling for the sanctity of a vowed life against very human obstacles: their own fatigue, apathy, jealousy, pride, spiritual dryness, anger, and sexual concupiscence.[33]

In recent years such scholars as Jean Leclercq and Caroline Walker Bynum have looked to Bernard's historical audience for a solution to what is perhaps the most vexing problem in Bernardine studies: the apparent contradiction between his matter (spiritual love) and his manner of conveying it (the *amor* of the Song).[34] Leclercq argues that Bernard consciously incorporates amatory images into his preaching in order to help the members of his order recognize and accept "the more or less hidden impulses, motives, and memories of the infra-conscious" and raise them "to the supraconscious levels of the psyche where basic human needs become freely chosen op-

32. See Leclercq, "New Recruitment—New Psychology," in *Monks and Love*, pp. 8–26. I am summarizing his findings here.

33. In Sermon 48, for instance, Bernard warns against envy. In Sermon 7 he expresses regret that the monks sleep instead of praying during the night vigils.

34. Freudian critics such as Marvin Pope explain the combination in terms of an obsessive sexual repression, whereas scholars like Peter Dronke, who associate Bernard as a theologian primarily with dialectical analysis, conclude that Bernard "is unafraid to use the sexual imagery of the Song of Songs because it need not even for one moment be understood in its foul human sense." See Pope, ed. and trans., *The Song of Songs* (1977), p. 123; Dronke, *Medieval Latin and the Rise of European Love-Lyric*, vol. I (1965), p. 62.

tions."[35] Adapting Leclercq's basic method, which correlates the imagery Bernard uses to the psychological needs and experiences of his audience, Bynum sees the *Sermones* as reflecting not so much the attitude of Cistercian men toward women and marriage, but rather their conception of the feminine domain, the contrasexual, within themselves.[36]

This chapter builds on these psychohistorical studies of the *Sermones* by noting specific parallels between Bernard's exegetical method and the process of spiritual formation he advances in his auditors. There is a definite tropological relationship between what he says and how he says it. The way Bernard joins letter and spirit, interpretation and exhortation, mirrors and promotes the coupling of the masculine and feminine principles within the soul, the union of the Hero and the Hetaira, as a necessary psychological means for the soul's mystical marriage with the Word. Here as always, Bernard looks to grace for the perfection of nature, even as he presupposes a natural basis for its operation.

In the rhetorical analysis that follows, I delineate a three-part pattern of ascent/descent/ascent in Bernard's approach to his text which unites opposing movements along a single vertical axis in order to promote the psychological integration, the wholeness and holiness, of his auditors. The ascending movements from the carnal to the spiritual are intimately associated with the masculine principle in the process of sanctification. The central motion of descent, on the other hand, evokes the feminine principle in both the objective plan of salvation (defined by the allegory) and the affective response of Bernard's auditors. It is the descending line, proceeding from *allegoria* to *littera*, that reliteralizes the Song of Songs in Bernard's discourse, essentially defines its rhetorical appeal, and informs the final, imageless ascent.

The Primary Ascent: From the Letter to Its Allegory

Saint Bernard definitely affirmed a historical referent for the Song, associating it with Solomon's marriage to Pharaoh's daughter

---

35. Leclercq, *Monks and Love*, p. 104.
36. See Caroline Walker Bynum, *Jesus as Mother: Studies in the Spirituality of the High Middle Ages* (1982).

and the events recorded in the Books of Paralipomenon.[37] His exegesis regularly begins with the *sensus litteralis* and frequently takes the calculated rhetorical risk of dwelling on the *amores* described, adding details that feed the imagination of his auditors. For instance, Bernard expands upon the Bridegroom's praise of the Bride's cheeks ("Your cheeks are beautiful as the turtle-dove's"), even as he urges his listeners to cling to the allegorical *sententia*:

> Vide autem ne carnaliter cogites coloratam carnis putredinem, et purulentiam flavi sanguineive humoris, vitreae cutis superficiem summatim atque aequaliter suffundentem: e quibus sibi invicem moderate permixtis, ad venustandam genarum effigiem rubor sub-pallidus in efficientiam corporeae pulchritudinis temperatur. Alioquin incorporea illa animae invisibilisque substantia. . . .[38]

> [You must not give an earth-bound meaning to this coloring of the corruptible flesh, to this gathering of blood-red liquid that spreads evenly beneath the surface of her pearly skin, quietly mingling with it to enhance her physical beauty by the pink and white loveliness of her cheeks. For the substance of the soul is incorporeal and invisible. . . .][39]

In another sermon Bernard paints a vivid picture of the Bridegroom's approach to his beloved, couching it in rhetorical questions, before discounting it as an inappropriate act of imagination:

> Quid igitur? Pingemus nobis, sive in Psalmis ista legentes, sive in praesenti Cantico, virum gigantem procerae staturae, absentis cuiuspiam mulierculae amore captum, et dum properat ad cupitos

---

37. Cf. William of St. Thierry, *Exposition on the Song of Songs*, trans. Mother Columba Hart (1970), pp. 10, 117. William and Bernard discussed the Song together, especially when they were both ill and confined to the infirmary. See William, *Vita Prima* I.xi.59, PL 185, c258–59.

38. *Sermo* 40: I.1 in *Sermones super Cantica Canticorum*, vol. II, ed. J. Leclercq, C. H. Talbot, H. M. Rochais (1958), p. 24. Volume I contains Sermons 1–35; volume II, Sermons 36–86. I use this edition of the Latin text throughout, citing parenthetically only the sermon, volume, and page numbers.

39. Sermon 40: I.1 in *On the Song of Songs* II, trans. Walsh, p. 199. Hereafter, longer Latin quotations are followed by the previously cited Cistercian Fathers Series translations by Kilian Walsh (Vols. I, II, III) and Irene Edmonds (Vols. III and IV), with the volume and page numbers given parenthetically.

amplexus, transilientem montes collesque hos, quos videmus mole corporea super plana terrae tanta altitudine eminentes, ut et supra nubes aliqui illorum verticem extulisse cernantur? Verum non decet istiusmodi corporeas phantasias imaginari, praesertim tractantes hoc Canticum spirituale; sed nec licet omnino nobis, qui meminimus legisse nos in Evangelio, quia / SPIRITUS EST DEUS, ET EOS QUI ADORANT EUM OPORTET IN SPIRITU ADORARE. (*Sermo* 53: II.3, vol. II, pp. 97–98)

[What then? Whether our reading be in the psalms or in the present song, shall we imagine for ourselves a powerful man of great stature, captivated by the love of an absent girl-friend and hastening to her desired embraces by bounding over those mountains and hills whose massive bulk we see towering to such heights above the plain that the peaks of some seem to penetrate the clouds? Surely it will not do to fabricate physical images of this kind, especially when treating of this spiritual song; and it is certainly not legitimate for us who recall reading in the Gospel that "God is a Spirit and those who worship Him must worship in spirit."] (III, p. 61)

In a third passage the saint actually invites his monks to imagine a seduction scene, dramatizing the lover's speech for them before discounting it as a word play ("litteralis lusus"):

Puta ergo sic dicere sponsum: "Ne timeas, amica, quasi haec, ad quam te hortamur, opera vinearum, negotium amoris impedire seu interrumpere habeat. Erit certe et aliquis usus in ea ad id quod pariter optamus. Vineae sane macerias habent, et hae diversoria grata verecundis." Hic litteralis lusus. Quidni dixerim lusum? Quid enim serium habet haec litterae series? Ne auditu quidem dignum quod foris sonat, si non intus adiuvet Spiritus infirmitatem intelligentiae nostrae. Ne ergo remaneamus foris, ne et turpium, quod absit, amorum videamur lenocinia recensere, afferte pudicas aures ad sermonem qui in manibus est de amore; et cum ipsos cogitatis amantes, non virum et feminam, sed Verbum et animam sentiatis oportet. (*Sermo* 61: I.2, vol. II, p. 149)

[Imagine the bridegroom therefore saying: "Don't be afraid, my love, that this work in the vineyard to which we are urging you will prevent or interrupt the business of love. It will surely provide opportunities for that which we both equally desire. The vineyards have walls, of course, and these are welcome shelters for the shy." This is a word play. Why shouldn't I call it a play? For where is the seriousness in these words? The external sound is not worth hearing unless the Spirit within helps our weak understanding. Therefore let us not dally outside, lest we seem preoccupied with the allurements of lust, but listen with modest ears to the sermon on love that is at hand. And when you consider the lovers themselves, think not of a man and a woman but of the Word and the soul.] (III, p. 141)

In each of these three passages the imaginative identification for Bernard's auditors is clearly with the Bridegroom as he gazes on the face of his beloved, hastens to her embraces, and speaks with her about lovemaking. The woman is objectivized, whereas the thoughts and emotions of her male lover are sympathetically articulated. The expansive freedom with which Bernard plays upon the literal meaning of the text suggests that his method is directed by pastoral motives. By first unfolding the carnal meaning of the Song in an appealing way and then rejecting that same physical imagination as inappropriate, he enforces upon his auditors the painful awareness of their own cupidity. That awareness, moreover, precipitates a renewed conversion, a turning away from the self as unlikeness. As Etienne Gilson puts it, "the starting point" for Bernard is "the factual state of man"[40] and his ingrained *cupiditas*.

As a regular pattern in the *Sermones*, Bernard begins with an explanation of the letter of the *versus* before proceeding to the allegorical and moral meanings. In its literal meaning the *locus* of audience identification for Bernard's male auditors is invariably a masculine placement with the Bridegroom. After using the text *ad litteram* to awaken in his auditors a desire for the feminine (exteriorized in the Bride), Bernard leaves the literal/carnal meaning abruptly behind in an ascent to the spiritual sense of the passage. At this level the place of audience identification is redefined allegorically in terms of the feminine. The shift in placement provides

40. Gilson, p. 87.

Bernard's celibate auditors with an objective frame within which the legitimate need for feminine complementarity can be satisfied inwardly through bridal identification with their own *anima*.

In his unfolding of the allegorical meaning of the Song, Bernard redirects the yearning for sexual complementarity which the letter of the text has evoked by leading his monks to discover the feminine within themselves: "Who is this 'she'?" The allegory defines the Bride no longer as the exterior object of male desire, but rather as the inward complement of the masculine principle within the psyche, the affective domain that answers to reason, the soul that loves and enables one's receptive self-surrender to God. The exegetical movement from letter to allegory thus promotes a psychological movement from the projected feminine to the feminine that is self-possessed.

The allegorical *logos* that identifies the Bridegroom with God and the Bride with the individual soul not only affirms the sacramentality of marriage as the highest expression of love in the natural order ("excellit in naturae donis affectio haec amoris"); it also gives meaning to the need for sexual complementarity as an impulse toward ultimate completion by the otherness of God. Virginity, with its voluntary renunciation of a natural complement, thus intensifies a natural longing which, sublimated, finds its psychological fulfillment at a higher level in a bridal relationship to the divine Spouse. Bernard typically defines this relationship in terms of its affective quality:

> Quis dicit? Sponsa. Quaenam ipsa? Anima sitiens Deum. Sed pono diversas affectiones, ut ea quae proprie sponsae congruit distinctius elucescat. Si servus est, timet a facie domini; si mercenarius, sperat de manu domini; si discipulus, aurem parat magistro; si filius, honorat patrem; quae vero osculum postulat, amat. Excellit in naturae donis affectio haec amoris, praesertim cum ad suum recurrit principium, quod est Deus. Nec sunt inventa aeque dulcia nomina, quibus Verbi animaeque dulces ad invicem exprimerentur affectus, quemadmodum sponsus et sponsa: quippe quibus omnia sunt communia, nil proprium, nil a se divisum habentibus. Una utriusque haereditas, una mensa, una domus, unus thorus, una etiam caro. . . . Si ergo amare sponsis specialiter principaliterque

convenit, non immerito sponsae nomine censetur anima quae
amat. (*Sermo* 7: II.2, vol. I, pp. 31–32)

[Now who is this "she"? The bride. But why bride? Because she is
the soul thirsting for God. In order to clarify for you the charac-
teristics of the bride, I shall deal briefly with the diverse affective
relationships between persons. Fear motivates a slave's attitude to
his master, gain that of a wage-earner to his employer, the learner is
attentive to his teacher, the son is respectful to his father. But the
one who asks for a kiss, she is a lover. Among all the natural
endowments of man, love holds first place, especially when it is
directed to God, Who is the Source whence it comes. No sweeter
names can be found to embody that sweet interflow of affections
between the Word and the soul, than bridegroom and bride. Between these all things are equally shared, there are no selfish reser-
vations, nothing that causes division. They share the same inheri-
tance, the same table, the same home, the same marriage bed, they
are flesh of each other's flesh. . . . Therefore, if a love-relationship is
the special and outstanding characteristic of the bride and groom, it
is not unfitting to call the soul that loves God a bride.] (I, pp. 38–
39)

Noting that the church is the unique Bride of Christ, Bernard
goes on to stress that "each single one of us undoubtedly possesses
by participation"[41] a share in that brideship. In his concern to feminize his auditors, to lead them into a personal identification with the
Sponsa of the Song of Songs, Bernard explicates the allegorical
meaning with a certain impatience, "passing quickly through that
shadowy wood where allegories lurk unseen" until he reaches "the
open plain of moral truths."[42] As he says, his purpose in delivering
the *Sermones* "is not so much to explain words as to move hearts."[43]
The allegorical exposition, which deliteralizes the Song and shifts
the place of audience identification from the masculine to the feminine, is important in the *Sermones* mainly because it provides an
objective justification for a rhetorical use of the text *ad litteram*.

41. Sermon 12: VII.11, vol. I, p. 86.
42. Sermon 16: I.i, vol. I, p. 115.
43. Ibid., p. 114.

The Tropological Descent: From the Allegory to the Letter

Having taken up and dismissed the literal meaning of the Song as a "lustful allurement," Bernard returns to the letter—this time not as an isolated sign but as a metaphoric vehicle joined to its tenor. The Bridegroom does not stand alone; he is now identified with Christ and becomes his transparency, revealing Jesus to be a Lover. Because both the heavenly *amor carnalis* and lust, as its sinful counterpart, set the affections in motion in response to something sense-perceptible, Bernard imitates the divine pedagogy that sets the two in competition with each other. The rhetorical strategy Bernard employs in setting the letter of the Song in opposition to the literalized allegory aims at activating an emotive, and distinctly feminine, desire for God that "makes the carnal sense taste flat"[44] in comparison. In the process he converts the literal meaning into a sacramental, a *symbolum* that is a source of actual grace for his auditors.

Commenting on the "strange manner of speech and extraordinary disregard for names" in the Song—features that make it "quite different from the rest of the Scriptures"—Bernard concludes that "it is not the words which are to be pondered, but the affections behind them."[45] He consistently affirms the value and the necessity of the full range of human emotions in each person's total relationship with God. All those affections that belong to us as bodily creatures are to be directed to God who is Spirit, but such a transmittance is possible only through the mediation of sacraments and sacramentals, the outward signs of God which touch our senses and involve our feelings. Aware that the *littera* of the Songs, and his own words, can be such *signa*, Bernard points to the incarnate Word in a way designed to touch the hearts of his listeners.

The most developed metaphor in the *Sermones* is that which presents Jesus as the Bridegroom. Urging his audience to "look steadily" at the Lord, marked with the wounds of his Passion, Bernard describes him with such ardor that he ends by exclaiming "How beautiful you are, Lord Jesus!"[46] He tells his fellow monks, "Your affection for your Lord Jesus should be both tender and

---

44. Sermon 85: III.8, vol. IV, p. 204.
45. Sermon 79: I.1, vol. IV, pp. 137–38.
46. Sermon 25: IV.9, vol. II, p. 57.

intimate, to oppose the sweet enticements of sensual life. Sweetness conquers sweetness as one nail drives out another."[47] Bernard recognizes that strengthening the feminine domain, the Hetaira-self, within his monks through a bridal response to Christ-as-Hero serves to immunize them against lustful desires for the feminine exteriorized and objectified in sexual fantasies. At the same time, the Christ-Hero provides a redeeming model for the masculine side of themselves, elevating the *animus* (in relation to the *anima*) from a Seducer to a Savior, from a Ravisher to a Rescuer. Far from repressing or denying the fundamental feelings of attraction, Bernard evokes them and places them at the service of God, asking his listeners, "What human affections have you ever experienced, any of you, that are sweeter than is now expressed to you from the heart of the Most High?"[48]

The feminine, which figures so strongly in the relationship Bernard cultivates between his auditors and Christ, is also directly evoked in tropological exhortation when Bernard urges his monks to follow the Bride's example in their ascetical striving. Like her, they should meditate on Christ's passion.[49] Imitating the Bridegroom's dovelike beloved ("ut imitator castissimae volucris"), they should withdraw into the solitude of prayer.[50] When experiencing spiritual aridity, they should follow the Bride's example and beg for divine assistance.[51] Like the Bride, they should spread the odor of the best ointments ("fragrant unguentis optimis") through works of charity.[52] They should bestrew the marriage couch with the flowers of practiced virtue.[53]

The stress on an active, as well as contemplative, *imitatio* of the Bride leads Bernard to develop the maternal aspects of the feminine in his appeal to his Cistercian audience. "Remembering the breasts" of the Bride, for instance, should move the abbots of the order to follow her in nursing the life of the community:

47. Sermon 20: III.4, vol. I, p. 150.
48. Sermon 52: I.1, vol. III, p. 50.
49. See *Sermo* 43: II.2, vol. II, p. 42.
50. See *Sermo* 40: III.4, vol. II, p. 26.
51. See *Sermo* 21: III.5, vol. I, p. 124.
52. See *Sermo* 12: II.5, vol. I, p. 63.
53. See *Sermo* 46: I.2, vol. II, p. 56.

Discite subditorum matres vos esse debere, non dominos; studete magis amari, quam metui: et si interdum severitate opus est, paterna sit, non tyrannica. Matres fovendo, patres vos corripiendo exhibeatis. Mansuescite, feritatem ponite, suspendite verbera, producite ubera: pectora lacte pinguescant, non typho turgeant. (*Sermo* 23: I.2, vol. I, p. 140)

[Learn that you must be mothers to those in your care, not masters; make an effort to arouse the response of love, not that of fear; and should there be occasional need for severity, let it be paternal rather than tyrannical. Show affection as a mother would, correct like a father. Be gentle, avoid harshness, do not resort to blows, expose your breasts: let your bosoms expand with milk, not swell with passion.] (II, p. 27)

Calling the Song "the book of our own experience,"[54] Bernard works to establish a series of parallels between the affective love life of the Bride and the lives of the monks listening to him. Again and again he invites his auditors to see whether their "inward experience reechoes"[55] the psychological processes he describes, insisting that "only personal experience can unfold"[56] the meaning of Canticles.

The Final Ascent: Beyond Words and Images

The virtuous life to which Bernard calls his auditors, a life of conformity to the will of God, predisposes them for the reception of special graces during moments of contemplative *unitas* with God, when they can pretaste, however briefly, the joys of the afterlife. To kindle longing in his fellow monks for such intimacy with God, Bernard speaks out of his own *historia*, illustrating for his auditors how the word of the Song can become flesh, how its allegory may be literalized in personal experience. Bernard has become the Bride, and others, following him, can also enter into marriage with the Word:

54. Sermon 3: I.1, vol. I, p. 16.
55. Sermon 21: III.4, vol. II, p. 7.
56. Sermon 1: VI.11, vol. I, p. 6.

Sed prodar sane ut prosim, et, si profeceritis vos, meam insipientiam consolabor; si non, meam insipientiam confitebor. Fateor et
mihi adventasse Verbum—in insipientia dico—et pluries. Cumque
saepius intraverit ad me, non sensi aliquoties cum intravit. Adesse
sensi, affuisse recordor; interdum et praesentire potui introitum
eius, sentire numquam, sed ne exitum quidem. (*Sermo* 74: II. 5, vol.
II, p. 242)

[But I make this disclosure only to help you, and if you derive any
profit from it, I shall be consoled for my foolishness; if not, my
foolishness will be revealed. I admit that the Word has also come to
me—I speak as a fool—and has come many times. But although he
has come to me, I have never been conscious of the moment of his
coming. I perceived his presence, I remembered afterwards that he
had been with me; sometimes I had a presentiment that he would
come, but I was never conscious of his coming or his going.] (IV,
pp. 89–90)

The *Sermones* envision a final ascent of ecstatic prayer which, like
the first rising up, is imageless. Unlike the allegorical ascent, however, it is not a journey of the mind defined by the dialectic of *logos*
alone. Rather, it is an ascent to the divine Bridegroom which includes the affections, which couples the masculine with the feminine
principle within the soul, even as it joins the soul to God.
    William of St. Thierry, whose personal conversations with Ber-
nard about the Song influenced both his own exposition and Bernard's *Sermones*, describes the process of divine descent and human
ascent behind the writing and the reading of Canticles:

Therefore the Holy Spirit, when He was about to deliver to men
the canticle of spiritual love, took the story which inwardly is all
spiritual and divine, and clothed it outwardly in images borrowed
from the love of the flesh. Love alone fully understands divine
things; therefore the love of the flesh must be led along and transformed into the love of the spirit so that it may quickly comprehend things like to itself. Since it is impossible that true love,
pining for truth, should long rest content with images, it very
quickly passes, by a path known to itself, into that which was

imagined. But even after a man becomes spiritual, he still shares in the delights of fleshly love which are natural to him; but when they have come into the possession of the Holy Spirit, he devotes them all to the service of spiritual love.[57]

God descends to man, incarnating his divine Idea in corporeal images accommodated to human nature. The auditor is expected to know that the human *amor* that gains literal expression is an image of God's love. At the same time, the proper response to God includes delight, rooted in the auditor's sense-nature and stimulated by the concrete imagery of the text, but transferred through and beyond the vehicle to its tenor. The mind's journey eventually leads it beyond every image, but the original *affectus* evoked by the image remains in force, qualifying the soul's relationship to God.

In Sermon 41, Bernard himself links the scriptural word to the images conceived by the contemplative man in prayer and thereafter used by him in preaching. In his exposition of the gold and silver ornaments fashioned for the Bride (Cant. 1:10), Bernard describes how an ecstatic experience of God ("spiritu excedenti") is frequently followed by an influx of earthly images into the mind, images well adapted to the wordless truth that has just been imparted ("infusis divinitis sensis convenienter accommodatae"). Inspired by angels, these *similitudines* make the radiance of divine reality more bearable for the mind ("ipsi animae tolerabilior") and enable the person to communicate the truth he has experienced to others ("quibus communicare illum voluerit capabilior"). Not only do the angels produce these mental images within the mind; they also inspire the elegance of diction which renders the embellished truths easily understood and delightful to hear: "quo congrue atque decenter ornatae et facilius ab auditoribus capiantur et delectabilius" (*Sermo* 41: III.4, vol. II, p. 31). Thus the ascent of the mind and the descent of the Word unite in the wisdom and eloquence ("sapientiam cum eloquentia") employed in preaching: "ad praedicationis opus."

Significantly, Bernard uses a feminine metaphor—that of a mother suckling her babes—to characterize the preacher's descent to

57. William, *Exposition*, pp. 18–19.

his auditors in imagistic discourse. In Bernard's understanding, the feminine principle embodies the spirit and gives it the moving power of corporeal substances, engaging the emotions. Paradoxically, it is this descending line from *res* to *signa* which makes possible the heartfelt attachment to God, the bridal *affectus*, which gains its purest expression in ascent, *alienatio mentis*, ecstatic and sacrificial detachment from everything earthly.

In his definition of contemplative experience as imageless ("et similitudinibus exuat") and bodiless,[58] Bernard sharply contrasts the incarnational rhetoric that serves to fill the soul with a longing for spiritual marriage, and the actual realization of that desire, superimposing the line of ascent over the line of descent. Paradoxically, for Bernard the way down is the way up. The rapturous fulfillment of the soul's *desiderium*—which comes as a grace, as a result of divine initiative—depends on the degree of human longing. Humility and transcendence, self-knowledge and the knowledge of God, limitation in one's own being and completion by the Other, descent and ascent belong together in Cistercian *ascesis*.

In Bernard's understanding, the end point of the Song is clearly beyond its literal vehicle, whether one considers the moments of ecstatic prayer or *aeternitas* itself. His *Sermones*, however, will have served their purpose of *translatio* if they kindle the love and longing of their auditors for God and engage the human *affectus* in the soul's movement toward him. No *signum* of the divine Bridegroom— neither Jesus in his earthly existence, nor a dearly beloved friend like Bernard's brother Gerard, nor the poetic image of the *Sponsus* presented in the Song—can be perfectly equated with the One encountered in the wedding feast of the afterlife, but the likeness they bear to him has its indispensable power of attraction over the feminized human heart:

> Sic, sic in caelo esse non ambigo, ut lego in terra, sentietque pro certo anima quod continet pagina, nisi quod sufficit ista omnino exprimere, quantum capere illa tunc poterit, sed nec quantum iam potest. (*Sermo* 52: I.2, vol. II, p. 91)

58. See *Sermo* 52: II.5, vol. II, pp. 92–93.

[That in Heaven it is like this, as I read on earth, I do not doubt, nor that the soul will experience for certain what this page suggests, except that here she cannot fully grasp what she will there be capable of grasping, but cannot yet grasp.] (III, p. 51)

Taken together, the Cistercian and Victorine treatments of the Song realize to the full the tropological potential of the historicizing strategies we have seen in the ecclesiastical and Marian commentaries. Bernard's reading of the Song resembles the Marian expositions in two ways. Like Rupert of Deutz and Alain de Lille, Bernard tends to historicize the Song by supplying a narrative line to connect its images—not the Gospel story primarily, but the life story of his auditors. Second, like the Marian Mother-Bride, the Bride in Bernard's *Sermones* orients herself toward the personal and subjective— her experience of the Bridegroom himself.

The Victorine texts, on the other hand, also encourage the auditor's immediate identification with the Bride, but they do so in an imagistic, not a narrative progression, letting the Song symbolically bespeak the relationship between the world and God. Their fascination with the Song *qua poetica* and their atomistic approach to its images recall Bruno's lyrical linkage of letter and truth. While Bruno's Virgin-Bride is a dynamic expression of the feminine, the Victorine seeress a static one, they share a common orientation toward the objective and nonpersonal—the world as a field of conquest and vision, cipher and epiphany, veil and revelation.

In the Victorine writings the emphasis is on the *anagoge*, the upward leading of the images themselves as traces ("vestigia") of the invisible Lover. The creaturely signs speak of the God manifested through them. Hence, for the mystics of St. Victor, the *historia* of the Song consists in its concrete literal images treated atomistically and collectively as a thesaurus of signs pointing beyond themselves. Bernard, on the other hand, emphasizes the descent of God, who enfleshes himself in corporeal images in order to raise up humankind. That descent and ascent defines the *historia* of the Song as a narrative of divine wooing and human *raptus*. The Victorine reading stops time, as it were, to enter eternity in a single lyric moment, while the Cistercian view places the Song in the flow of time. Both readings represent the self as Bride, using the Song to express the individual's experience of God. Their imaging of self in bridal terms brings to the fore the role of the feminine principle in their spiritual development—the seeress within them enabling intuitive vision and understanding; the Hetaira, a personal self-surrender to the Other sealed *in aeternum*.

4

Middle English Transitions:
The Case of Richard Rolle

The streams of affective interpretation—ecclesiastical, Marian, and mystical—which arose in the twelfth century essentially determined the way the later Middle Ages received and imitated the Song. That, at least, is the conclusion we can draw from an examination of Song-related Middle English texts in a wide variety of literary genres. As I will show, the rich, synthetic unfolding of the Canticles tradition in vernacular writings confirms and continues the rhetorical strategies we have been detecting in the earlier, exegetical texts.

The New Testament plays of the York cycle, for instance, realize the dramatic definition of the Song as a dialogue between the church and Christ through a structured series of lyric utterances that invite audience participation and evoke a devotional response to the divine call. In these plays Mary figures as Mother and Seeress, speaking on behalf of the community, realizing the church's destiny in the pattern of her own life, drawing the audience into her archetypal brideship.

The religious love lyrics of the fourteenth century popularize the images and implied narratives of the earlier Victorine and Cistercian treatments of the Song, making them expressive of the private devotional experience of men and women alike, lay and religious. Like the *versus* of Bruno of Segni, these lyrics derive their basic forms—prayer, prosopopoeia, and dialogue—from the dialogic structure of Canticles itself. Like the Song too (and unlike the courtly lyrics with which they are often compared), these religious love songs define a feminine placement for their auditors, either as speaker or as addressee.

Pearl, the ornate dream-vision of the Northwest Midlands, records a process of consolation which is at the same time a myth of *anima* development, as the feminine soul-life of the narrator unfolds in a bridal surrender to the divine will. The psychological narrative centered on the conversation between the mourner and the Maiden has a striking analogue in Saint Bernard's *Sermones super Cantica*, where he contextualizes his passionate eulogy for his brother Gerard in his exposition of Canticles 1:4. The black but beautiful Bride, mortal but raised to glory, inspires in Bernard an increase in his own mystical brideship as he struggles to accept Gerard's death. In this Bernardine Bride the Pearl-Maiden finds her pattern and precedent.

The feminine that emerges in *Pearl* and in the *Sermones* as a dynamic principle of personal development also manifests itself in Richard Rolle's tempestuous history. In his writings, the use of various feminine *figurae* registers definite growth in the mystical life by tracing key psychological processes involved in affective integration. Rolle's relationship to women and to his own bridal self reflects and conditions his experience of union with God.

In the chapters that follow I examine each of these Song-related texts, following a roughly chronological order. I begin with Rolle, a mystic whose scriptural exegesis associates him closely with the interpretive tradition I have already discussed. The narrative of *anima* development in Rolle's biography prepares the way for a discussion of similar psychological processes in *Pearl* and *Pearl*'s Bernardine analogue, Sermon 26. I then turn to the religious love lyrics and their imagistic evocation of the feminine principle, linking that discussion closely to a treatment of the York plays, in which lyric utterances are carefully contextualized within an unfolding drama of salvation. What is a private prayer in the isolated lyrics becomes a communal expression of devotion in the cycle performances.

The rhetorical power of these texts depends in large part on their appropriation of the Song *ad litteram* within literary, religious, and social contexts defined by the Song's allegory. That is to say, the allegorical *logos* (Christ's relationship to the church, to Mary, to the soul) justifies the *pathos* of the Song's language and even necessitates it as a way of rendering dogma practical and experiential. The spiritual meaning of the Song needs to be embodied; the Bride ("anima") needs to be accepted as a personal "I," as a communal "we." In Richard Rolle's scriptural and somatic mysticism we find perhaps the most extreme form of that literalization.

The Song, *Canor*, and *Anima* Development in Richard Rolle

In Richard Rolle's writings, the historical tendency to reliteralize the text of the Song of Songs reaches a certain climax. Rolle's mystical experiences are carnal as well as spiritual; his reading of the Song becomes a song (*canor*) and conditions his whole way of contemplation, even as his experiences of God seek validation not in the traditional categories of mystical theology (purgation, illumination, and union), but in the scriptural word itself. Citing the Bible as the source for his terms and the confirmation of his experience, Rolle writes: "As I forsooth, seeking in Scripture, might find and know, the high love of Christ soothly stands in three things: in heat; in song; in sweetness."[1]

No single biblical passage has been identified as Rolle's authority, but the evidence of his literary *corpus* points to the Song of Songs. The hermit of Hampole stands apart from the other English mystics—the *Cloud*-author, Walter Hilton, Dame Julian of Norwich, and Margery Kempe—in his strong predilection for the Song. According to John Alford, Rolle quotes Canticles "more frequently than any other book of the Bible,"[2] with the single exception of Psalms. Rolle describes even the Psalter, which he understands to be the earthly outward expression of *canor*, in language derived from the Song: "þis boke es called garth enclosed, wele enseled, paradys fulle of appelles."[3] Indeed, Rolle introduces the subject of the Psalms

1. Richard Rolle, *The Fire of Love* I.xiv, ed. and trans. Frances M. M. Comper (1914, repr. 1920), p. 66. Comper's translation is based on Richard Misyn's 1435 Middle English translation of *Incendium Amoris*.

2. John Alford, "Biblical *Imitatio* in the Writings of Richard Rolle," *ELH* 40 (1973): 18.

3. *English Writings of Richard Rolle*, ed. Hope Emily Allen (1931), p. 5.

in exactly the same way exegetes traditionally define the allegory of the Song of Songs: "þe mater of þis boke es Crist and his spouse, þat es, haly kirk, or ilke a rightwys mans saule."[4] The Psalter and the Song of Songs are, in fact, so closely related in Rolle's understanding that the two books are only one song, each an extension of the other.

Hope Emily Allen and Robert Boenig have drawn attention to Rolle's *Comment on the First Verses of the Canticle of Canticles* as an important expression of his central themes.[5] Two of Rolle's English writings, the *Ego Dormio* and the "Amore Langueo" section of *The Form of Living*, bear titles taken from the Song, and the Latin *Melos Amoris* and *Incendium Amoris* recall Rolle's description of Solomon's book as "þe sang of lufe."[6] Many a poem of Rolle's bears the derivative caption "Cantus [or Canticum] Amoris." Rolle also relies upon the Song of Songs to illustrate the two stages of the contemplative life—"Amore langueo" (Cant. 2:5) summing up the essential *affectus* of the "inseparabel lufe" that conditions the lower form of contemplation,[7] and "Ego dormio et cor meum vigilat" (Cant. 5:2) providing an imagistic expression of the affective quality of "syngulere lufe" accompanied by ceaseless *canor*.[8]

Rolle's tendency to understand and explain his own mystical experience in biblical terms and his overriding interest in the anagogic dimension of the Song result in a presentation of the contemplative life which emphasizes the bodily component to an unusual degree. As we have seen, particularly in the case of the Victorine mystics, an anagogic reading of the *Canticum* tends to fuse the carnal and spiritual meanings as a means of conveying the bliss of heaven. Rolle's anagogic emphasis in his presentation of the *vita contemplativa* leads him to include corporeal experience—hearing, tasting, feelings of warmth—in a similar way that is easily misunderstood but perfectly consistent with the biblical *imitatio* informing all his work.

In Rolle's reliteralization of the Song of Songs, his fusing of letter and allegory, he mimetically expresses the personal union of body

4. Ibid., p. 7.
5. See Robert Boenig, trans., *Richard Rolle: Biblical Commentaries* (1984), p. 2; Hope E. Allen, *Writings Ascribed to Richard Rolle* (1927), p. 92.
6. See *English Writings*, p. 103.
7. Ibid.
8. Ibid., pp. 61, 106.

and soul which results from contemplative *unitas* with God. Hope Emily Allen rightly observes that Rolle "has carried to its ultimate and logical conclusion the doctrine of the immortality of the body"[9] in his insistence that "body and sawle joys in God lyvand";[10] that the transfiguration of the physical and the purification of the affections must begin in this life if it is to be perfected in the *visio beata*. Citing Saint Augustine, Rolle defines contemplation as "a gastely dede of fleschly affeccions, thorow þe joy of a raysed thoght."[11] Similarly, in his prologue to *The English Psalter*, Rolle calls the joy of contemplation "þe heghest þat may be in man lyfand in body and feland."[12] In the *Incendium Amoris* Rolle differentiates between (1) the rapture that carries the soul out of the senses ("extra sensum carnis") and (2) that which lifts the soul together with the body ("in sensu carnis") to God, arguing that the latter is the higher *raptus*, the earthly rapture Christ himself experienced as a Man.[13]

Rolle's somatic mysticism, based in part on the belief that holiness enables participation already here on earth in the properties of the resurrected body,[14] leads him to reify the anthropomorphism of Scripture in the description of his experiences. In Rolle's writings, according to Rita Copeland, "'honey' and 'melody' are not simply affective terms employed as sensual icons for a meaning that defies discursive expression: the experience of love *is* supernatural sweetness and song."[15] As Copeland puts it, "song is at once the form of expression and the thing expressed," a single term in which the metaphoric distance between tenor and vehicle is so compressed that "the verbal image assumes literal force."[16]

The semantic consequence of Rolle's all-pervasive use of Scrip-

9. Ibid., p. xxx.
10. Ibid., p. 118.
11. Ibid., p. 116.
12. Ibid., p. 6.
13. *Incendium Amoris*, ed. Margaret Deanesly (1915), p. 255.
14. In a keynote address at the May 1988 International Medieval Congress in Kalamazoo, Mich. ("Bodily Miracles and the Resurrection of the Body in the High Middle Ages"), Caroline Walker Bynum has linked "the flowering of somatic miracles in western Europe in the twelfth and thirteenth centuries" to the lively theological consideration during this same period of the doctrine of bodily resurrection.
15. Rita Copeland, "Richard Rolle and the Rhetorical Theory of the Levels of Style," in *The Medieval Mystical Tradition in England: Papers Read at Dartington Hall, July 1984*, ed. Marion Glasscoe (1984), p. 71.
16. Ibid., pp. 65, 72.

ture to record his experiences is that his words have an inescapable truth value participatory in revelation itself. Hearing the heavenly *canor* depends upon singing the psalms, even as the Psalter provides an earthly embodiment (the "verba") of that song. As Rolle expresses it in his prologue to the *English Psalter*: "Grete habundans of gastly conforth and ioy in God comes in þe hertes of þaime þat says or synges devotly þe psalmes in lovynge of Jhesu Crist . . . . And þam þat lastes in þaire devocioun he rayses þam in to contemplatif lyf and ofte syth in to soun and myrth of heuen."[17] Rolle's account of the conversion experience in which he himself received the gift of *canor* draws a similar link between the scriptural word and celestial audition. As he describes it, his meditation on Scripture disposed him to hear an angelic sound ("delectabilissimam armoniam"), which entered into him and which he now utters in his own prayers and psalm saying: "eciam oracionibus ipsis et psalmodia eundem sonum edidi."[18]

Rolle's profoundly biblical mysticism—with its body/soul, letter/spirit nexus—leads him to use a fairly stable and limited lexicon (mainly derived from the Song and the Psalter) in describing the inner life. The repetitiveness in Rolle's accounts, together with his tendency to reify the physical imagery of Scripture through claims of actual sensation, has led scholars to deny any genuine development in Rolle in the years following his famous chapel experience. Despite his popular reputation for sanctity and widespread influence during his own day,[19] the scholarly consensus is that Rolle remained, as David Knowles says, "a beginner"[20] in the contemplative life.

---

17. *English Writings*, p. 4.

18. *Incendium Amoris*, p. 190.

19. Hope Emily Allen notes that "Rolle's influence was very great during the later generations of the Middle Ages," pointing out that the writings of the *Cloud*-author and Walter Hilton demonstrate in part a reaction against him. See *English Writings*, p. lvi. Gabriel M. Liegey calls Rolle "probably the most influential English writer of the late Middle Ages." See "The 'Canticum Amoris' of Richard Rolle," *Traditio* 12 (1956): 369. Raymond W. Chambers reports that "investigation of English wills and of documents bearing on the ownership of books seems to show a dozen manuscripts of Rolle for one or two of *The Canterbury Tales*." See *On the Continuity of English Prose from Alfred to More and His School* (1932, repr. 1957), p. ci.

20. David Knowles, *The English Mystical Tradition* (1961), p. 54. See also George Wood Tuma, *The Fourteenth-Century English Mystics*, vol. I (1977), pp. 26–27.

Rolle's very concrete (because reliteralized) identification with the Bride of Canticles, however, provides a basis for a positive evaluation of his progress toward wholeness and holiness. As we have seen, commentaries on the Song of Songs indicate that a coupling of the higher and lower, rational and affective, masculine and feminine powers within the soul takes place as a condition for the simultaneous anagogic marriage, the soul's bridal union with God in contemplative experience.[21] Indeed, beginning in the twelfth century, the classification of the Song of Songs as affective literature brought to the fore not only the power of the literal text to engage the emotions, but also the *necessity* of affective integration as a basis for contemplative *unitas*.[22] Only if the *affectus* can be won over from carnal desires to the love of spiritual things through an organic transference can the natural disharmony between the intellect and the will be overcome, giving the psyche access to the deeper truths that can only be known through the combined, concentrated power of intellect and emotion. The "inner woman," the feminine self, must be wedded if God is to wed the soul.

If the hermit of Hampole attained to the unitive state in his mystical relationship with God, his own affective integration at the moral level should be evident, the tropological "marriage" being expression, means, and security for the anagogical one. As we have seen, medieval psychology consistently associates feminine *figurae* with the affective domain that is part of every person. I hope to show, then, that the changing way Rolle writes about (and to) feminine figures bears witness to a gradual personal assimilation of the feminine principle with its power to make Rolle, in truth, God's bride.

Through the various feminine *figurae* that appear in the writings of Richard Rolle, we can chart not only Rolle's psychological growth but also the stages in his spiritual development as a mystic. His youth is marked by an externalization and projection of the *anima* onto powerful feminine figures—temptresses (representing

---

21. See, for instance, Honorius of Autun, *Expositio in Cantica Canticorum*, PL 172, c349–50.

22. See A. J. Minnis, "Literary Theory in Discussions of *Formae Tractandi* by Medieval Theologians," *NLH* 11 (1979): 133–45; Vincent Gillespie, "Mystic's Foot: Rolle and Affectivity," in *The Medieval Mystical Tradition in England: Papers Read at Dartington Hall, July 1982*, ed. Marion Glasscoe (1982), pp. 203 ff.

the diabolic) and the Virgin Mary (representing the divine)—who attract him either to sin or to sanctity. As Rolle matures, he enters into a conscious relationship with his own *anima* by appropriating the words and attitudes of the Bride in the Song of Songs. In doing so, he opens himself, in the whole and holy way common to the great mystics, not only to the feminine principle within his own soul and to the women in his life, but also to God himself as the Bridegroom and Source of Song. In this matter of affective integration, which is closely related to that of mystical development, Rolle's commentary on his own life cannot be separated from his biblical exposition.

Projection: The Feminine "Other"

Rolle's autobiographical writings, included as digressions in his biblical commentaries and spiritual treatises, reveal that his greatest personal temptations were sexual. The Latin *Officium* prepared in anticipation of Rolle's canonization records one of his most serious trials in the seventh *lectio*, quoting the account Richard himself gives in his *Comment on the First Verses of the Canticle of Canticles* in a section that was later published separately in Middle English under the title *Nominis Iesu Encomium*:

It fell one a nyghte als I lay in my ryste in þe begynnynge of my conuersyone, þare appered to me a full faire ʒonge womane þe whilke I had sene before and þe whilke luffed me nogt lytill in gude lufe. And when I had beholdyn hyre and I was wondyrde why scho com swa on nyghte in þe wyldyrnes, sodanly withowttyne any mare speche, scho laid hire besyde me, and when that I felyd hir thare I dred þat scho sulde drawe me to iuell, and said þat I would ryse and bless us in þe name of þe Haly Trynytee, and sche strenyde me so stallworthely þat I had no mouthe to speke, ne no hande to styrre: and whene I sawe þat I perceyuede well þare was na womane bot þe devell in schappe of womane. Tharefore I turnede me to Gode and with my mynde I said "Ah Ihesu how precyous es thi blode," makand þe crosse with my fyngere in my breste, and als faste scho wexe wayke and sodanly all was awaye; and I thankked Gode. . . .[23]

23. "The Virtues of the Name of Jesus," in *English Prose Treatises of Richard Rolle of Hampole*, EETS 20, ed. George G. Perry (1866, repr. 1921), p. 5; quoted in *The*

This demonic visitation in the form of a beautiful woman (whom Rolle had known before his conversion) took place, as he says, in the early days of his hermitage. According to his confession in the *Incendium Amoris*, his conduct toward four different women in the Dalton household where he began his retirement earned him well-merited reproofs.[24] Looking back, Rolle says of himself, "my childhood was foolish, my boyhood vain, my youth impure" ("infancia mea stulta fuit, puericia mea vana, adolescencia mea immunda").[25]

In the *Incendium Amoris* and *Melos Amoris* Rolle frequently warns others aspiring to the contemplative life to avoid the company of women. He underscores his advice with references to his own experience as a beginner:

> Nichil namque ita neophitis nocet nec est aliquid quod tam cito a celica simphonia subtrahit sedentem aut quod humanum animum evertit ab amore eterno et repente reclinat a regimine rectitudinis sicut pulchritudo placens formose mulieris.[26]

> [For nothing so harms a novice, nor is there any thing that so quickly draws the one sitting in prayer away from the heavenly symphony, or that diverts the human mind from eternal love and causes it suddenly to bend back from the rule of rectitude, like the pleasing beauty of a beautiful woman.]

Women, whether present physically or *in memoria*, are especially dangerous to the young hermit, Rolle says, not only because their natural attractiveness tends to divert the *affectus* from its divine attachment, but also because women themselves are easily seduced ("faciliter seducuntur et cito vincuntur"), having a marked emotional propensity ("proniores ad delectacionem voluptatis") and being "less of reason" than men: "Minus quippe viget in eis racio."[27]

Rolle's youthful negative projection onto women of the darker passions within himself has its counterpart in a positive projection

---

Officium and Miraculum of Richard Rolle of Hampole, ed. Reginald Maxwell Woolley (1919), p. 7.

24. The account is given in Chapter 12 of the *Incendium*, pp. 178–79.
25. Ibid., p. 178.
26. Richard Rolle, *Melos Amoris*, ed. E. J. F. Arnould (1957), pp. 63–64.
27. *Incendium*, p. 263.

onto the Virgin Mary, whose femininity objectifies the noble (and as yet unrealized) possibilities of his own *anima*.

At the beginning of his life as a hermit, Rolle made his first public appearance in a church attended by his first patrons, the Daltons. It was the vigil of Mary's Assumption. At the invitation of the pastor, Rolle arose and preached an eloquent homily, presumably on the liturgical texts, which moved his auditors to tears.[28] There is, then, a definite link between Rolle's youthful acceptance of his vocation and his love for the Virgin. Images from the Song of Songs, included in the Assumption liturgy, permeate the *Canticum Amoris*, an early poem in which Rolle dedicates himself to Mary as her devotee: "Zelo tibi langueo, virgo speciosa!"[29] Twelve of the 156 lines of the poem praise the physical charms of the Virgin in an *effictio* that names her rosy lips, her golden hair, her lovely cheeks, her serene brow; the rest of the text describes her inner beauty in a rhetorical *notatio* that explains her power of attraction over him:[30]

> Virgo decora pari sine, vivens pure dilexi,
> Squalentis heremi cupiens et in aruis haberi.
> Per citharam sonui celicam subiectus amori.
> Virgo, quam cecini, animam sublima Ricardi.
>
> (ll. 153–56)

[Lovely Virgin without equal, I have loved you purely in my life, desiring a hermit's poverty and a life in the wilderness. Overcome by love, I have sounded a song on the heavenly lyre. Virgin, whom I have sung, lift up the soul of Richard.]

The *Canticum Amoris* is the only poem in the Rolle canon addressed to the Virgin. Dating from Rolle's youth, it reflects his struggle with sexual temptations and his need to dedicate himself to the one peerless woman ("pari sine") who could be a feminine object of his love without putting his vocation in jeopardy. Still unable to identify with his own affective domain, Rolle cannot identify with

---

28. See *Officium*, Lectio II, pp. 24–25.
29. Gabriel M. Liegey's article, cited above, includes an edition of the poem.
30. Cf. Liegey, p. 378.

the Virgin. She remains outside of him, the woman who inspires his manly worship and surpasses all other women in beauty and grace.

Identification: The Feminine "I"

Rolle's later writings continue to praise and honor Mary, but he no longer addresses her as his beloved. Instead, he accepts her life as a pattern for his own and sees her as an *exemplum* for his own bridal relationship to Jesus. It is no longer enough for Rolle to love Mary; he must *become* her and let her live within him as "Sponsa." The *Comment on the First Verses of the Canticle of Canticles* makes this clear when Rolle meditates on the mouth of the Virgin, kissed by God, and the breasts of the Virgin, touched and suckled by him;[31] and then proceeds to describe his own attachment to Christ in bridal terms: "I languish with the love of Jesus."[32]

Rolle's increasing conscious identification with the feminine principle within his own soul—and with it, an integration of *affectus* and *ratio*—is most evident in his appropriation of the words and sentiments assigned to the Bride of the Song:

> O Jesu iustissime, . . . veni qui vivificas; illabere languenti: en vulneror, nam viscera amore ardescunt; aperta est ianua animae amantis tui, quia Qui temperas adventum expecto et mortem non metuo, sed mallem quam mundum, ut graderer cum gaudio, quia amore langueo.[33]

> [O Jesus most just, come, you who give life; glide into the languishing one. For I am wounded; my wounds burn with love. The door to the soul of your lover is open. Because you keep back, I await your coming, and I do not fear death but rather I prefer it to the world so that I hasten with joy [towards you], because I languish for love.]

This passage is but one of many in the *Melos Amoris* and *Incendium Amoris* where Rolle describes the contemplative experience in terms of embraces and kisses ("adherens amplexibus, osculis anhelo")—

31. *Biblical Commentaries*, p. 96.
32. Ibid., p. 100.
33. *Melos*, p. 177.

images that express both his union with God and the redemption of
primal affections newly integrated within him. He compares this
state of psychic wholeness to a wedding feast ("cum epulis internis")
celebrated with music ("armonia audita") which anticipates the
Wedding Feast of the Lamb.[34]

Ordered Relationships: The Feminine "Thou"

Rolle's writings clearly indicate a mutual interdependence between his experience of mystical marriage with God and his growth
in personal integrity. As Rolle puts it, "the death of ill affections
belongs to him that takes heed to contemplation."[35] Sometimes he
speaks of a "heavenly shadow" or "cloud" that protects the contemplative "against all heat of lechery or filth."[36] At other times he
speaks of a languishing for God ("sapiencie increate et divine dul-
cedinis amore langueo") which overcomes the rival longings within
him for women or riches: "amore mulierum aut presencium di-
viciarum."[37] In his *Comment on the First Verses of the Canticle of
Canticles* he speaks about a mystical marriage with God which overcomes any disjuncture within the contemplative between his reason
and his affections, enabling him to live peacefully among women
without being tempted by them: "Therefore the ardor of eternal
love sweetly enkindles the mind divinely adamant so that now,
drunk with supernal sweetness, we are able indeed to live among
women and feel no delight of women in the soul."[38]

This final state, in Rolle's understanding, recalls the paradisal
order in which a certain natural love of man for woman, and woman
for man ("naturalis dileccio viri ad mulierem, et mulieris ad virum"),
untainted by lust, exists according to God's plan ("secundum naturam a Deo primo institutam"). This affectionate relationship between the sexes has its natural pleasures of exchange ("delectaciones
ut in mutuis colloquiis et tactibus honestis, grataque cohabitacione")
which can be meritorious if directed from within by charity ("cari-
tate informata").[39]

34. Ibid., p. 179.
35. *The Fire of Love* I.xi, p. 54.
36. Ibid., I.v, p. 30; I.viii, p. 41.
37. *Melos*, p. 175.
38. *Biblical Commentaries*, p. 78.
39. *Incendium*, p. 263.

When Rolle writes about the anagogic relationship between men and women which results from mystical marriage with God, he bases his words on his own experience. As Hope E. Allen has suggested, Rolle's last letters—*Ego Dormio*, addressed to a nun of Yedingham; *The Commandment*, seemingly composed for a nun of Hampole; and *The Form of Living*, written for the recluse Margaret Kirkby—support his claim that the gift of *canor* had gradually led him to an affective integration that enabled him to have friendships with women without moral danger or spiritual disquiet.[40] Rosamund Allen points out that the charitable exchange with a "solitary reader" in the epistles achieves a singleness of tone, a "clarification both of addressee and speaker,"[41] which is lacking in the earlier prose works. That horizontal relationship between Rolle and a particular human friend reflects in its depth and purity the vertical relationship of "singular love" the hermit now enjoys with God, and offers an indirect proof of an achieved mystical *unitas*. Rolle's ability to communicate with individual women in a whole and healthy way points to an affective integration within himself—the marriage of "vis inferior" with the "ratio"—as a precondition for, and fruit of, his mystical marriage with Christ.

The letters indicate that Rolle's identification with the Bride of Canticles has made possible a new relationship to the women in his life. Like him, they are called to be Christ's brides. Consciously acknowledged and directed according to the divine order, the affective domain is no longer a necessary cause for Rolle's separation from women; rather, it enables him to be effective as a spiritual director for his sisters. Joined to Christ as Christ's Bride, the hermit of Hampole can lead others to him. Thus, when Rolle writes *Ego Dormio* to woo the nun of Yedingham, he woos her for Christ:

> Forþi þat I lufe, I wow þe, þat I myght have þe als I walde, noght to me, bot to my Lorde. I will become þat messanger to bryng þe to hys bed, þat hase made þe and boght þe, Criste, þe keyng sonn of heven. For he wil with þe dwelle, if þou will lufe hym: he askes þe na mare bot þi lufe. And my dere syster in Criste, my wil þou dose

40. *English Writings*, pp. li–lii.
41. Rosamund Allen, " 'Singuler Lufe': Richard Rolle and the Grammar of Spiritual Ascent," in *The Medieval Mystical Tradition in England: Papers Read at Dartington Hall, July 1984*, p. 46.

if þou lufe hym. Criste covaytes noght els, bot þat þou do his wil, and enforce þe day and nyght þat þou leve al fleschly lufe, and al lykyng þat lettes þe til lofe Jhesu Crist verraly.[42]

This last text, in which Rolle freely woos a woman for Christ and with Christ, bears eloquent testimony to the inner marriage that has taken place within him, reconciling him to his own feminine otherness. The integrated *anima* has completed and perfected his masculine self, freeing him to be more fully a man among women because he has become himself a bride before God, *sponsa Christi*.

42. *English Writings*, p. 61.

5

Mourning and Marriage in Saint Bernard's *Sermones* and in *Pearl*

In the spiritual biography of Richard Rolle, I have traced key psychological processes leading to a full integration of the feminine principle in his contemplative practice. Those same processes of *anima* development find mythic expression in *Pearl*.[1] At the beginning of the poem, the mourner grieves for the loss of a girl-child as the feminine principle within him emerges from the undifferentiated subconscious. When he next sees her, she is a womanly projection, distant and distinct from himself, ideally beautiful. As she engages in dialogue with him, challenging and correcting him, answering his questions, he gradually comes to affirm her right to an existence apart from himself. Her accepted otherness becomes a desirable complement, and he yields to the longing to lose himself in her. That ecstasy, which leads him outside himself, ends abruptly in a return to himself. The disappearance of the projected *anima* forces the conscious discovery of the inner *anima*, the hidden pearl within himself that needs polishing through a practiced submission to God's will. Grieving over death (when the *anima*, at first uncon-

---

1. Ann Belford Ulanov provides a reading of the Psyche-Eros story as a myth of *anima* development in *The Feminine in Jungian Psychology and in Christian Theology* (1971), pp. 215–40. The stages she mentions roughly parallel the ones I detect in the *Pearl* narrative. The idea of *anima* development does not, of course, preclude the historicity of either the child or the visionary Maiden, but simply emphasizes the psychological response these *figurae* evoke and express.

scious and then projected, is lost to the ego) marks the stages of
growth and prepares for spiritual marriages, the mourner's successive reunions with the Maiden—at first in the Dream-Garden (*historia*); then in the mutual moral acceptance of God's will (*tropologia*);
and finally outside the limits of the poem in heaven itself (*anagogia*).

The psychological drama played out in *Pearl* unfolds in three parts
correspondent to the threefold movement—ascent/descent/
ascent—I have already charted in Saint Bernard's tropological approach to Canticles. In the masculine frame, which comprises the
opening and closing sections of the poem, the narrator struggles to
deal with the absence of the feminine, to discover the spiritual
meaning of the literal condition in which he finds himself. In the
dominant central panel (Sections II–XIX), the feminine is powerfully present in the Pearl-Maiden who descends from the New
Jerusalem as an allegory-made-literal in order to assist the narrator's
ascent. The central panel is delineated from the other two by the
Maiden's appearance and disappearance and by two symbolic
deaths. The first death occurs when the grieving narrator throws
himself upon the grassy mound to weep and sleep; the second, when
he plunges into the river that divides the living from the dead. In
both cases the Maiden's death and/or disappearance precipitates a
parallel dying to self that proves salvific.

Beyond this three-part structural similarity, however, other more
telling analogies link Bernard's *Sermones super Cantica Canticorum* to
Pearl. Both evoke the feminine as a dynamic, Hetaira-like principle
of personal development and treat the experience of loss and mourning as an essential part of a process of spiritual growth. In Sermon 26
Bernard commemorates the death of his brother Gerard, giving
passionate expression to his grief. He carefully incorporates his
elegy into his exegesis of Canticles 1:4 ("I am black but beautiful,
daughters of Jerusalem, like the tents of Kedar, like the curtains of
Solomon") and thus joins the experience of human loss to the mood
of love-longing that permeates the Song.[2] Like the sufferer in *Pearl*,

2. G. R. Owst reports that a funeral sermon was delivered in the cathedral church
at Worcester, c. 1390–1410, in which the speaker chose the same text from Canticles
("Nigra sum et formosa"), applying it to the *vanitas* theme. In it the preacher
dramatically addresses the ghost of a deceased woman, who had been beautiful in life
and whose body is now black and decaying. Owst associates the tyrannical image of
Death with Saint Bernard. See *Literature and Pulpit in Medieval England* (1952, repr.
1961), pp. 530–33.

Bernard comes (through an imaginary dialogue with the departed) to accept the beloved's right to a separate existence. That acceptance heightens Gerard's power to mirror the otherness of God and the anagogic fulfillment of Bernard's own being. Bernard describes Gerard in feminine terms as the Bride of God and as his own *sponsa*. As he enters into a new relationship with the departed, Gerard's brideship increases his own. Longing for Gerard, now wedded to God, thus becomes a desire for them both in the New Jerusalem through the mediation of the feminine principle.

In both *Pearl* and the *Sermones*, the loss of a human beloved initiates the narrator's inner struggle to accept God's will and eventually leads him to a deeper moral and mystical union with God. The human Other (a feminine or feminized figure) mediates the divine otherness for the mourner, who is changed through the interaction. *Anima* development, as a natural psychological process, thus finds its metaphysical meaning in the soul's relationship to God. Bernard goes beyond the insight of the Victorine mystics, who stress the power of Canticles, as an anagogic marriage song, to console the virtuous in their suffering through the promise of heavenly rewards: "per considerationem praemiorum," as Richard says.[3] It was Bernard's genius, and that of the *Pearl* poet following him, to convert the pain of separation from a beloved individual into celestial *desiderium*, assimilating the departed soul to the Eternal City, uniting an elegy with an epithalamium.[4]

The psychological movement—from grieving over loss, to reconciliation and ecstatic union, to longing for reunion—dictates the precise combination of literary genres peculiar to the two works: elegy, didactic dialogue, and visionary epithalamium. According to Laurence Eldredge, the unanswered critical question about *Pearl* "is fundamentally one of generic assignment: someone needs to devise or discover the definition of a genre that will include both the static view of the symbols and the dynamic view of the narrator's progress."[5] Bernard's elegy, in its Song of Songs context, provides that

3. Richard of St. Victor, *Benjamin Minor* XXII, PL 196, c15.
4. In the *Commedia* Dante accomplishes a similar fusion of human and divine love in the person of Beatrice. He does not, however, link the beginning of his spiritual journey with Beatrice's death.
5. Laurence Eldredge, "The State of *Pearl* Studies since 1933," *Viator* 6 (1975): 194.

definitional key. As a new (and controversial) form of *consolatio mortis*, Bernard's Sermon 26 anticipates *Pearl* in its use of imagery from Canticles, in its specific combination of literary genres, and in its psychological action. The sermon's own novelty helps to explain the relative singularity of *Pearl* in its generic mixture and define the spirituality common to both works.

Scholars have long recognized that *Pearl* is replete with images taken from the Song of Songs.[6] They have, however, overlooked any specific link between the poem and Bernard's widely circulated *Sermones super Cantica*,[7] largely because of the mistaken assumption that Sermon 26, as Patricia Kean says, "interrupts the sequence"[8] of ongoing exposition and does not actually belong to the sermon series.[9] A careful examination of Sermon 26 in the context of the preceding and succeeding sermons makes it abundantly clear that the Bernardine *consolatio* is carefully integrated into the *Sermones* as a whole. The elegy serves to amplify Bernard's exposition. Kean's passing comment that Bernard's words about mourning in Sermon 26 "could stand as a commentary on *Pearl*"[10] needs to be taken more seriously than she herself takes it, given the context in which those words appear: *In Cantica Canticorum*.

The complaint raised against Bernard by Berengar of Poitiers, Peter Abelard's ardent disciple and vociferous supporter, indicates that Bernard's contemporaries viewed Sermon 26 as an integral part

6. See Jefferson B. Fletcher, "The Allegory of the *Pearl*," *JEGP* 20 (1921): 1–21; Marie P. Hamilton, "The Meaning of the Middle English *Pearl*," *PMLA* 70 (1955): 805–24; Elizabeth Petroff, "Landscape in *Pearl*: The Transformation of Nature," *Chaucer Review* 16 (1981): 181–93; and Patricia M. Kean, *The Pearl: An Interpretation* (1967), pp. 17, 21, 55, 75, 84, *et passim*.

7. Jean Leclercq reports that twelfth-century monasteries of every observance possessed copies of the *Sermones*. See *The Love of Learning and the Desire for God*, trans. Catharine Misrahi (1962), p. 91. Kean observes that "there is no inherent improbability in the suggestion that [the *Pearl* poet] knew St. Bernard's work, since it is likely that no single writer had a greater influence on Middle English devotional literature" (p. 39).

8. Kean, p. 234.

9. Jean Leclercq has demonstrated that the *Sermones* are not, as formerly believed, transcriptions of talks given orally, but rather literary compositions carefully prepared for a reading audience. See Leclercq, "Were the Sermons on the Song of Songs Delivered in Chapter?" in *On the Song of Songs* II, trans. Kilian Walsh (1976), vii–xxx; "The Making of a Masterpiece," in *On the Song of Songs* IV, trans. Irene Edmonds (1980), ix–xxiv.

10. Kean, p. 234.

of the *Sermones*. Berengar criticized Bernard as a Latin stylist for mixing incompatible genres in his sermons on the Song, combining a death song with an epithalamium: "tragoedia risum procerit nuptiarum."[11] The peculiar combination of literary kinds chosen by the abbot of Clairvaux was, therefore, novel enough in his time to excite notice.

Bernard himself hints at the unusual nature of his passionate elegy by repeated reflection on his own feeling and speaking. He relates that he had "stood with dry eyes at the graveside" of his brother and "kept up a pretence" of emotional calm "lest [his] affection should seem stronger than [his] faith."[12] Realizing that his suppressed feeling was "growing all the more bitter . . . because it found no outlet" (p. 61), he finally decides to pour out his grief in the sympathetic presence of his fellow monks, his spiritual sons. In the course of the therapeutic lament that follows, Bernard vents his feelings, weeps without restraint, enters into dialogue with his listeners and Gerard himself, and eventually finds the grace of consolation "without ceasing to mourn" (p. 67), integrating his human emotions of loss and longing into the scriptural frame and the process of his personal salvation.

Saint Augustine's manner of dealing with his grief at the time of Saint Monica's death stands in sharp contrast to Bernard's and confirms the newness of the Cistercian *consolatio*. In the *Confessions* Augustine writes that he kept himself from weeping at his mother's bedside "by a powerful command of [his] mind," deeming that it was not fitting to solemnize her funeral "with tearful cries and groans," because her virtuous life offered the assurance of her eternal happiness.[13] Distressed by the force of his feelings, which opposed "due order," Augustine "sorrowed over [his] sorrow with an added sorrow,"[14] going first to the baths, and then to bed, in an attempt to calm himself. In the end, however, Augustine broke down in private and "took comfort in weeping" for her and for himself "for a

11. Quoted by G. R. Evans in *The Mind of St. Bernard of Clairvaux* (1983), p. 97. For Berengar's letter, see PL 178, c1863–64.
12. Bernard, Sermon 26, in *On the Song of Songs* II, p. 60. This translation, cited in full above, is used throughout, with page numbers given parenthetically hereafter. Sermon 26 dates from 1138.
13. *The Confessions of St. Augustine* IX.12, trans. John K. Ryan (1960), p. 224.
14. Ibid., p. 225.

small part of an hour."[15] Augustine asks his reader to interpret his weeping "as he wants" and pray for him "if he finds a sin in it." Uncomfortable with his own emotional response, which wars with both his reason and his faith, Augustine yields to weeping only as a concession to the weakness of his nature, excusing it with the memory that his mother Monica had wept for him before his conversion.[16]

Bernard, on the other hand, affirms the positive, God-willed value of grieving, making "public the depth of [his] affliction" (p. 69). He insists that his intense grief only superficially resembles the uncontrolled mourning of those without faith: "My emotional outburst is certainly like theirs, but the cause, the intention, differs" (p. 68). He then explains that the expression of one's feelings, as a psychological outlet, can keep one free from the bitterness produced by suppression. The flow of tears may actually "wash away the stains of those sins" (p. 67) that incurred God's anger. Mourning merits the grace of consolation from God and men, "for those who mourn shall be comforted" (p. 67). Finally, mourning, as a measure for the degree of mutual love, can intensify the emotional experience of human loss and thus increase our heartfelt longing for heaven and the personal reunion in Christ it promises.

The *Sermones* themselves dramatize the truth of Bernard's rationale for expressive mourning. Bernard's own grieving process becomes a means to marriage—within himself (in the union of *ratio* with *affectus*); with the soul of Gerard; and with God. Marked by Bernardine influence in its structure and spirit, *Pearl* too validates mourning as part of a positive psychological process that leads, through the power of love-longing associated with the feminine principle, from the experience of loss to the possibility of ultimate union.

Mourning over Loss

At the beginning of Sermon 26, Bernard applies the idea of a dark mortality to the tents of Kedar which enclose the soul. Digressing to

15. Ibid., p. 226.
16. See book III, chapters 11–12 of *The Confessions* for the famous account of Monica's weeping over her wayward son, and a bishop's assuring words to her that "it is impossible that the son of such tears should perish."

speak of Gerard's death and his own afflictive bereavement, he asks aloud: "I, whose life is bitterness, what have I to do with this canticle?" (p. 60). His rhetorical question finds an answer in his personal experience of death. Gerard's dying literalizes the allegory of the Bride's blackness: her earthly body, her human susceptibility to suffering, death, and decay.

Bernard's process of consolation begins with a depiction of himself at his brother's grave, casting clay over the body "soon to be at one with the clay" (p. 60) ("terram mox futurum").[17] Similarly, the mourner in *Pearl* starts his spiritual journey on the spot where his dear one "drof in molde3 dunne."[18] He addresses the earth, which claimed his treasure and deprived him of joy: "O moul, þou marre3 a myry iuele" (l. 23). Bernard reports that, at the time of Gerard's burial, he was striving to reconcile his emotions with his creed, consoling himself with commonplaces:

> At ego, quibus poteram viribus, fidei reluctabar affectui, nitens vel invitus non moveri frustra addictione naturae, universitatis debito, conditionis usu, potentis iussu, iudicio iusti, flagello terribilis, Domini voluntate. (p. 171)

> [With all the force of faith that I could muster I resisted my feelings, striving, against my will, not to be vainly upset by what is but our natural destiny, a debt that all must pay by the law of our condition, by the command of God and his just judgment.] (p. 61)

The passage could stand as a prose rendition of the confession in *Pearl*, in which the bereaved finds his heart warring with his reason, his will unable to rest in God's:

> A deuely dele in my hert denned,
> þa3 resoun sette myseluen sa3t.
> I playned my perle þat þer wat3 spenned,
> Wyth fyrce skylle3 þat faste fa3t;

17. *Sermones super Cantica Canticorum* in *Sancti Bernardi Opera*, vol. I, ed. J. Leclercq, C. H. Talbot, H. M. Rochais (1957), p. 171. The Latin citations from the sermons are taken from this edition. Hereafter I give the page numbers parenthetically.

18. *Pearl*, ed. E. V. Gordon (1953, repr. 1963), l. 30. This edition is used throughout, with lines cited parenthetically.

þaȝ kynde of Kryst me comfort kenned,
My wreched wylle in wo ay wraȝte.

(ll. 51–56)

Like the speaker in *Pearl*, who declares, "I dewyne, fordolked of luf-daungere" (l. 11), and who calls death "a þef" (l. 273), Bernard expresses his experience of loss in the language of a lover robbed by death:

Quo mihi avulsus est? Quo mihi raptus e manibus, homo unanimis, homo secundum cor meum? Amavimus nos in vita: quomodo in morte sumus separati? (p. 172)

[Why has he been torn from me? Why snatched from my embraces, a man of one mind with me, a man according to my heart? We loved each other in life: how can it be that death separates us?] (p. 61)

Even as *Pearl*'s narrator justifies the intensity of his mourning by the singular worth of the one he has lost—"Ne proued I neuer her precios pere" (l. 4)—Bernard invites his auditors to recall Gerard's great virtues and reminds them that no one was dearer to him:

Scitis, o filii, quam intus sit dolor meus, quam dolenda plaga mea. Cernitis nempe quam fidus comes deseruit me in via hac qua ambulabam, quam vigil ad curam, quam non segnis ad opus, quam suavis ad mores. Quis ita mihi pernecessarius? Cui ego aeque dilectus? (p. 172)

[You, my sons, know how deep my sorrow is, how galling the wound it leaves. You are aware that a loyal companion has left me alone on the pathway of life: he who was so alert to my needs, so enterprising at work, so agreeable in his ways. Who was ever so necessary to me? Who ever loved me as he?] (p. 61)

When the poet pictures the mourner sitting on the very hill where he lost his pearl, sleeping near her grave in an autumnal atmosphere of harvest and in-gathering, spices and stillness, he provides an imagistic representation of Bernard's sentiment: "I live, and I die in living: and shall I call this life?" (p. 62) (p. 172: "Vivo, ut vivens moriar: et hoc dixerim vitam?"). The spiritual death into which both speakers are drawn as a result of the actual death of a beloved facilitates the dying to self, the losing of self, that (in accord with the laws of nature and grace) necessarily precedes a new personal integration.

Reconciliation and Ecstatic Union

When the mourner in *Pearl* awakens in the Dream-Garden, he startles to see the girl-child he lost in a new form of womanly beauty. Dressed in white and gold, studded with pearls, she resembles the image of the soul in bliss which Bernard sketches in Sermon 27. Beginning with the words "My brothers, our friend has gone back to his homeland" (p. 74), Bernard goes on to depict Gerard (and every holy soul) as God's Bride. Like the *Pearl* poet, Bernard strains the limits of language in his attempt to speak of the ineffable:

> Quid, inquam, tale in se ostendit ea quae praeterit figura huius mundi, quod aequare speciem animae possit illius, quae exuta terreni hominis vestutatem, eius qui de caelo est decorem induit, ornata optimis moribus pro monilibus, ipso purior, sicut et excelsior aethere, sole splendidior? (p. 182)

> [What qualities can we find within the framework of this passing world that can equal the radiance of a soul that has shed its decrepit, earthly body, and been clothed in heaven's loveliness, graced with the jewels of consummate virtue, clearer than mountain air because of its transcendence, more brilliant than the sun?] (p. 75)

In his presentation of the Bride's eternal beauty as "an image of eternity" (p. 76), Bernard resorts (as the *Pearl* poet does) to using the enduring hardness and brightness of metals, gems, and stars.[19] After depicting the soul clad in virtues, he exclaims, "What are they but pearls in the jewelled raiment of the Bride, shining with unceasing

---

19. See Theodore Bogdanos, *Pearl: Image of the Ineffable* (1983), for a fine treatment of the poem's apocalyptic imagery.

radiance?" (p. 76) (p. 183: "Quid nisi margaritae quaedam sunt in sponsae ornatu, splendore perpetuo coruscantes?").

The projected otherness of the Bride—in both the *Sermones* and in *Pearl*—prompts initial feelings of estrangement in the mourners. When Bernard imagines himself in Gerard's presence, the abbot's first words to him express resentment over the dissimilarity of their fates, Gerard enjoying bliss, and he plunged into grief:

> Solum me divisio vulneravit. Commune, quod libuit; quod triste et lugubre, meum: in me transierunt irae, in me confirmatus est furor. Erat ambobus alterutrum gratia praesentia, dulce consortium, suave colloquium; sed tantas utriusque delicias ego perdidi, tu mutasti. Et quidem immutatis illis retributio multa. (pp. 172–73)

> [Only I am wounded by the parting. All that was pleasant we rejoiced to share; now sadness and mourning are mine alone; anger has swept over me, rage is fastened on me. Both of us were so happy in each other's company, sharing the same experiences, talking together about them; now my share of delights has ceased, and you have passed on, you have traded them for an immense reward.] (p. 62)

In a striking parallel, the first words the narrator speaks to the Pearl-Maiden after her appearance dwell upon the difference in their conditions. He half-reproaches her for her happiness in the face of his misery:

> Much longeyng haf I for þe layned,
> Syþen into gresse þou me agly3te;
> Pensyf, payred, I am forpayned,
> And þou in a lyf of lykyng ly3te,
> In Paradys erde, of stryf vnstrayned.
> (ll. 244–48)

Her seeming indifference to his suffering presents to his mind the possibility of a double loss: not only has she died; in her glorified state, in her utter transcendence, she has ceased to love him. The Maiden responds to this doubt, telling him, "Sir, 3e haf your tale mysetente, / To say your perle is al awaye" (ll. 257–58), lost—not in the earthly arbor—but "in þis gardyn gracios gaye" (l. 260) where mourning is unknown. She assures him that the Prince of Heaven preserved her for him when he placed her "in cofer so comly clente" (l. 259). Her transformation is meant, in God's plan, to be his gain. He has lost "bot a rose" (l. 269), and now a "perle of prys" (l. 272) is in store for him.

The psychological action played out in *Pearl* has a haunting antecedent in Sermon 26. Bernard tells his dead brother, "How I long to know what you now think about me, once so uniquely yours, as I sink beneath the weight of cares" (p. 63) (p. 173: "Quam vellem scire quidnam sentias nunc de me illo unico tuo, mediis nutante curis et poenis"). Reflecting on the heavenly joys Gerard experiences in God's presence, Bernard wonders aloud whether his brother still remembers him: "It is possible that though you once knew us according to the flesh, you now no longer know us" ("Forte enim, etsi nosti nos secundum carnem, sed nunc iam non nosti"). Dismissing his fear, Bernard expresses his belief that Gerard loves him more than ever, that their mutual affection has, through a wonderful transformation, become a thing of eternity:

Affectus proinde tuus non est imminutus, sed immutatus; nec, quando Deum induisti, nostri cura te exuisti: et ipsi enim cura est de nobis. Quod infirmum est abiecisti, sed non quod pium. Caritas denique numquam excidit: non oblivisceris me in finem. (p. 173)

[Your love has not been diminished but only changed; when you were clothed with God you did not divest yourself of concern for us, for God is certainly concerned about us. All that smacks of weakness you have cast away, but not what pertains to love, and since love never comes to an end, you will not forget me forever.] (p. 63)

In the fervor of his faith, Bernard imagines that he actually hears Gerard speaking to him in the words of Isaiah 49:15: "Can a woman forget the son of her womb? And if she should forget, yet I will not forget you" (p. 64).

In the spiritual assurance of an enduring mutual love, both Bernard and the narrator in *Pearl* are made even more painfully aware that death separates them from the beloved. The dreamer cannot cross the mysterious river without dying himself, and his appointed hour has not yet come. The prospect of a continued separation from the Maiden fills him with dismay and he asks, "Now haf I fonte þat I forlete, / Schal I efte forgo hit er euer I fyne?" (ll. 327–28). Similarly, Bernard observes that Gerard has been "transplanted into life" (p. 67) through a gateway that remains "simply death" to himself: "Aut quod illi vitae ianua fuit, mihi plane est mors" (p. 176). Unable to follow him through that route of passage, Bernard bursts into a river of tears: "Flow on, flow on, my tears. . . . Let my tears gush forth like fountains" (p. 67) (p. 176: "Exite, exite lacrimae. . . . Erumpant fontes aquarum").

Accepting the otherness of the beloved (as a condition for genuine complementarity) requires the two mourners to see God's justice in the disparity of their respective conditions. Bernard praises Gerard's virtues at length, recalls his own imperfection, and concludes: "I have no wish to repudiate the decrees of God, nor do I question that judgment by which each of us has received his due; he the crown he earned, I the punishment I deserved" (p. 69) (pp. 177–78: "Nec tamen contradico sermonibus Sancti, nec reprehendo iudicium, quo recepit quisque quo dignus est, ille coronam quam meruit, ego quam debui poenam"). *Pearl*'s first-person narrator has much more difficulty understanding the divine justice that underlies the Maiden's glorification, recalling that she died a mere two-year-old, able to recite "nawþer Pater ne Crede" (l. 485). Using a series of scriptural passages—the parable of the laborers in the vineyard (Matt. 20:1–16), Psalm 23:3–4, Luke 18:15–17—the Maiden explains that the innocent are deserving of a heavenly reward. Her summary comment provides a place for both holy men like Gerard and babes like herself in the heavenly realm:

> Two men to saue is god by skylle:
> þe ry3twys men schal se hys face,
> þe harmle3 haþel schal com hym tylle.
> (ll. 674–76)

When the narrator has come to a deeper understanding and acceptance of God's justice, when he is able to forget himself and rejoice in the Maiden's happiness, he is granted the vision of the New Jerusalem that is her dwelling place: "As John þe apostel hit sy3 wyth sy3t, / I sy3e þat cyty of gret renoun" (ll. 985–86). Ravished with delight, he beholds the bejewelled city itself, the wounded and wonderful Lamb, the virgins in his train; he hears the mystical "nwe songe" (l. 882), which has become an epithalamium for all those "arayed to þe weddyng in þat hyl-coppe" (l. 791). Finally he sees the Pearl Maiden herself in the procession behind the Lamb, and at that moment the desire to follow her awakens with great intensity within him: "þat sy3t me gart to þenk to wade, / For luf-longying in gret delyt" (ll. 1151–52).

Similarly, Bernard's meditation on the beauty of Gerard's soul in bliss turns into a mental image of the New Jerusalem "prepared as a bride adorned for her husband" (Rev. 21:2–3). In answer to his own questions about the relationship between the individual soul and the bridal city, Bernard explains—in an argument echoed in *Pearl*, stanza 66—that the church is the unique Bride of Christ ("My dove is the only one") in whose brideship many souls participate (p. 79). The beauty of the 144,000 is the splendor of "þe nwe cyté o Jerusalem" (l. 792).

The assimilation of Gerard into heaven itself, of the Maiden into the City, accomplishes imagistically the psychological transference of love for a human being into love for God and intensifies it. In *Pearl* the mourner's wish to be with the Maiden quickly turns into a mad resolve to plunge into the river that separates them: "Quen I se3 my frely, I wolde be þere, / By3onde þe water þa3 ho were walte" (ll. 1155–56). His attempt to do so marks the end of the dream-vision, the abrupt return to the world of transience.

This sequence in *Pearl* also has its counterpart in Bernard's sermon. Toward the end of his consolatory elegy, Bernard recalls how, on the night of Gerard's death, he was summoned to his brother's bedside. Gerard was filled with the bliss that is often granted to dying saints when their inner vision already beholds the celestial realm that beckons to them. Experiencing a happiness that is a foretaste of heaven, Gerard was singing ("sic cantabat") the praises of God: "Quanta . . . dignatio Dei" (p. 179).

Recalling Gerard's ecstasy inspires Bernard's own. His mind "fixed" on Gerard in his transfiguration ("intentus gloriae ejus"), he almost forgets himself and his earthly condition: "propriae fere miseriae obliviscor." Contemplating his brother's glory, Bernard longs to be with him in the heavenly city: "Would that I have not lost you, but have sent you on before me! Would that one day, however far off, I may follow you wherever you go!" (p. 70). In a bold appropriation of the passage from Apocalypse which describes the Virgins following the Lamb (Rev. 14:4), Bernard—like the *Pearl* poet after him—envisions himself following a holy and human beloved in the train of Christ, thus stressing the importance of an intermediary figure who directly engages the natural affections that are to be divinized in the marriage with God.

The inner vision of Gerard's beatitude, however, is a fleeting one. Bernard describes his return to earthly realities as an awakening from a dream:

> Sed revocat me ad me pungens dolor, facileque a sereno illo intuitu, tamquam a levi excitat somno perstringens anxietas. Plangam igitur, sed super me, quia super illum vetat ratio. Puto enim, si opportunitas daretur, modo diceret nobis: "Nolite flere super me, sed super vosmetipsos flete." (p. 179)

> [But the pang of sorrow quickly recalls me to myself from that serene vision; I am roused, as from a light sleep, by a gnawing anxiety. I continue to lament, but over my own plight, because reason forbids me to mourn for him. I feel that, given the occasion, he would now say to us: "Do not weep for me, but weep for yourselves."] (p. 71)

Longing for Reunion

In both *Pearl* and Sermon 26, the second, visionary separation from the beloved forces the mourner to see his own moral struggle to accept God's will not so much as a "yes" to loss, but as a means to overcome loss, division, and death itself. Conformity with the divine will expresses and secures one's union with the Beloved-in-God—at first tropologically, and then in eternity. The natural pain of separation belongs to God's will as a way of intensifying the longing that bridges the gap between earth and heaven.

The sentiments Bernard expresses as he rouses himself from the waking dream of Gerard—anxiety, uneasiness, and continued grief—provide a striking analogue to the emotions of *Pearl*'s narrator when he finds himself alone in the arbor, deprived of his dream, assenting with a troubled heart to God's will: "I raxled, and fel in gret affray, / And, sykyng, to myself I sayd, / 'Now al be to þat Prince3 paye'" (ll. 1174–76).

Scholars have often been disturbed by the troubled emotions that condition the ending of *Pearl*, noting that the narrator's final state is little better than his initial one.[20] What they fail to understand is the degree to which both Bernard and the *Pearl* poet affirm the necessity of longing in the salvific process, and the possibility of a tender and intense human sorrow in combination with a perfect acceptance of God's wish and will. As Bernard puts it,

> numquid, quia sentio poenam, reprehendo sentiam? Humanum est illud, hoc impium. Humanum, inquam, et necesse affici erga caros, sive delectabiliter, cum praesto sunt, sive, cum absunt, moleste. Non erit otiosa socialis conversatio, praesertim inter amicos; et quid effecerit mutuus amor in sibi praesentibus, horror indicat separationis, et dolor de invicem in separatis. (p. 178)

> [shall I find fault with his judgment because I wince from the pain? This latter is but human, the former is impious. It is but human and necessary that we respond to our friends with feeling, that we be happy in their company, disappointed in their absence. Social intercourse, especially between friends, cannot be purposeless; the reluctance to part and the yearning for each other when separated indicate how meaningful their mutual love must be when they are together.] (p. 69)

In Bernard's understanding, the strong bond of affection between his brother and him is actually a divine gift, a work of grace, revealing, promising, and safeguarding his eventual spiritual mar-

<hr />

20. See, for instance, Ann Chalmers Watts, "*Pearl*, Inexpressibility, and Poems of Human Loss," *PMLA* 99 (1984): 33–34; Bogdanos, pp. 140–47; Kean, *The Pearl*, pp. 213, 227–42; A. C. Spearing, *The Gawain-Poet: A Critical Study* (1970), pp. 167–70.

riage with God in *aeternitas*. Therefore he uses the language of lovers to describe his relationship to Gerard—"my soul cleaved to his" (p. 68)—and parallels that human oneness with Gerard's union with the Holy: " 'He who is united to the Lord becomes one spirit with him,' his whole being is somehow changed into a movement of divine love" (p. 63).

If Bernard's own eternal marriage with God is to be consummated, he must endure on earth a purgatory of longing—a *desiderium* for the Divine which is intensified by the human longing it assimilates and includes. Because Gerard is one with God, Bernard's longing for them both becomes a two-in-oneness. As he expresses it, "All by myself I experience the sufferings that are shared equally by lovers when compelled to remain apart" (p. 70) (p. 178: "Solus ego patior quod solent pariter pati qui se diligunt, cum se amittunt"). Like the Bridegroom of the Song, who declares, "Vulnerasti cor meum, soror mea sponsa," he confesses, "I feel it, the wound is deep" (p. 69) (p. 177: "Sentio, laesus sum, et graviter").

As Bernard uses amatory language in relation to his brother, *Pearl*'s narrator responds to the babe who has been transformed into God's virginal bride with the words and sentiments of "luf-longyng" (l. 1152)—his human desire finding its ultimate meaning in his own espousal to God. Knowing that his treasure is in heaven, the mourner continues to grieve—"A longeyng heuy me strok in swone, / And rewfully þenne I con to reme" (ll. 1180–81)—but his human response to the death of a dear one has become a hunger for her-in-heaven that reconciles him with the Prince and sublimates the pain of separation, turning it into a means of purification: "He gef vus to be his homly hyne, / Ande precious perleȝ vnto his pay" (ll. 1211–12).

Becoming a pearl like the Pearl, a bride like the Bride, represents the end point of *anima* development in the two mourners who die to themselves by submitting to God's will. That tropological dying secures their own integrity, opens the way for reunion with the departed, and prepares them for the eternal Wedding Feast.

In *Pearl*, Bernard's Sermon 26, and the extrapolated spiritual biography of Richard Rolle, we find narratives of *anima* development in which the male protagonists encounter the feminine at first outside themselves and then within their own consciousness as an integral dimension of self. Reading the bridal figure—be it Mary, or the Pearl-Maiden, or Gerard—as an allegory of the self necessitates in each case an identification with the latent feminine principle within the psyche. The integrated *anima* then gradually manifests itself in a new personal attitude toward God and his providential ordinance of things.

The various stages in these narratives are marked, as we have seen, by lyrical moments in which the speaker expresses intense emotions ranging from grief to love-longing to ecstatic praise. My main focus, however, has been, not on these lyric moments, but on the narrative line connecting them. In the next chapter I consider a set of religious love songs in which the characteristic affects of both the Song of Songs and the bridal spirituality inspired by that text gain expression in the devotional forms of popular piety.

6

Religious Love Lyric
and the Feminine "I"

In *The Form of Living* Richard Rolle advises the recluse Margaret
Kirkby not only to read the psalms and pray by calling the names
"Jesus" and "Mary," but also to recite the "cantus amoris" he has
composed for her.[1] Scholars frequently point to Rolle's epistolary
poems, Thomas of Hales's "Love Rune," the *Ancrene Wisse*, and *þe
Wohunge of ure Lauerd* as evidence that a considerable portion of the
religious love songs were, as Rosemary Woolf says, "composed for
pious women of noble birth or for women in religious orders."[2] Be
that as it may, the metaphoric identification of the individual Christian with a woman in love is an essential feature of many other
works—biblical, mystical, and liturgical—which were certainly
composed for male or mixed audiences.[3] The important point is not
the gender of the intended auditors but the feminine principle, the
anima, which exists in both men and women and to which these
poems appeal.

The Middle English religious poems that may properly be called
love songs are, in general, of two types: (1) those in which the
Virgin Mary figures, in Peter Dronke's words, "as a romantic hero-

---

1. *English Writings of Richard Rolle*, ed. Hope Emily Allen (1931), p. 107.
2. Rosemary Woolf, *The English Religious Lyric in the Middle Ages* (1968), p. 63.
3. One need only recall Bernard's *Sermones super Cantica Canticorum*, Hugh of St.
Victor's *De Amore Sponsi ad Sponsam*, Richard Rolle's autobiographical *Incendium
Amoris*, and the many *O vos omnes* complaints uttered by the crucified Christ to
passersby in popular lyrics and sermon tags.

ine in her own right,"[4] and (2) those in which Christ appears as the soul's Bridegroom. Dronke, Patrick Diehl, and Woolf all associate the Marian lyrics closely with the courtly tradition, while connecting the love poems directed at Christ with the mystical tradition and the Song of Songs as a model text.[5] None of them, however, explores the masculine/feminine polarity implicit in such a division of texts and traditions; nor do they examine the tropological implications of this polarity for the symbolic structuring of the religious poems. Let me begin pursuing this line by making some broad generalizations.

In the secular love songs the central consciousness and voice is almost invariably masculine.[6] The lover speaks *about* his beloved, not to her. She is present only in her absence, unnamed, unattainable. The speaker exteriorizes her as a goal to be achieved, an ideal to be realized; objectivizes her as a "bote for bale," a source of pleasure, and a panacea for pain. Essentially static, she inspires desires in her lover which motivate his exterior deeds and fill him with inner restlessness. The dominant pattern of movement is one of ascent, the humble lover being moved by eros to approach the remote and sovereign lady with whom he identifies his own happiness and self-fulfillment.

The audience of such poems is forced, both by the rhetorical distancing and depersonalizing of the feminine element and by the fictive (and/or historical) preclusion of an "I-thou" relationship between the lover and his lady, into an identification with the *animus*, the masculine principle represented by the speaker. Whether or not the historical audience was male or mixed is irrelevant. The rhetoric of the poems tends to masculinize its listeners. The postur-

---

4. Peter Dronke, *The Medieval Lyric* (1968), p. 69.

5. Ibid. See also Woolf, pp. 274–308; Patrick S. Diehl, *The Medieval European Religious Lyric: An Ars Poetica* (1985), p. 74. For a related discussion, see Patrick J. Gallacher, "The Annunciation Pattern in Amorous Persuasion," in *Love, the Word, and Mercury: A Reading of John Gower's "Confessio Amantis"* (1975), pp. 26–43.

6. Woolf observes, "It is, of course, the lover, not his mistress, who complains of love in the medieval lyric" (p. 63). The exceptions she cites are *chansons de mal mariee*. Dronke reports that he knows of only one *alba* in which the woman's voice is central, and that poem strongly echoes the Song of Songs. See *The Medieval Lyric*, p. 175. Dronke includes two Latin love lyrics based on the Song of Songs in *Medieval Latin and the Rise of European Love-Lyric*, vol. II (1966), pp. 335–38, 364. They are among the few in which a woman speaks.

ing of the poet as lover aims less at moving a woman to respond to
the poet's lament by granting him her favors than at winning general
approval of his performance as a lover, judged according to the
conventional rules of the game. Indeed, every enactment of the role
in the lyrics tends to be paradigmatic, offering would-be lovers in
the audience a linguistic framework for organizing and expressing
their own real or imagined experience.

Unlike the secular songs, which write out the feminine by defining it as nameless, absent, exterior, and unattained, the religious
lyrics enforce the constant rhetorical presence of the feminine as a
role to be played. In the lyrics of Richard Rolle and his followers, for
instance, the "I" of the speaker articulates an appropriate human
response of love-longing for the Savior in the form of apostrophe or
prayer. In the religious love songs that exhibit prosopopoeia, Christ
himself appears to woo the soul. Sometimes, too, the lyric is a
divine/human dialogue of lovers which combines prosopopoeia
with paradigmatic utterance.[7] In every case, however, the occupiable "ego" of the poem, like the central consciousness of the Song of
Songs, is feminine. The audience's "I" is invariably that of the Bride,
whether she herself speaks (as in the paradigmatic poetry of prayer)
or whether she is addressed directly by Christ. The audience's identification with the feminine principle in the form of a receptive
surrender to the Divine is expected and encouraged, moreover, by
the symbolic structuring of the poems themselves, in which the
dominant pattern of movement is that of descent, entrance, and
opening.

Whereas the Christ-centered love songs directly feminize their
auditors, the Marian poems do so indirectly, in a rapid mimesis of
the usual process of *anima* development. They typically begin with a
masculine alignment for the reader, who approaches the heavenly
Lady as an idealized projection of the feminine. Unlike the distant
courtly mistress with her "daunger" and inaccessibility, however,
Mary is responsive and welcoming, bending down from her en-
thronement. Her mildness quickly enables the reader to identify
with her. The speaker then modulates away from addressing her to

---

7. Diehl makes these formal distinctions in *The Medieval European Religious Lyric*,
pp. 141, 158.

addressing Christ with, in, and through her feminine mediation. Mary thus becomes the "other self," the embodied "feminea natura" of her male admirer.[8]

Both the profane and the devotional songs draw upon the same set of conventions: the springtime setting; the lover's complaint at the beloved's absence and inaccessibility; expressions of insatiable longing; references to the wounds of love; encomia of the beloved's body; the imagery of gems, gardens, sleeplessness, and burning; the lover's posture of humble vassalage; the association of consummated love with heaven and heavenly bliss. As Dronke puts it, "The language is the same."[9] Indeed, confronted with the overt similarity between the two *ad litteram* and the complexity of their mutual influence, scholars have seldom gone beyond the notation of common motifs and metaphors. Distinguishing features of the two traditions are usually discussed in other-than-literary terms of content alone which stress the difference in the love object: Christ substituting for an earthly lover, Mary taking the place of a beloved lady.

As I hope to show, however, the elements of the secular love songs which appear in the religious poems are assimilated according to the definitive pattern of the divine/human relationship established by the biblical Song of Songs and the *Brautmystik* associated with it. That pattern presupposes: (1) mutual affection between the lovers, (2) an association of the Bridegroom with Christ, (3) an identification of humankind with the feminine voice and, as a consequence of the latter, (4) the centrality of the feminine principle in the audience response engendered by the symbolism and rhetorical

---

8. Saint Hildegard of Bingen calls woman the "embodiment" of man's love. As a radiant reflection of God's essence (love), she has the power to lead man back to God through the attraction she exerts upon him. Men in whom the feminine principle has been integrated have a comparable power to elevate the women they love. Unlike other men who look upon women lustfully with eyes like arrows ("oculi aliorum ad eas velut sagittae sunt"), these men have beautiful and peaceful eyes ("pulchris et sobriis oculis") that harmonize with a woman's pure gaze ("ad ipsas honeste symphonizant"). Their actions are controlled. They have a woman's power to endure suffering, to be moderate, and to exercise a sensitive understanding: "Saepe autem multas poenas sustinent, ubi in possibilitate sua se continent, sed in eis est temperata prudentia, quam feminea ars habet, quae bonam continentiam ex feminea natura contrahit, et etiam intelligibilem intellectum habent." Dronke quotes the relevant passages from *Causae et Curae* in *Medieval Latin*, vol. I, pp. 66–69.

9. Ibid., p. 62.

strategies of the poem. Even as the secular love songs tend to masculinize their audience, the religious lyrics aim—directly (in the Christ poems) or indirectly (in the Marian lyrics)—at feminizing theirs.

The same analogy which links the literal/carnal *Sponsa* of the Song of Songs to her allegorical significance (the church or the individual soul) in the vertical frame of reference also operates horizontally in these religious love songs to assimilate the auditor in a particular dimension of his or her psyche: the *anima* or feminine principle with its characteristic tendencies. As we have seen, Saint Bernard of Clairvaux emphasizes that God reveals himself as a Bridegroom rather than as Master, Teacher, or Father in the text of the biblical *Canticum* in order to elicit a specifically bridal response, an *affectus* of loving surrender, from his auditors.[10] Similarly, the religious love lyrics that present Christ as a Wooer aim at kindling the same affection in their listeners. Frequently they focus attention on the body of Christ, naked and lacerated on the cross, as a proof of his love.[11] Christ himself speaks again and again to encourage a meditation on his sufferings with a personal application: "Lo! Lemman swete, now may þou se / þat I have lost my lyf for þe."[12]

Unlike the secular songs, these religious lyrics affirm an "I-thou" relationship between the lover and his beloved (however sinful and unresponsive she may be), encourage the reader's immediate and intimate identification with the feminine partner, and unequivocally approve her yielding to her divine-and-human lover. The Marian commentaries on the Song of Songs help to place the Marian love lyrics in this same scheme by underscoring the Virgin's exemplary character for her human lovers whom she incorporates into herself as *femina*, giving them a share in her own bridal/motherly relationship to Christ.

A complex coalescence with the Christ poems and the feminine principle animating them sets the Marian lyrics apart from the

10. See Bernard, Sermon 7:2 in *On the Song of Songs* I, Cistercian Fathers Series 4, trans. Kilian Walsh (1976), pp. 38–39.
11. Among the poems of this sort, see nos. 1, 2, 3, 4, 15, 46, 48, 52, 66, 68, 70, 74, 76, 77, 78, 83, and 91 in *Religious Lyrics of the Fourteenth Century*, ed. Carleton Brown, 2d ed., revised G. V. Smithers (1952).
12. Ibid., no. 78, p. 94, ll. 1–2.

courtly love songs with their masculine ethos.[13] As I hope to show, Mary's function in these poems as Mediatrix along the vertical line of human ascent (masculine) and divine descent (feminine) typically elicits a contrasexual (first masculine, then feminine) response in the auditor. The love poems addressed to her thus represent a merging of the two traditions—courtly and Christo-mystical—and reflect the polaric (and often unresolved) tensions between the two. The complexity of response engendered by the Marian lyrics serves not only to highlight the relatively simple feminization achieved by the Christological love poems, but also to define the general difference between the religious lyrics and their courtly counterparts in terms of a masculine/feminine reader alignment.

Mary the Lady

The fourteenth-century love songs addressed to the Virgin dwell upon her closeness to the Savior and frequently modulate into prayers to Christ. The Harley lyric "Blessed be þou, Levedy"[14] includes the speaker's repeated petition that Mary lead him to Jesus: "Prey3e Iesu þy sone þat he me rede ant wysse" (l. 3); "þy deore suete sones love þou lere me to winne" (l. 6); "wisse me to þi deore sone" (l. 12); "preye Iesu Crist, þi sone, þat he me grace sende" (l. 26). The speaker himself also prays directly to Jesus twice in the poem in abrupt changes of address which underscore the two-in-oneness of Jesus and Mary, and Mary's role as a teacher of prayer. Her action is to be imitated, her proximity to Christ appropriated. Thus the ascent of the *animus* to the beloved lady ("Bryhte ant shene sterre cler," "suete flur of parays") in the form of a knightly service and surrender ("þou here me for þi man . . . for þyn euer ycham") becomes, through her mediation, an identification with the femi-

13. As Dronke has shown, the secular love songs at their most sublime ascribe a genuinely religious function to the beloved woman who reveals something of God's love to her human partner and thus effects his transformation. Dronke points to Dante's Beatrice, and other scholars have characterized Chaucer's Criseyde in a similar way. In such cases, the secular relationship typically modulates into a sacred one that leaves the courtly sphere behind. See *Medieval Latin*, vol. I, pp. 69, 75, 87–97.

14. *The Harley Lyrics*, ed. G. L. Brook, 2d ed. (1956), no. 26, pp. 64–65.

nine principle in its capacity to receive the divine Bridegroom: "Iesu, mid þi suete blod þou bohtest me so dere" (l. 20).

Another Harley lyric, "Ase y me rod þis ender day,"[15] begins with the secular convention of a lover riding through the green wood, thinking of an unnamed, sweet maiden, and seeking "play." Only in the twelfth line does it become clear that the lady is Mary. Unlike the unattainable and distant women in the secular complaints, she is the speaker's "solas nyht ant day" (l. 14), his "ioie" (l. 15), his "dayes blis" and "nyhtes rest" (l. 20). His pleasure in her modulates into a meditation on *her* five joys, culminating with the Assumption into heaven. At this point the poem about Mary turns into a prayer to Christ: "Crist, leue vs alle wiþ þat wymman / þat ioie al forte sene" (ll. 53–54). Once again the masculine principle, with its pattern of ascent and conquest, finds its complement in a feminine receptivity to grace through the Marian mediation: "wiþ þat wymman."

The characterization of Mary in the religious love lyrics generally helps to unite the movements of ascent and descent along a single vertical axis by coupling her nobility with humility, her incomparable beauty with kindness and benignity. The Harley lyrics celebrate her "milde mod."[16] The fifteenth-century lyric "Upon a Lady my Love is Lente"—which, like many of the later Marian poems strongly influenced by the courtly tradition with its masculine consciousness,[17] does not modulate into a direct address to Christ— combines an absolute knightly vassalage before Mary ("to serve this lady we all be bounde") with an awareness that she is readily attainable ("never fer to seke, / Nother too grete ner too small") and available to help her children ("Redy she is night and day").[18] Serving such a lady, named and near, indirectly feminizes her lover and, with him, the reader who identifies with his "I." She herself is not the goal, but represents the way to the goal through her mediation: "Pray we to this lady bright, / In the worship of the Trinite, / To bring us alle to heven light" (ll. 25–27).

15. Ibid., no. 27, pp. 65–66.
16. The phrase occurs in both nos. 26 and 27.
17. See Woolf, p. 2.
18. No. 188 in *Middle English Lyrics*, ed. Maxwell S. Luria and Richard L. Hoffman (1974), p. 177. This poem also appears in Carleton Brown's edition of fifteenth-century lyrics.

"Quia Amore Langueo" (c. 1400), probably the most famous of the Marian love songs, illustrates the general pattern I have been delineating.[19] The initial reader placement is masculine. A moon-struck lover envisions Mary as a "crouned quene" (l. 3) who appears high above him at a tower window. He hears her express her love-longing in the words of the Song of Songs. Her languishing for Christ has extended into "loue of man" (l. 9), whom she wishes to unite to herself. She address the listener in second person: "I loue the soo" (l. 62); begs him to turn from his sin; and calls herself his "moder" (l. 33), "suster" (l. 47), "frende" (l. 63), and "loue" (l. 90). "Hygh in heuen" (l. 84), she invites his ascent to claim the noble heritage in store for him: "come þer-to" (l. 94). Finally she proposes a marriage that will turn him into herself: "Take me for þy wyfe and lerne to synge, / *Quia amore langueo*" (ll. 95–96). The imagined consummation of a union with Mary necessarily feminizes her lover, who now shares in her languishing for Christ and for man-kind. Thus the refrain from Canticles shifts from prosopopoeia to prayer as the lover first hears her words and then appropriates them, to become himself a mother and bride.

Christ the Lover

The Marian love songs eventually lead to Christ, shifting the reader gradually from a masculine to a feminine placement; but the Christological lyrics evoke the *anima* directly and immediately. Sometimes the feminine self speaks to Christ in prayer: "Suete ihesu, kyng of blysse, / myn huerte loue, myn huerte lisse."[20] Sometimes Christ himself professes a Bridegroom's love: "Mi loue is falle vp-on a may, / For loue of hire i defende þis day."[21] More rarely, the divine and human voices join in dialogue. Taken together, these three lyrical kinds—prayer, prosopopoeia, and dialogue— reflect the dialogic structure of the Song itself and thus continue in the vernacular the imitative trend we have already seen in Bruno of

19. *Religious Lyrics of the Fourteenth Century*, no. 132, pp. 234–37.
20. Ibid., no. 7, p. 7, ll. 1–2.
21. Ibid., no. 73, p. 90, ll. 1–2.

Segni's Latin *versus*. A close look at an example of each kind will clarify the feminizing rhetorical strategies they typically employ.

Prayer: The Feminine "I"

> Ihesu, als þow me made & boght,
> þou be my lufe & all my thoght,
> and help þat I war to þe broght—
> with-owten þe may I do noght.
>
> Ihesu, als þou may do þi wille,
> and nathyng es þat þe may lette,
> With þi grace my hert fulfill,
> my lufe & my lykyng in þe sette.
>
> Iesu, at þi wille I pray þat I mot be;
> All my hert fulfill with perfyte lufe to þe.
> þat I haue done ill, Ihesu, forgyf þow me,
> And suffer me neuer to spill, Ihesu, for þi pyte.
> Amen.[22]

This prayer is included among the "cantica divini amoris" attributed to Richard Rolle by the scribe of the Cambridge University manuscript (Dd. 5.64, III) in which it is extant. Although, as Carleton Brown observes, it exhibits the "fervid mysticism"[23] of Rolle's attested writings, it cannot be called erotic in the sense of any explicit sexual (or even sensual) imagery. Nevertheless it gives an affective expression to the feminine principle within the psyche as it calls out for completion by the otherness of Christ, and thus implicitly sacramentalizes sexual difference as the outward sign of humankind's need for God and innate attraction to him as *telos*.

The first stanza opens with the bridal self's recognition of the two main pledges (*arrhae*) of Jesus's love: "als þow me made & boght." Creation and redemption warrant a generous return of love, the speaker's total self-giving to Christ. This, however, is impossible without the Bridegroom's taking possession of her. The soul admits her powerlessness ("with-owten þe may I do noght") and, like the

22. Ibid., no. 80, p. 95.
23. Ibid., p. xix.

Bride of Canticles who begs to be drawn to her Spouse ("trahe me post te"), she asks to be taken to Jesus.

Increased intimacy characterizes the second stanza. In the Bridegroom's presence the *anima* actively surrenders to his will, placing herself in his power. In a petition analogous to a request for intercourse, the bridal self begs Jesus to fill her heart with his grace and transfix her love and liking.

To the extent that the Bridegroom *does* his will with her, she is *at* his will. Complemented and completed by the masculine principle represented in Jesus through union with him, the soul becomes stronger and more capable of action. In the third stanza the speaker aspires to "perfyte lufe," confesses the evil she has done as an independent agent, and requests eternal life: "suffer me neuer to spille." The divine/human marriage thus effects an inward integration that contains the hope of immortality and total divinization.

As a paradigmatic utterance the prayer assimilates its auditors into the feminine "I" and thus directs their spiritual formation through the threefold movement of the poem: (1) the recognition of helplessness, (2) receptive surrender to the Beloved, and (3) active coordination with him. To the extent that the audience occupies the bridal ego, they are, in turn, entered by Christ and filled with his grace. The repeated address to "Ihesu" and the rhetorical focusing on "thou" fashion an atmosphere of intimacy in which the self can be lost in the Other in an imitation of *ecstasis*. Without the imagery of sex, this simple poem virtually achieves a metaphysics of sexuality by invoking the feminine in relation to a masculine and divine otherness. At the same time it engages the emotions that characterize the feminine principle and places them at the service of Christ as a motivating force for moral action: "Ihesu, at þi wille I pray þat I mot be."

Prosopopoeia: The Feminine "Thou"

The sixteen-stanza lyric "In a valey of þis restles mynde"[24] is perhaps the finest of the vernacular poems inspired by the *Canticum*.

24. "Quia Amore Langueo" in *Political, Religious, and Love Poems*, EETS 15, ed. F. J. Furnivall (1866, reedited 1903, repr. 1965), pp. 180–89. I use the version found in Lambeth Ms. 853. Furnivall names the poem by its refrain. I have referred to it by its first line to avoid confusing it with the Marian lyric, cited above, which has the same refrain.

It literalizes the traditional allegory that identifies Christ with the Bridegroom of the soul through his visionary appearance as a lover-knight wounded in the search for his spouse. The poem's refrain, "Quia amore langueo," is taken from Canticles 2:5 and 5:8. The lyric incorporates key images of the Song—the cleft rock, the latticed window, the bridal chamber—and paraphrases the sensuous biblical invitation to enter the lover's garden, abounding in ripe apples, and there to dine and drink "mylk, hony, & wiyn" (l. 84). Even more important, perhaps, it imitates the poetic technique of the Song which minimizes the distinction between present experience and memory, the actual and the imaginary presence of the beloved, the world without and the world within.[25]

Rosemary Woolf has called attention to the mixture of images in the poem which identify Christ as the brother and lover, as well as the mother of the soul. She explains this inconsistency in terms of the "variety of sources"[26] informing the lyric—in particular, the Good Friday *improperia*, the allegory of the lover-knight, and the Song of Songs—and justifies it aesthetically on a twofold basis. First of all, however incongruous the vehicles may be when considered paratactically, they have a common reference to a single tenor that subsumes (and unifies) them all: the love of God revealed on Calvary. Second, "the sustained intensity of tone" in the poem supports the multiplicity of images as "a fine poetical expression of the complexity and variety of love."[27] In the context of the present discussion I want to add a third, rhetorical justification to the two Woolf offers and show how the poet's imagistic technique aims at the progressive unfolding of the feminine principle in the auditors' devotional response.[28]

There are two speakers in the poem: the paradigmatic "I" of the Everyman figure who speaks in the first two stanzas about his encounter with Christ and thus introduces him, and the "I" of the wounded King who utters his lament in the prosopopoeia of the remaining fourteen stanzas. The audience within the poem—the

25. Cf. Douglas Gray, *Themes and Images in the Medieval English Religious Lyric* (1972), p. 144.

26. Woolf, p. 189.

27. Ibid., p. 191.

28. Stephen Joseph Manning, considering the lyric in scholastic categories, also sees a definite pattern of spiritual growth. See *Wisdom and Number: Toward a Critical Appraisal of the Middle English Religious Lyric* (1962), pp. 59–62.

speaker who meets Christ and hears his complaint—gradually enters into an "I-thou" relationship with the Crucified which facilitates the assimilation of the outer audience into the same espousal. The rhetoric of the poem includes three main movements: (1) the visionary's gradual identification first with the Bride Christ is seeking, and then, through her, with Christ himself; (2) Christ's modeling of the response he desires from his Bride by his assumption of specifically feminine roles in an imagistic sequence from languishing to receptive lovemaking to pregnancy, nursing, and rearing; (3) a shift in Christ's address from talking *about* his beloved to speaking *to* her, which reinforces repentance as a precondition for the intimacy of the "thou."

The first two stanzas provide a dramatic introduction to the lament that follows. In his restless inner search for a faithful lover, the ego of the speaker encounters a man who seems to be his alter ego, someone who searches and languishes for love even as he does. Wounded, seated beneath a tree on a hill, the stranger assumes Christ's features:

(1)
In a valey of þis restles mynde
   I souȝte in mounteyne & in myde,
Trustynge a trewe loue for to fynde.
     Vpon an hil þan y took hede;
     A voice y herde—& neer y ȝede—
       In huge dolour complaynynge þo,
     "Se, dere soule, how my sidis blede,
       Quia amore langueo."

(2)
Vpon þis hil y fond a tree;
   Vndir þe tree a man sittynge,
From heed to foot woundid was he,
     His herte blood y siȝ bledinge:—
     A semeli man to ben a king,
       A graciouse face to loken vnto;—
I askide whi he had peynynge,
       He seide "*quia amore langueo.*"
          (ll. 1–16)

At the beginning of the third stanza, in a statement fraught with dramatic irony, Christ identifies himself not with the speaker but with the one the speaker seeks: "I am treu loue, þat fals was neuere" (l. 17). The declaration promotes an immediate feminizing of the first "I" in relation to Christ, a conscious inclusion of the *anima*.

> (3)
> I am true loue, þat fals was neuere;
>> Mi sistyr, mannis soule, y loued hir þus;
> Bi-cause we wolde in no wise disceuere,
>> I lefte my kyngdom glorious.
>> I purueide for hir a paleis precious;
>>> Sche fleyth, y flolowe, y souȝte hir so,
>> I suffride þis peyne piteuous
>>> *Quia amore langueo.*

The listener cannot, however, enter fully into his own bridal self until he has been purified. Therefore he must listen to Christ complain, in the spirit of the liturgical reproaches, about the hardheartedness of his beloved:

> (4)
> My fair spouse, & my loue briȝt,
>> I saued hir fro betynge, & sche haþ me bet;
> I cloþid hir in grace & heuenli liȝt,
>> þis bloodi scherte sche haþ on me sette,
>> For longynge of loue ȝit wolde y not lett;
>>> Swete strokis axe þese; lo,
>> I haue loued hir euere as y hir het,
>>> *Quia amore langueo.*

> (5)
> I crowned hir wiþ blis, & sche me with þorn;
>> I ledde hir to chaumbir, & sche me to die;
> I brouȝte hir to worschipe, & sche me to scorn;
>> I dide her reuerence, & sche me vilonye.
>> To loue þat loueþ, is no maistrie;

Hir hate made neuer my loue hir foo,
Axe me no questioun whi,
   Quia amore langueo.

        (ll. 33–40)

The third-person treatment of the Bride enforces the rhetorical distance that still separates the auditor from Christ and from his own *anima*, a rhetorical distance corresponding to the separation by sin.

Already in this first section of the complaint (stanzas 3–5), feminine elements in the portrayal of Christ help to effect a similar *anima* integration in the person of the reader. In the Song of Songs it is the Bride who languishes for love, the Bride who leaves her chamber and searches for the Bridegroom, the Bride who is beaten and stripped (Canticles 5:2–8). In the poem, however, Christ incorporates all these features in the *historia* of his passion and death as a way of expressing his Incarnation, his full identification with the humanity symbolized by the Bride.

In the second section of Christ's lament (stanzas 6–9), he draws attention to his wounded body ("loke vnto myn hondis, man!") and presents his bloody hands and feet, his open side and outstretched arms, as a "baite" to entice his Bride. At the same time that the rhetoric of the poem is promoting a highly emotive response in the feminine self of the auditor, Christ unfolds the feminine principle within his own personality to a higher degree, moving beyond searching and languishing to receptive self-surrender. He stresses that he has opened his members to his Bride (l. 54); that his wounded side is a sacred space to be filled, a bridal chamber, and a nest (ll. 57–60) into which she may come.

(6)
Loke vnto myn hondis, man!
   þese gloues were ȝoue me whan y hir souȝte;
þei ben not white, but rede & wan,
    Onbroudrid with blood my spouse hem brouȝte.
þei wole not of, y loose hem nouȝte,
    I wowe hir with hem where-euere sche go;
þese hondis for hir so freendli fouȝte,
    Quia amore langueo.

(7)

Merueille nou3te, man, þou3 y sitte stille;
    Se, loue haþ sched me wondir streite,
Boclid my feet, as was hir wille,
        With scharp naile, lo, þou maiste waite.
        In my loue was neuere desaite,
            Alle myn humours y haue opened hir to,
        þere my bodi haþ maad hir hertis baite,
            Quia amore langueo.

(8)

In my side y haue made hir neste;
    Loke in! how weet a wounde is heere,
þis is hir chaumbir, heere schal sche reste,
        þat sche & y may slepe in fere.
        Heere may sche waische, if ony filþe were,
            Heere is sete for al hir woo;
        Come whanne sche wole, sche schal haue chere,
            Quia amore langueo.

(9)

I wole abide til sche be redy,
    I wole hir sue if sche seie nay;
If sche be richilees, y wole be gredi,
        And if sche be daungerus, y wole hir praie.
        If she wepe, þat hide y ne may,
            Myn armes her hired to clippe hir me to.
                (ll. 41–70)

Having led his auditor circuitously through the knowledge of his sins to a firmer faith in God's love and forgiveness, Christ suddenly completes the identification of the listener with the Bride at the end of stanza nine with an imperative addressed to them as two-in-one: "Crie oonys: y come: Now, soule, asay, / *Quia amore langueo*" (ll. 71–72). Now he no longer speaks to the man about his Bride; rather, he speaks to his Bride in the man. The re-vision this implies is symbolically expressed in the tenth stanza when Christ, in an echo of the introduction, describes himself sitting on the mount: "I sitt on þis hil, for to se fer, / I loke into þe valey, my spouse to se" (ll. 73–

74). In the beginning the searcher in the valley gazes up to the hilltop; now Christ looks down into the lowland and sees in the seeker his Spouse:

> (10)
> I sitte on þis hil, for to se fer,
>   I loke into þe valey, my spouse to se;
> Now renneþ sche a-wayward, ȝit come sche me neer,
>   For out of my siȝte may sche not flee.
>   Summe wayte hir prai to make hir to flee,
>   I renne bifore, and fleme hir floo;
>   Returne my spouse aȝen to me,
>   Quia amore langueo.

In the imaginative (and rhetorical) presence of the Bride, Christ begins to woo her directly in stanza eleven, addressing her as "thou" and paraphrasing the Song of Songs:

> (11)
> Fair loue, lete us go pleye!
>   Applis ben ripe in my gardayne,
> I schal þee cloþe in a newe aray,
>   þi mete schal be mylk, hony, & wiyn.
>   Fair loue, lete us go digne,
>   þi sustynaunce is in my crippe, lo!
>   Tarie þou not, my faire spouse myne,
>   Quia amore langueo.
>   (ll. 81–88)

The Eucharistic reference, which makes his own Body in the crib "sustynaunce" for his Bride and links the wine of the Song to the wine of the altar, recalls the total sacrifice that is the proof of Jesus's love. Promising his beloved cleansing, healing, and mercy, Christ finds himself frustrated by her reluctance to surrender herself completely to him: "Whi wolt þou not, faire loue, with me dele?" (l. 92).

> (12)
> Iff þou be foul, y schal þee make clene;
>   If þou be sijk, y schal þee hele;

If þou moorne ou3t, y schal þee meene;
> Whi wolt þou not, faire loue, with me dele?
> Foundist þou euere loue so leel?
>> What woldist þou, spouse, þat y schulde do?
> I may not vnkyndeli þee appele,
>> *Quia amore langueo.*

>>>>>>> (ll. 89–96)

He takes counsel within himself and resolves to wait patiently until she looks out of the window of her earthly enclosure and sees both him and her true, heavenly home. The rhetorical distancing produced by the third-person deliberation about the Bride is immediately countered by Christ's direct appeal to her: "Loke out on me at þe wyndow of kyndenes / *Quia amore langueo*" (ll. 103–4).

> (13)
> What schal y do with my fair spouse,
>> But a-bide hir of my gentilnes
> Til þat sche loke out of hir house
>> Of fleischli affeccioun? loue myn sche is.
>> Hir bed is maade, hir bolstir is blis,
>>> Hir chaumbir is chosen; is þer non moo.
>> Loke out on me at þe wyndow of kyndenes,
>>> *Quia amore langueo.*

>>>>>>> (ll. 97–104)

In order to activate the feminine principle still more fully in the devotional response of his auditors, the poet intensifies the feminine in his characterization of Christ. Not only does Christ languish like a bride and open his body to be entered by his beloved; he also becomes a mother whose wounds are a womb, who waits quietly for his loved one to awaken, and who nurses her with his breast:[29]

> (14)
> My loue is in hir chaumbir: holde 3oure pees,
>> Make 3e no noise, but lete hir slepe:

---

29. For a summary of the biblical, patristic, and mystical usage of this kind of feminine imagery to describe God, see Jennifer P. Heimmel, "*God is our Mother*": *Julian of Norwich and the Medieval Image of Christian Feminine Divinity* (1982).

My babe, y wolde not were in disese,
   I may not heere my dere child wepe.
   With my pap y schal hir kepe.
      Ne merueille ȝe not þouȝ y tende hir to;
   þis hole in my side had neuere be so depe,
      But *quia amore langueo.*

                  (ll. 105–12)

Once again Christ's overheard meditation on the Bride in the third person is followed by his address to her in the second. Having made himself a mother to soften the hard heart of his Bride, to awaken the *anima* in her, Christ calls attention to the feminine principle animating them both: "Longe þou for loue neuere so hiȝ, / My loue is more þan þin may be; / þou wepist, þou gladist, y sit þee bi" (ll. 113–15). Mid-stanza, however, Christ asks the Child-Bride sitting beside him to look at him and attend to his question:

ȝit woldist þou oonys, leef, loke vnto me!
   Shulde y alwey fede þee
      With children mete? nay, loue, not so!
   I wole preue þi loue wiþ aduersite,
      Quia amore langueo.

                  (ll. 116–20)

Christ thus points to the need for feminine complementarity by the paternal, masculine principle which tests, strengthens, and "proves" love, and which secures not only their mutual relationship but also the Bride's personal integrity and endurance. Thoroughly feminized, the Bride can enter into a complementary relationship with the Bridegroom which strengthens her inwardly and brings her into coordination with him. Paradoxically, in weakness she is strong, able to endure tribulation, persevering unto death. Her outward marriage to Christ is the effective sacrament of the inner psychological marriage of *animus* and *anima*:

(16)
Wexe not wery, myn owne wijf!
   What mede is it to lyue euere in coumfort?
In tribulacioun I regne moore rijf
   Ofttymes þan in disport.

> In wele & in woo y am ay to supporte;
>   Myn owne wijf, go not me fro!
> þi meede is markid whan þou art mort,
>   *Quia amore langueo.*

(ll. 121–28)

The poem, like the Song of Songs, has its anagogy, its anticipation of the eternal Wedding Feast. Beyond the mortal body there is another, more perfect bridal chamber. After death there is the reward of faithful love. Having left father, mother, and home for her Husband, the Bride finds everything anew in him who has made himself all things for her. The poem, like the Bride's life, depends for its closure and completion upon the response given to the Bridegroom's repeated "amore langueo." It has no end in itself. It is a love song that requires an answer, even as closure for the bridal self is a matter of being completed by the Other.

Dialogue: "I" and "Thou"

> Vndo þi dore, my spuse dere,
> Allas! wy stond i loken out here?
>   Fre am i þi make.
> Loke mi lokkes & ek myn heued
> & al my bodi with blod be-weued
>   For þi sake.
> Allas! Allas! heuel haue i sped,
> For senne iesu is fro me fled,
>   Mi trewe fere.
> With-outen my gate he stant alone,
> Sorfuliche he maket his mone
>   On his manere.
> Lord, for senne i sike sore,
> Forȝef & i ne wil no more,
> With al my mith senne i forsake,
> & opne myn herte þe inne to take.
> For þin herte is clouen oure loue to kecchen,
> þi loue is chosen vs alle to fecchen;
> Min herte it þerlede ȝef i wer kende,
> þi suete loue to hauen in mende.

Perce myn herte with þi louengge,
þat in þe i haue my duellingge. Amen.[30]

The early-fourteenth-century lyric "Vndo þi dore" is, according to Woolf, "both the earliest and the best of the lover-knight complaints."[31] Woolf's praise of the poem is certainly merited, but her description of the text is misleading. There is no indication that the lover is a knight, and only the first six lines are devoted to his lament. Although the superscript "Ecce sto ad hostium et pulso" is a quotation from Apocalypse 3:20, the poem itself vividly recalls the scene recorded in Canticles 5:2 and its associated allegory:

Ego dormio et cor meum vigilat:
Vox dilecti mei pulsantis:
Aperi mihi, soror mea, amica mea, columba mea,
   immaculata mea;
quia caput meum plenum est rore, et cincinni mei
   gluttis noctium.

[I sleep, and my heart watcheth:
the voice of my beloved knocking:
Open to me, my sister, my love, my dove, my
   undefiled;
for my head is full of dew, and my locks of the
   drops of the night.]

Indeed the poem is best understood not in the tradition of the knightly complaint but as belonging to the set of devotional poems that paraphrase the Song of Songs and literalize its spiritual meaning.

The closest analogue to "Vndo þi dore" is probably the famous eleventh-century Latin *rhythmus* attributed to Saint Peter Damian.[32] Like the Middle English poem, the Latin lyric "Quis est hic qui

30. *Religious Lyrics of the Fourteenth Century*, no. 68, p. 86.
31. Woolf, p. 189.
32. According to Dronke, the poem is extant in an eleventh-century miscellany in the Beneventan script. Migne attributes it to Peter Damian (PL 145, c939). The poem also appears in Bruno of Segni's *Expositio in Cantica Canticorum*, PL 164, c1266. I quote and translate the full text in Chapter 2.

pulsat ad ostium" devotes the first two stanzas to Christ's dramatic appearance, his call to the Bride to open the door, and his reference to his wounds. In the Latin lyric, however, Christ's call is answered by the Bride's immediate response. She runs to lift the latch, only to discover that her royal lover has already gone. Weeping, she follows him, searching for him by night in the city streets where watchmen find, beat, and strip her, before giving her a new cloak and a new song with which to make her appearance before the king. As Dronke notes, the action subsequent to the lover's call is characterized by "passionateness, excitement, and swiftness"[33] as the poet closely follows the letter of his source, inserting the allegory almost incidentally with a few well-chosen phrases.[34]

The Middle English poem presents the same scene from Canticles not as a narrative recounted by the Bride but as a dialogue between the lover and his beloved, a combination of prosopopoeia and prayer.[35] The words of Christ inspire the Bride's meditation and are answered by her self-surrender to him. Unlike the Latin lyric, which uses the introductory stanzas to establish the theological context directly ("Ego sum summi Regis Filius"), "Vndo þi dore" does not immediately name the lover who speaks. Instead of referring in a general way to Christ's sufferings ("passus mortem et multas injurias"), replacing the letter of the Song with its *sententia*, the poet literalizes the allegory.[36] The Bridegroom's locks are wet, not with the dew of the night ("gluttis noctis") but with blood. The question "Wy stond i loken out here?" (l. 2) confronts the Bride with a fact that must be explained in personal rather than objective/dogmatic terms.

Unlike the Bride of Canticles, who runs to draw the latch, the Bride of the Middle English poem must go through a whole process of conversion which includes her own effort to open her heart (by forsaking sin) and her petition to be opened (by the piercing force of Christ's love). The allegory of the door is so literalized in the poem

---

33. Dronke, *Medieval Latin*, vol. I, p. 270.

34. Those phrases include "novum canticum" and the epithet "cujus manus plasmaverunt hominem."

35. Cf. Edmund Reiss, *The Art of the Middle English Lyric* (1972), p. 125.

36. The poet's technique resembles that of Bruno of Segni, in whose lyrics Solomon literally becomes Christ, and soldiers saints, while retaining their original imagistic position within the source text as transparencies, or types, of their allegorical referents.

that Christ's flight from the Bride paradoxically becomes his standing alone outside the gate, waiting for her and separated from her by
her sin. Christ's stasis slows the pace of the poem and allows its
symbols to develop a full semantic resonance as the poet shifts their
context (sometimes with paronomastic force), applying them first
to Christ and then to the Bride.

The opening address "my spuse dere" immediately feminizes the
"I" of the listener, both the Bride within the poem and the bridal self
of the auditor who identifies with her. Christ's declaration "fre am i
þi make" (l. 3) reminds the Bride of the two great pledges of his love
(arrhae): creation (he is her Maker) and redemption (he is her Mate,
having purchased her with his blood). His free and generous action
("fre am i") is paradoxically limited by his Bride's lack of acceptance;
he is locked outside. The pun on "loken," "loke," and "lokkes"
recalls the efficacy of Christ's passion, his bloody hair becoming a
synecdoche for the whole Calvary sacrifice with its power to unlock
the gates of heaven and sway the hearts of those who meditate upon
it: "Loke mi lokkes" (l. 4).[37] The closing words of Christ's address,
"for þi sake" (l. 6), mark the intimacy of the exchange.

The Bride speaks to herself before she answers the Bridegroom.
Her "allas! allas!" (l. 7) echoes his as she, on the other side of the wall,
considers the situation. Unlike the Bride of Canticles, who exclaims
at finding her lover has already left, she laments at seeing him
standing there alone. "Flight" is simply separation, all the more
terrible because she has caused it: "for senne iesu is fro me fled" (l. 8).
Sin is the wall that keeps them apart, keeping her from her "trewe
fere" (l. 9). The allegorical sententia is thus included in the letter of
the lyric as a metaphoric tenor along with the vehicle that sustains it:
"with-outen my gate he stant alone, / Sorfuliche he maket his
mone" (ll. 10–11).

In the third and last section of the poem (ll. 13–22), set off from
the first two by its use of simple couplets, the bridal "I" mediates the
audience's response to Christ's call. The dialogue (despite the inter-
vening wall) is maintained by the Bride's assumption of the Bridegroom's own terms. She grieves over her sin ("for senne i sike sore")

37. Bernard makes a similar pun in his sixty-first sermon on the Song: "The
piercing nail (clavus) has been turned into a master key (clavis) to show me the Will of
the Lord." See Sermo 61: II.4 in Sermones super Cantica Canticorum, vol. II, ed. J.
Leclercq, C. H. Talbot, H. M. Rochais (1958), p. 150.

in answer to the Bridegroom's suffering and sighing ("he maket his mone"). She "forsakes" sin because of what he has endured "for [her] sake" (l. 6). She flees evil even as he has fled "for senne" (l. 8). In fulfillment of his request ("Vndo þi dore") she opens her heart.

The barrier of sin having been removed through confession and contrition, the lovers enter into an intimate in-one-anotherness, which the Bride describes as a mutual in-dwelling. Opening her heart to him, she finds herself entering his pierced heart: "for þin herte is clouen oure loue to kecchen" (l. 17). Like the biblical "dove in the clefts of the rock" (Cant. 2:14) she finds her home in his wounds.[38] His lanced side immediately inspires her request to be pierced through with a compassionate understanding of his love: "þi suete loue to hauen in mende" (l. 20). The closing couplet eloquently expresses the paradox of her double petition: "Perce myn herte with þi louengge, / þat in þe i haue my duellingge" (ll. 21–22). Entered by him, she can enter into him and find her true home in heaven with its many mansions. Thus the poet links the feminine principle—defined in its essence by the impulse toward receptive self-surrender—with divinization, coupling the descent of God with human ascent, mirroring a marriage that is simultaneously ana-gogic—the union of God and man—and tropological: the *integritas* of the human faculties.

The feminizing rhetorical strategies I have traced in these representative lyrics serve to engage the auditor in an intensely personal religious experience of Christ as a Bridegroom. Best suited for an individual's use in private devotion, these simple love songs recall the mystical treatments of the Song in their evocation of a spousal "I." As we shall see, the public, performative setting of the Corpus Christi cycle plays gives a different valence to the rhetoric of religious lyric. In the dramas, the bridal speaker gives voice to communal sentiments, either as an inclusive *figura* reminiscent of *ecclesia* herself, or as an exemplary, Marian figure modeling an appropriate audience response. Thus the bridal "I" becomes a bridal "we."

38. Traditional *allegoresis* associates the clefts of the rock with the wounds of Christ. See Bruno, *Expositio*, PL 164, c1249; Bernard, *Sermo* 61: II.4 in *Sermones*, p. 150.

7

Biblical Drama, Devotional
Response, and the Feminine "We"

Despite the efforts of Rosemary Woolf and others to "recon-
struct the medieval understanding of biblical drama,"[1] the
historical definition of the genre has remained elusive—and, with it,
the reasons for the apparent affinity between the dramatic and lyric
kinds in the minds of fourteenth- and fifteenth-century playwrights
and players. Woolf has contended that "quite a number of lyrics
were later incorporated into the mystery plays: not because the plays
were lyrical, but because the lyrics were dramatic."[2] Her neatly
balanced statement clearly requires some qualification—first of all,
because the number of lyrics known to have been taken from other
sources does not, by any means, account for all the songs, prayers,
praises, and laments found in the plays; second, because whether or
not the cycle plays can be called lyrical depends on the definition of
that term.

Using the narrow definition of lyric as an "isolable" poem expressing a unified emotion and corresponding in its theme to that of
independently existing lyrics, George C. Taylor attests that easily
"one-fourth of the great body of material found in the York and
Towneley plays" is lyrical, while the Chester and Hegge plays are
"very considerably" influenced by the lyric mode.[3] Judged by Tay-

1. Rosemary Woolf, *The English Mystery Plays* (1972), p. 101.
2. Woolf, *The English Religious Lyric in the Middle Ages* (1968), p. 19.
3. George C. Taylor, "The Relation of the English Corpus Christi Play to the

lor's standards, the plays themselves cannot be considered lyrical in the sense that every speech can be isolated from its dramatic context. On the other hand, the significant number of lyrics which appear in the mysteries strongly suggests that the lyric subgenre is essential to them as a formal constituent. If, as Woolf, V. A. Kolve, Richard J. Collier, and others have argued, the vernacular biblical cycles consciously aimed at evoking an affective response in their audience through the on-stage expression of emotion,[4] then the lyric formulation necessarily furthered what Collier calls "the devotional motive of the drama"[5] and made possible its achievement.

The generic mixture found in the cycle plays corresponds to the combination of genres attributed to the Song of Songs (as a drama, lyrical in kind) and suggests that the medieval reading of the Song as *dramaticon* influenced the historical definition of biblical drama and informed its artistic development in ways hitherto unnoticed. Although the *Canticum* is the only book in the canon which was perceived to have been written, as Origen says, "in modum dramatis,"[6] its model character for the biblical cycle plays has never been studied.

In some ways the omission is understandable. None of the Corpus Christi cycles includes a Play of Solomon, and direct verbal allusion to Canticles is rare.[7] Even the four New Testament scenes most closely assimilated to the Song in the commentary tradition— the Annunciation, the Crucifixion, the Appearance to Mary Magdalene, and the Assumption of the Virgin—reveal surprisingly little evidence of verbal borrowings. The York play of the Assumption includes six songs in which selected texts from the *Canticum* are set to music, but the liturgy of the Marian feast, not the Song itself, clearly provides the immediate inspiration for the dramatic usage.

Middle English Religious Lyric," *MP* 5 (1907): 15. See also Taylor, "The English 'Planctus Mariae,' " *MP* 4 (1907): 605–37; Lu Emily Pearson, "Isolable Lyrics of the Mystery Plays," *ELH* 3 (1936): 228–52.

4. See V. A. Kolve, *The Play Called Corpus Christi* (1966), p. 5; Woolf, *English Mystery Plays*, pp. 88–90 *et passim*.

5. Richard J. Collier, *Poetry and Drama in the York Corpus Christi Play* (1978), p. 121.

6. Origen, *Prologus in Canticum Canticorum*, trans. Rufinus, PG 13, c63.

7. In the York *Purification*, for instance, the prophet Simeon hails the Christ Child as "floscampy and flower vyrgynall," thus briefly incorporating Canticles 2:1 into his litany of praise. See *The York Plays*, ed. Richard Beadle (1982), p. 158.

Scholars, moreover, usually contend that the allegorical reading of the Song impeded the full recognition of its dramatic character until long after the close of the Middle Ages. To be sure, Origen had classified the Song of Songs as *dramaticon* in the third century and, as we have seen, twelfth-century exegetes associated the Song's separate dialogues with appropriate evangelical scenes (the Annunciation, the Visit to the Tomb, the Assumption). William of St. Thierry even outlined the "argumentum" of the play. It was not until the Renaissance, however, that writers began supplying a continuous, fully developed, amatory plot to match the Song's dialogue.[8] In 1729 Samuel Croxall's play *The Fair Circassian* incorporated the verses of the *Canticum* into an oriental love story. In 1772 J. F. Jacobi outlined a three-character plot, later adapted for performance by H. Ewald (1826), Ernest Renan (1860), and A. Hazan (1936), in which King Solomon, a royal lecher, tries to steal a beautiful shepherdess away from her beloved country swain, only to be converted in the end by the couple's constancy to one another. In 1885 the German scholar Franz Delitzsch placed the lyric utterances of the Song within a simple plot line in which there are only two main characters, Solomon and Shulamith, the country lass whose virtue elevates the carnally minded king from mere physical attraction to pure love.[9] Clearly none of these dramatic readings, which assign the role of lecher to Solomon, has much in common with the allegorical interpretation that associates Solomon with Christ, the Bride with the church, and the biblical love songs with multiple signs of their mutual relationship.

Yet, as Michael V. Fox has recently insisted, the scholarly assump-

8. The Spanish poet Fray Luis de Leon (1527–1591) translated the Song into the vernacular and wrote a commentary in which he depicts Solomon and his beloved playing the parts of a shepherd and a shepherdess in a pastoral retreat. Cornelius à Lapide (1567–1637) enlivened the dramatic theory by dividing Canticles into five acts. In *The Reason of Church Government Urg'd against Prelatry* (1642), John Milton reminded his readers that "Scripture also affords us a Divine pastoral Drama in the Song of Solomon consisting of two persons and a double chorus, as Origen rightly judges." See *Complete Poems and Major Prose*, ed. Merritt Y. Hughes (Indianapolis: Odyssey Press, 1957, repr. 1980), p. 669.

9. For summary discussions of the dramatic view of the Song of Songs, see Morris Jastrow, Jr., *The Song of Songs* (1921), pp. 95–113; Marvin Pope, ed. and trans., *The Song of Songs* (1977), pp. 34–35; Michael V. Fox, *The Song of Songs and the Ancient Egyptian Love Songs* (1985), pp. 256–58.

tion of a late, postmedieval realization of the Song as drama depends upon an unnecessarily restrictive definition of the dramatic mode. According to Fox, the attempt to impose upon the *Canticum* a linear plot developing "in a straight line toward a single goal"[10] stems from a narrow Western concept of drama which ignores the possibility of reiterative structures. External evidence supports the likelihood that the text of the Song was originally recited by different singers representing the various characters and accompanied by mimetic action.[11] As Fox observes, however, whether or not the Song was performed before an audience, its dramatic mode of presentation remains assured "insofar as the poems create their world through *personae*"[12] represented as engaged in dialogue. The reader encounters "this world without preparation, thrown *in medias res*, guided by the speakers' words alone."[13]

Fox's argument, based on a comparative study of Egyptian love songs, echoes the early commentaries on the *Canticum*. Recognized as an epithalamium, the biblical love lyrics were perceived to have an occasional setting (historically considered, the nuptials of Solomon and Pharaoh's daughter) with a dramatic potential. Isidore of Seville expressed the generally accepted view when he wrote that the Gentiles had derived the epithalamium as a lyric genre ("istius generis carmen assumptum est") from Solomon's *Canticum*, first performing it on stage ("in scenis"), afterward reciting it at marriage feasts in the wedding chamber of the couple ("in thalamis decantetur").[14]

The essential feature of the Song which led to its classification as *dramaticon* was not, however, its ability to be performed, but rather its implied dialogue in which alternating voices spoke to one another without any of the temporal connectives, descriptions, or commentary usually provided by a third-person narrator. That dialogue was the key feature becomes clear from an examination of the discussion

10. Fox, p. 257.

11. Fox cites the depictions of similar performances of poetry by singers in Egyptian paintings, stelae, and statuettes. See p. 256.

12. Ibid., p. 258. Fox observes that "the Song of Songs makes extensive use of dialogue" whereas "dialogue was not among the forms of Egyptian love poetry." See pp. 263–64.

13. Ibid., p. 255.

14. Isidore of Seville, *Etymologiarum* I, PL 82, c120.

of the three voices of poetry—expository, dramatic, and narrative—found in Isidore of Seville, Bede, and Rabanus Maurus. I quote the relevant passages in full because of their importance to our present consideration of medieval dramatic theory, and also because of their relative neglect in comparable studies. Sandro Sticca cites the three-fold *distinctio* only as evidence that the Middle Ages misconceived the drama of the classical past.[15] Kolve mentions the theory of the "three voices of poetry" in passing, only to dismiss its applicability to actual dramatic practice in the Corpus Christi play.[16] Collier uses a closely related triad of relevant categories—homiletic, lyric, and narrative—in his presentation of the York cycle's "poetic drama,"[17] but he himself never refers to the medieval sources in question, nor does he use them as a basis for his discussion.

Isidore of Seville provides a brief listing of the "tres characteres dicendi" found in the writings of the poets:

> Apud poetas autem tres characteres sunt dicendi: unus in quo tantum poeta loquitur, ut est in libris Virgilii Georgicorum. Alius dramaticus, in quo nusquam poeta loquitur, ut est in comoediis et tragoediis. Tertius mistus, ut est in Aeneide. Nam poeta illic et introductae personae loquuntur.[18]

> [Among the poets, moreover, there are three manners of speaking: one in which the poet alone speaks, as in the books of Virgil's *Georgics*; a second, dramatic mode in which the poet never speaks, as in the tragedies and comedies; a third, mixed form, as in the *Aeneid* (for there the poet, as well as introduced characters, speaks).]

Isidore lists only classical works as examples of the three styles of poetic discourse. Bede and Rabanus Maurus vary the order of the listing (in accord with the fourth-century presentation of the Latin grammarian Diomedes) and add literary examples from the biblical canon to offset those of pagan authorship. To quote Bede:

15. See Sandro Sticca, *The Latin Passion Play: Its Origins and Development* (1970), pp. 12–13.
16. See Kolve, pp. 27–28.
17. Collier, p. 16.
18. Isidore of Seville, *Etymologiarum* VIII.vii, PL 82, c309.

Poematos genera sunt tria; aut enim activum vel imitativum est,
quod Graeci dramaticon vel micticon appellant; aut enarrativum,
quod Graeci exegematicon vel apangelticon nuncupant; aut com-
mune vel mixtum, quod Graeci coenon vel micton vocant. Dramaticon est, vel activum, in quo personae loquentes introducuntur, sine poetae interlocutione, ut se habent tragoediae et fabulae
(drama enim Latine fabula dicitur). Quo genere scripta est: "Quo
te, Moeri, pedes? An, quo via ducit in urbem?" Quo apud nos
genere Cantica Canticorum scripta sunt, ubi vox alternans Cristi et
ecclesiae, tametsi non in hoc interloquente scriptore, manifesta
reperitur. Exegematicon est vel enarrativum in quo poeta ipse
loquitur sine ullius interpositione personae, ut se habent tres libri
Georgici toti, et prima pars quarti; item Lucretii carmina et his
similia. Quo genere apud nos scriptae sunt Parabolae Salomonis et
Ecclesiastes, qua in sua lingua, sicut et Psalterium, metro constat
esse conscripta. Coenon est vel micton in quo poeta ipse loquitur et
personae loquentes introducuntur, ut sunt scripta Ilias et Odyssia
Homeri et Aeneidos Virgilii et apud nos historia beati Job, quamvis
haec in sua lingua non tota poetico, sed partim rethorico, partim sit
metrico vel rithmico scripta sermone.[19]

[There are three kinds of poems. Either the poem is enacted or
mimetic (which the Greeks call *dramaticon* or *micticon*); or it is
expository (which the Greeks designate as *exegematicon* or *apangelticon*); or it is joint or mixed (which the Greeks call *coenon* or
micton). In a dramatic or enacted poem, speaking characters are
introduced without any commentary by the poet, as in the case of
tragedies and fables (for a drama is called a *fabula* in Latin). That
eclogue which begins, "Where do your feet lead you, Moerius, or
where does the road lead into the city?" is written in this literary
kind. Among our works, the Song of Songs belongs to this genre,
for in it the voice of Christ, alternating with that of the church, is
clearly found; nor does the writer speak in between. In an expository or descriptive poem the poet himself speaks without the
interposition of any *persona* as, for example, in the whole first three

19. Bede, *De Arte Metrica* I.xxv, in *Opera Didascalica*, CCSL 123A, ed. C. B.
Kendall (1975), pp. 139–41; PL 90, c174. The gloss indicates that "mictos" is syn-
onymous with "fabula"; "micticon" and "dramaticon" with "carmen fabulosum."
See also Rabanus Maurus, *De Universo* XV.ii, PL 111, c419–20.

books of the *Georgics* and the first part of the fourth, as well as in
the songs of Lucretius and poems similar to these. This genre is
exemplified among us by Solomon's Proverbs and Ecclesiastes
which, it is commonly agreed, were written in the original language in meter (as were the Psalms). In a combined or mixed kind
of poem the poet himself speaks, and characters speaking in their
own voices are also introduced. Homer's *Iliad* and *Odyssey* and
Virgil's *Aeneid* were written in this genre; and, among our works,
the history of holy Job—although in the original language this was
not written entirely in poetry, but partly in rhetorical, partly in
metrical or rhythmic speech.]

A careful reading of this passage reveals, among other things, that
Kolve erroneously describes the threefold classification as distinguishing "the dramatic from the lyric and epic voices."[20] Lyric
poetry cannot be equated with the expository mode (*exegematicon*) in
which the poet speaks in his own voice ("poeta ipse loquitur"). In
the latter, as P. B. Salmon puts it, "The poet does all the talking, but
his talk is descriptive, explanatory, hortative, or narrowly narrative."[21] Indeed, what Fox calls "expressive lyric" (defined as a short,
poetic utterance in which the poet articulates his personal feelings)[22]
is utterly neglected in the discussion. Salmon observes:

It is at least clear from these texts that the voice which was to
become *exegematicon* or *apangelticon* in the Middle Ages was not the
lyric, as we understand the term now, but a manner of utterance in
which the poet presents objects and persons as they appear before
his eyes. It would thus cover didactic and explanatory texts; indeed, any form which does not at any point specifically represent
the words of fictitious (or historical) characters as direct speech.[23]

On the other hand, what Fox defines as the "dramatic lyric"—
that is, an emotive speech or song uttered by a created *persona*—is
implicitly included in the discussion of the three voices of poetry by

20. Kolve, p. 27.
21. P. B. Salmon, "The 'Three Voices' of Poetry in Mediaeval Literary Theory,"
Medium Aevum 30 (1961): 15.
22. See Fox, p. 254.
23. Salmon, p. 12.

the choice of the Song of Songs to exemplify the dramatic mode. The Song's very name points to its lyric character.[24] Indeed, the descriptive title "Cantica Canticorum" with its nominative neuter plural had encouraged the commentators to see the work as a set of love songs thematically united.[25] In addition, the notion of personation is evident in Bede's designation of speakers: "vox alternans Christi et Ecclesiae."

Beginning in the third century with Origen, Christian commentators on the Song distinguished four different speakers: the Bride, the Bridegroom, the Bride's attendants, and the Groom's companions. The members of the wedding party, however, were conceived to be *dramatis personae* in a twofold sense that exceeds Fox's formal definition of created, literary voices distinct from the poet's own. Not only were they considered dramatic in the literal meaning as speaking parts that could be appropriated by readers assuming their roles; they were viewed as dramatic in the allegorical sense, for Christ and the church were heard speaking through the mask, the outward form, of the Bridegroom and Bride ("sub specie sponsi sponsaeque"). The *Glossa* provides us with a summary of this double dramatization:

> Quatuor mihi in hoc opere invenisse videor personas, sponsum et sodales ipsius, sponsam et adolescentulas cum ea. Alia a sponso, alia dicuntur a sponsa: nunnulla a juvenculis, quaedam a sodalibus sponsi. Congruum quippe est ut in initiis sit adolescentularum multitudo cum sponsa, juvenum turba cum sponso. Sponsum,

24. The *Glossa* indicates that the Song of Songs takes precedence over all the other biblical canticles, surpassing them in dignity: "sua dignitate omnia alia excellens cantica" (PL 113, c1127). Pseudo-Richard of St. Victor speaks of scriptural canticles of victory, of exhortation, of exultation, of assistance, and of union with God, listing as examples two Mosaic songs from Exodus and Deuteronomy, the hymn of Anna in 1 Kings 2, David's Psalm 27, and the *Canticum Canticorum* (PL 196, c408). Rupert of Deutz compares the Song of Songs to six other biblical canticles, all of them hymns of thanksgiving for specific favors ("beneficia"), and observes that the Song of Songs differs from the others in celebrating the greatest of God's gifts, the gift of himself to his beloved (PL 168, c838–40). Similarly, Honorius of Autun declares that the Song of Songs is preferred to all the other canticles because of its exalted subject matter: the nuptials of Christ and the church (PL 172, c350).

25. See Rupert of Deutz, *Commentaria in Cantica Canticorum*, PL 168, c839–40. There he discusses how the Song of Songs is divided into four periochae by the repeated refrain "Adjuro vos." According to Rupert, the four periochae constitute four songs, each celebrating the same sacrament of marriage ("idem sacramentum").

Christum intelligo, sponsam Ecclesiam sine macula et ruga. An-
gelos vero, et eos qui pervenerunt in virum perfectum, intelligo
amicos sponsi. Adolescentulae sunt sponsarum incipientium tur-
bae, juxta modum quemdam salutem adeptae.[26]

[It seems to me that four *personae* have been discovered in this
work: the Bridegroom and his comrades, the Bride and the maidens with her. Some things are said by the Groom, some by the
Bride, a few things by the young women, certain things by the
companions of the Groom. It is fitting indeed that in the beginning
there be a company of maidens with the Bride, a throng of youths
with the Groom. I understand the Bridegroom to be Christ, the
Bride the church without spot or wrinkle. I understand the
Groom's friends to be, in truth, the angels and those who have
attained perfect manhood. The maidens are a group of brides-to-
be, according to the degree of salvation they have attained.]

The *dramatis personae* thus include roles that the *Canticum's* audience is encouraged to assume on the basis of not only the emotions
articulated by the literal text with its power to evoke an emotional
response, but also the objective assignment of parts provided by the
allegorical analysis. These parts, in turn, have already been played
by God himself, who has spoken through the prophets, revealed
himself in the typology of kings and patriarchs, incarnated himself
in Jesus Christ, and joined himself to the church as his body. Audience identification with one or more speakers of the Song, then, is
virtually an *imitatio Dei*.

In summary, both the discussions of the three voices of poetry and
the list of speakers given above provide evidence that the Middle
Ages was especially sensitive to personation in the Song of Songs,
not merely in the formal sense defined by Fox (who distinguishes
between the expressive mode, spoken in the authorial voice, and the
dramatic mode, spoken by a created *persona*), but also in its rhetorical definition. As *dramaticon*, the Song was perceived virtually to
require personation, that is, the appropriation of the Bride's words
by the audience (taken collectively to be the church and, within that
choral body, the individual member) in response to the appropria-

26. *Glossa Ordinaria*, PL 113, c1128.

tion of the Bridegroom's utterance by Christ.[27] As a typical discourse (in the sense of typology), the bridal utterance defines a linguistic structure of identification through which individuals find and define themselves by assuming certain parts for which they have been cast in the divine scheme of things. Thus the medieval auditor of the Song could never be a mere listener, objectifying the discourse of the *Sponsa et Sponsus*; he or she had to become a speaker in its dialogue.

As I hope to show, the theoretical understanding of the Song as a drama in which Christ and his church speak in dialogue ("vox alternans Christi et Ecclesiae") offered the Middle Ages a scriptural model for a decidedly participatory kind of playacting which virtually included the audience-as-church in the cast,[28] and which structured itself rhetorically on the human responses given to God's repeated call. Although the Song of Songs cannot be said to have influenced the texts of the Corpus Christi plays in any appreciable way (measured quantitatively by instances of allusion and paraphrase), its qualitative influence can nevertheless be inferred from the deep structure of the dramas. Like the Song, they minimize the auditor/actor distinction through a rhetoric of personation. Like the Song, they aim at kindling a devotional response, at drawing the church into intimacy with God. Finally, like the Song, they evoke the feminine principle (as the principle of receptive self-surrender to God) within their auditors through the use of on-stage feminine *figurae* who articulate the desired affective response to the person of Christ.

The figure of Mary, in particular, plays a key role in directing the response of the audience and, as we shall see, she tends to represent the feminine under the archetypes most appropriate to corporate

27. For a historical perspective on personation, see Mary Hatch Marshall, "Boethius' Definition of *Persona* and Mediaeval Understanding of the Roman Theater," *Speculum* 25 (1950): 471–79.
28. The participatory nature of the plays is their hallmark. See Harold C. Gardiner, S.J., *Mysteries' End: An Investigation of the Last Days of the Medieval Religious Stage* (1946, repr. 1967), for a detailed account of the popular support for the plays. As Alan H. Nelson has shown, the method of staging the plays often drew the audience spatially into the action. See "Some Configurations of Staging in Medieval English Drama," in *Medieval English Drama*, ed. Jerome Taylor and Alan H. Nelson (1972), pp. 116–47; "Principles of Processional Staging: York Cycle," *MP* 67 (1970): 303–20.

experience—the Medium and the Mother.[29] The Medium gives expression to the community soul, bringing the collective unconscious into consciousness, providing a prophetic channel for prayerful response. Her characteristic genre (exemplified in the liturgical sequences of Adam of St. Victor) is the sacramental lyric, with its paratactic listing of images to name and rename the One. The Mother, on the other hand, actually embodies the ecclesial community and therefore enacts its role in a prefiguration of everything her children—as extensions of herself—are called to be and do. Like the Mother-Bride in the Marian commentaries on the Song, she stands as teacher and model. In the York New Testament plays, Mary takes the double part of Medium and Mother to increase the brideship of the audience (and the on-stage circle of disciples) as a feminine "we."

The Medial Woman and the Lyrics

The structure of call and response which defines the relationship between Christ and the church ("vox alternans Christi et Ecclesiae") is easily discernible in the York plays if one traces the reciprocal pattern in the lyrics of salutation. Christ initiates the call with the "Hail" addressed to the Virgin by Gabriel in *The Annunciation*: "Hayle Marie, full of grace and blysse."[30] Mary then models the church's response to Christ by starting the series of worshipful "Hail" speeches which appear in the various plays dealing with his earthly life. In the final movement of the cycle, Christ, together with his angels, once again addresses Mary with "Hail," this time repeatedly and with multiple titles of praise, as he calls her into paradise.

The repetitive quality of all these lyrics of love and praise underscores their unity of sentiment and works to stir the emotions of the

---

29. Ann Belford Ulanov, quoting Toni Wolff, describes the Medial Woman as being " 'immersed in the psychic atmosphere of the environment and the spirit of her period, but above all in the collective (impersonal) unconscious' " (p. 208). The Mother type, on the other hand, "represents a collective orientation to people" (p. 198). See *The Feminine in Jungian Psychology and in Christian Theology* (1971).

30. *The York Plays*, ed. Richard Beadle (1982), p. 114. Hereafter all quotations from this edition are cited parenthetically by page number.

auditors. At the same time, the lyric speeches slow down the action
of the plays in a significant *mimesis* of the eternal present. The
inclusion of a lyric regularly signals some kind of divine encounter, a
contemplative moment when the many and the One are united. It
marks the intersection of the vertical dimension with its timelessness
and the horizontal line with its historical progression, human meeting God, and God, human.

Mary, as the type of *ecclesia*, initiates the church's worship of
Christ in *The Nativity*. Kneeling to adore her newborn child, she
prays:

> Hayle my lord God, hayle prince of pees,
>   Hayle my fadir, and hayle my sone;
> Hayle souereyne sege all synnes to sesse,
> Hayle God and man in erth to wonne.
>   Hayle, thurgh whos myth
> All þis worlde was first begonne,
>   Merknes and light.
>
>   (p. 126)

Joseph then joins her in adoration with the words: "Hayle my
maker, hayle Crist Jesu, / Hayle riall Kyng, roote of all right" (p.
127). In *The Magi* each of the three Wise Men honors the Christ
Child with a "Hail" speech echoing that of Mary and Joseph. The
prophetess's song of welcome to Christ is followed in *The Purification* by Simeon's worshipful salutation:

> Haill floscampy and flower vyrgynall,
> The odour of thy goodnes reflars to vs all.
> Haill, moost happy to great and to small
>   For our weyll.
> Haill ryall roose, moost ruddy of hewe,
> Haill flour vnfadyng, both freshe ay and newe,
> Haill the kyndest in comfort that ever man knewe
>   For grete heyll.
>
>   (p. 158)

A certain climax in the series of "Hail" lyrics addressed to Christ
comes in *The Entry into Jerusalem*, when various citizens acclaim the

Lord under multiple titles in eight stanzas of praise culminating in a sung anthem. The homage offered to Jesus in this sequence is so marked and moving that it later inspires both the sincere worship of Bedellus in *Christ before Pilate I* ("They worshipped þe full holy on hy") and the mockery of the soldiers in *Christ before Pilate II*: "Ave, riall roy and *rex judeorum*" (p. 304).

The love and praise offered to Christ during his earthly life in the series of "Hail" lyrics are answered by him after his Ascension in the form of the angelic homage paid to Mary. In *The Death of the Virgin* Gabriel summons Mary to heaven, where she will reign beside Christ as his queen, in a speech reminiscent of the "Ave" of *The Annunciation*:

> Hayle, myghfull Marie, Godis modir so mylde,
> > Hayle be þou, roote of all reste, hayle be þou, ryall.
> Hayle floure and frewte noȝt fadid nor filyd,
> > Haile, salue to all synnefull.
>
> > > > (p. 386)

In *The Assumption of the Virgin* the apostle Thomas sees a vision of Mary's *transitus* and raises his voice in praise of her, joining the choir of angels: "Hayle jentilest of Jesse in Jewes generacioun, / Haile welthe of þis worlde all welthis is weldand" (p. 395). Finally, in *The Coronation of the Virgin*, Jesus sends to Mary an embassy of angels who greet her with another set of "Hail" speeches: "Haile, þe doughtir of blissid Anne" (p. 401).

In the total structure of the New Testament mysteries, then, the homage paid to Mary in the "hail" lyrics balances rhetorically the earlier acclamations of Christ, as the divine and human partners rejoice in a mutual exchange of love and admiration. Mary is the Medium through whom Christ directs his love for humankind and in whom humanity's worship gains its peak expression. The dynamic of call and response ("vox alternans Christi et Ecclesiae") is unmistakable. At the same time the sentiments articulated in the salutations recall the love and longing of the Song of Songs—an association that, in the three Marian plays, is underscored by direct quotation from the Song in the text of the hymns: "Veni de Libano" (Cant. 4:8) and "Surge proxima mea" (Cant. 2:10). Although none of the "Hail" lyrics, strictly speaking, can be called paraphrases of the Song, the collocation in them of images of paradise, lilies, roses, flowers, and kingship clearly reflects the contemplative *visio* of Canticles with its approach to the Beloved through multiple signs, all of them naming the One.

The Mother–Bride and Exemplification

The Doctor's prologue to *The Annunciation* prepares the audience to see in Mary the New Eve, who represents the human race and whose obedience to God works to reverse the Fall. The *logos* for audience identification with her is supported by the distinctly feminine *pathos* of the early New Testament plays. Mary alone encounters Gabriel. Mary and Elizabeth join in voicing the joy that is the proper human response to the Incarnation. In the Christ-Child plays, Mary is the first to kneel in adoration, the first to voice homage to the Savior. Joseph, the Shepherds, and the Magi assimilate their worship to hers. It is she who accepts the Wise Men's gifts and mediates their love to the Child in her arms. The subsequent worship of Christ by Anna, Simeon, and the priest also conforms to the pattern of Mary's first lyrical "hayle." Through Mary the audience can give emotive expression to their own love for Christ.

At the same time, Mary's sensitive, human qualities as a woman allow her to voice emotional responses to human suffering which require a masculine complement in the form of reasoned judgment and heroic endurance. Mary's on-stage education thus becomes a means for the dramatist to channel the energy of compassion, awakened in the audience and articulated through her, into the service of God. In *The Flight into Egypt* Mary's excitement and fear are tempered by Joseph's calm courage until she finally voices her simple surrender to God's will: "Amen as He beste may" (p. 166). In *Christ and the Doctors* Jesus himself corrects her maternal anxiety: "Wherto shulde 3e seke me soo? / Ofte tymes it hase ben tolde you till, / My fadir werkis, for wele or woo, / Thus am I sente for to fulfyll" (p. 180). Similarly, in the plays enacting the passion sequence, Mary's intense compassion for her crucified Son is supported by John's calm presence and divinized through Jesus's firm adherence to his Father's will.

Mary's feeling response to Christ's agony is represented in the plays as an answer on behalf of the assembly to his call from the Cross. In the York *Crucifixion* Jesus begs the bystanders to mark his wounds and meditate on suffering (p. 321). In *The Death of Christ* he makes two similar speeches that are clearly addressed not merely to the on-stage *personae* but to the larger audience:

> þis teene for thi trespase I take.
>> Who couthe þe more kyndynes haue kydde
>>> Than I?
>>>> þus for thy goode
>>>> I schedde my bloode.
>>>> Manne, mende thy moode,
>>> For full bittir þi blisse mon I by.
>>>>>> (p. 326)

Mary's lamentation, immediately following this first outcry of Christ, rhetorically confirms her role as the exemplar and exponent of the audience-as-Church. Christ's plea for a compassionate human response is answered directly by Mary's:

> Allas for my swete sonne I saie,
>> þat doulfully to ded þus is diȝt.
> Allas, for full louely he laye
>> In my wombe, þis worthely wight.
>> Allas þat I schulde see þis sight
>>> Of my sone so semely to see.
>> Allas, þat þis blossome so bright
>>> Vntrewly is tugged to þis tree.
>>>>> (p. 326)

Christ responds to Mary's *dolor* by giving her a second son, the apostle John—an action that, both traditionally and in the unfolding rhetoric of the cycle, confirms Mary in her role as Mater Ecclesiae. On the cross Christ divests himself of all his earthly treasures—including his mother and the home life she represents—in order to bequeath them to the church. His second monologue, addressed to the audience in the intimacy of the second person singular, asks each one to consider the depth of his love which is proven by absolute sacrifice: "With bittirfull bale haue I bought, / þus, man, all þi misse for te mende. / On me for to looke lette þou noȝt, / How baynly my body I bende" (p. 327).

Christ's appeals from the cross clearly aim at stirring an emotive response in his auditors. The on-stage enactors of that desired response are almost exclusively feminine *figurae*. In *The Road to Calvary* the daughters of Jerusalem, all of them designated "Maria," offer Jesus their pity and compassion. Maria III cleanses Jesus's bloody face with her veil. In *The Death of Christ* the Virgin Mary grieves for her Son. In *The Resurrection* the pious women continue to lament Christ's passion and death on the way to the tomb, recalling his innocence and the sins of humankind.

Another feminine *figura*, Mary Magdalene, facilitates the emotional shift from grief to joy through her enacted response to Christ's Resurrection from the dead. In *The Resurrection* and *Appearance* plays of the York cycle, she typifies the church both in her mourning for her sins as the cause of Christ's death and in her bridal rejoicing over his Resurrection. Magdalene has particularized the Calvary sacrifice as an atonement for her own sins: "þe woundes he suffered many one / was for my misse. / It was my ded he was for slayn, / And nothing His" (p. 351). Thus she stands "in typo Ecclesiae" as a converted sinner.[31] The ardent love she expresses for Christ, moreover, associates her, like Mary, with the *Sponsa* of the Songs.[32] Jesus, who finds her weeping in the garden, addresses her in bridal terms as "þou faithful fere" (p. 356) and "my loue" (p. 358). She, in turn, welcomes him as "mi joie, my luffe" and says that his love is sweeter than intoxicating mead ("swetter þanne þe mede"),

31. See Clifford Davidson, "The Digby *Mary Magdalene* and the Magdalene Cult of the Middle Ages," *Annuale Medievale* 13 (1972): 70–87, for a discussion of her model character.

32. Medieval hymns applied to Mary Magdalene, in her relationship to Christ, titles clearly derived from the *Canticum*: "sponsa," "dilecta," "Deo dilectissima," "dilectrix," "uncta sponsa," "Deo concupiscibilis," "Dei amica," "amica Jesu." See J. Szövérffy, "'Peccatrix Quondam Femina': A Study of the Mary Magdalene Hymns," *Traditio* 19 (1963): 93. Alain de Lille identifies her with the turtledove of the Song: "Through the turtledove which, as it is said, inconsolably grieves for her lost mate, Mary Magdalene is figured who, bereaved of her spiritual husband, mourned tremendously" ("Per turturem quae, ut dictum est, inconsolabiliter dolet amisso pari, figuratur Maria Magdalene, quae maxime doluit viduata viro spirituali"). See his *Elucidatio in Cantica Canticorum*, PL 210, c70.

even as the *amor* of Canticles is better than wine ("super vinum," "meliora vino"). In a courtly development of the biblical word "Set me like a seal on your heart, like a seal on your arm" (Cant. 8:6), Jesus asks her to write the "armoure" of his suffering on her heart. Magdalene responds by calling him the "crowned kyng" of love, an appropriate title for the New Solomon whose love "passis all erthely thyng" (p. 359).

As a pardoned and redeemed sinner, Mary Magdalene prepares the way for the markedly feminine portrayal of the early church in the last plays of the cycle. Once again the Virgin Mary (not Peter or any other disciple) takes a central position as the moral exemplar and emotional register for the on-stage and off-stage church—the apostles and the audience, respectively. In *The Ascension* Mary speaks first to articulate the mixed feelings of the multitude:

> A, myghtfull God, ay moste of myght,
>> A selcouth sight is þis to see,
> Mi sone þus to be ravisshed right
>> In a clowde wendande vppe fro me.
> Bothe is my herte heuy and light,
>> Heuy for swilke twynnyng schulde be,
> And light for he holdis þat he hight
>> And þus vppe wendis in grette poste.
>> (p. 377)

Immediately afterward John recalls Christ's Calvary commission and accepts Mary anew as his mother, thus confirming her maternal role for the neophyte church, Christ's mystical body.

That maternity is enacted in the remaining plays. In *Pentecost* Mary takes the leadership in the council of Apostles, urging them to unite in prayer. After the descent of the Holy Spirit, she is the first to speak in praise of God, articulating the appropriate affect of wonderment and grateful joy. In *The Death of the Virgin* the apostles all gather around her in the last hour, while she prays for them to Jesus, interceding for them in a motherly way, identifying herself with their needs and concerns. The sight of Mary's girdle in *The Assumption* confirms the apostolic circle anew in their faith and kindles their zeal to preach the Gospel to the nations. Finally, in *The Coronation*,

Mary's exaltation not only typifies and anticipates that of *ecclesia* as the bridal New Jerusalem; her queenly status is specifically linked to the church's destiny through the power of intercession Jesus bestows upon her.

The rhetorical identification of the church with Mary is confirmed in *The Last Judgment*, where her personal *transitus* is paralleled by the passage of the just souls into paradise. God's invitation to the upright parallels the "veni" addressed to the Virgin:

> Mi chosen childir, comes vnto me,
> With me to wonne nowe schall 3e wende
> þere joie and blisse schall euer be,
> 3oure liffe in lyking schall 3e lende.
>
> (p. 415)

The journey of the just ("transiens a loco ad locum") is accompanied, as Mary's was, by music ("cum melodia angelorum"), and the play ends with a hymn of praise ("et sic facit finem").

There is no more fitting *finis*. The York play in its entirety has been a "song of songs"—not merely in the literal sense supported by the constituent lyrics, but also in the dramatic meaning formulated by the theorists of the three voices of poetry. The direct feminization of the church in the York portrayal and the inclusive feminization of the audience in its emotive response to Christ help to define the inner dynamic of the cycle as "vox alternans Christi et Ecclesiae," as a series of divine calls and devotional responses, for which the biblical model is the Song of Songs, written "in modum dramatis."

Epilogue

This book examines medieval reader response—both interpretive and imitative—to the Song of Songs. Modern reception theory has accustomed us to the idea that the reader cocreates a text by filling in its gaps and incongruities, supplying contexts that render it meaningful.[1] Origen, as we have seen, did just that—passing over the erotic stumbling blocks ("offendicula") of the Song *ad litteram* to find a loftier, spiritual meaning, an allegorical *sensus* appropriate to God and predetermined by Origen's own theology. What he found reflected his preconceptions, the dogmas he sought to see. Indeed, as Rowan Greer says, "his hermeneutical principle is really nothing more than his theological view";[2] his ascent from the carnal letter to the spiritual *sensus* mirrors his idea of holiness as a Neoplatonic flight from the body to the realm of pure spirits, a process of enlightenment, a masculine quest for a recovered *logos*.

1. The new importance attached to the reader's part in the cocreation of a text by such critics as Roman Ingarden, Wolfgang Iser, Stanley Fish, Michael Riffaterre, Erwin Wolff, and Walter Ong has contributed to our understanding of medieval tropology, rhetoric, and audience assimilation. For a useful summary of the various schools of approach to the subject of reader response, see Iser, *The Act of Reading: A Theory of Aesthetic Response* (1978), pp. 27–36. The influential work of Hans Robert Jauss (*Alterität und Modernität der mittelalterlichen Literatur: Gesammelte Aufsätze 1956–1976* [1977]; "The Alterity and Modernity of Medieval Literature," *NLH* 10.2 [Winter 1979]: 181–229) has stimulated particular interest in the medieval reader's horizon of expectations and our ability to approximate it.

2. Rowan A. Greer, "Introduction," in *Origen*, trans. Rowan A. Greer, Classics of Western Spirituality Series (1979), p. 32.

In the twelfth century a different concept of holiness and of human nature provided an altered cultural context for the reading of the Song. Readers brought to the text a holistic view of human nature as a composite of body and soul, as well as a theological understanding of redemption which ultimately included corporeal transfiguration. These two preconceptions fostered a way of reading the Song that joined together in a tenor/vehicle unit the carnal and spiritual meanings, the letter and the gloss, which Origen's *a priori* assumptions and methodology had separated. Even more important, perhaps, the prime substance ("elementa") of holiness was understood to be the *affectus* of love and desire, not the *ratio*; the proof of holiness was practiced virtue, not intellectual enlightenment. This valorization of the *affectus* disposed readers to respond emotionally to the sensual images of the Song as an answer to a divinely authored rhetorical appeal. In the intent of God, the *pathos* of literal meaning, combined with the *logos* of authoritative interpretation, should motivate a personal surrender to him sealed in good works.

Unlike Origen, whose belief in two loves—carnal and spiritual, demonic and divine—led him to disassociate the literal and allegorical meanings of the Song, twelfth-century exegetes upheld a unitary concept of love. They therefore approached the erotic images of the Song in a way that rendered them transparent to their divine tenor, sacramentalizing them, making them vehicles for an organic transference of the *affectus* to Christ the Bridegroom.

Medieval psychology and theology, as we have seen, associated the *affectus* of love with the feminine principle in human nature and personified it in feminine *figurae*. This provided a new basis for an emotive identification with the Bride of the Song, who represented not so much the *mens* of Origen as the lower, affective powers of the soul (*anima*). Identifying with the Bride thus provided a means of self-knowledge, a way for male auditors to recognize their own veiled, recessive femininity and draw on its power in multiple relationships—to God, to the world, to others.

In addition to these general twelfth-century contexts, exegetes supplied other, more specific backgrounds against which they read and responded to the Song. Bruno of Segni brought to the Song his own involvement in the investiture controversy and read its ecclesiastical allegory in the pressing terms of contemporary politics and pastoral responsibility. Rupert of Deutz, filled with Marian devotion, discovered Mary's life story to be the Song's historical *fundamentum*. The Victorine and Cistercian expositors brought their own mystical experience to bear upon the Song and found in its images the outward expression of their contemplative exercise.

In these specific contexts—ecclesiastical, Marian, mystical—the "bridal self" takes on a variety of forms correspondent to the rhetorical situation and the action ("tropologia") being urged. The archetypes named by Jung—Virgin, Mother, Medium, and Hetaira— embrace the multiplicity of constellations the *anima* assumes in these commentaries as the *affectus* is evoked and directed "sub specie Sponsae" in different ways to achieve different ends. To oppose heresy and tyranny, Bruno calls forth the virginal *affectus* with its love of truth and independence. To encourage compassion for Christ's suffering and awaken anagogical longing, Rupert prompts identification with a maternal Bride, Mary. To secure a symbolic vision and appreciation of the world, the Victorine writers characterize the Bride as a seeress. To promote conformity with the Word and a fearless self-surrender to him, Bernard evokes within his followers the attitude of the Hetaira-Handmaid.

The perceived tropological goal of the Song determines, to a large extent, its manner of exposition. In the twelfth century, one read the Song primarily not to discover its veiled truth (as Origen did), but to apply its message, live its love. This emphasis on the moral application of the text in history, in space and time, drew support from a new, figural understanding of Solomon's literary *materia*. As a real, historically consummated marriage, the union of Solomon and Pharaoh's daughter reifies other marriages, which serve to sacramentalize their own. Solomon's nuptials foreshadow the Incarnation of Christ and the anagogic Wedding Feast of the Lamb, and these Christological couplings, in turn, affirm the holiness of the human marriage as a *figura* through which we come to know the affective quality of God's love for us. The "factum" enables the discovery of "faciendum"; what has been accomplished inspires the hope and the striving for new realizations in people's lives, here and in eternity.

The quest for a new realization of the Song, for a repetition of its love story, inspired not only the rhetoric of the commentaries but also the practice of poets and playwrights who sought to imitate the Song as an eminent example of biblical poetry, to use its images and duplicate its rhetorical strategies in their own compositions. As we have seen, Richard Rolle, the *Pearl* poet, the anonymous lyricists, and the playwright(s) of the York cycle all draw inspiration from the Song, exploit the moving power of its images, and feminize their auditors in relation to Christ through bridal identification. They invite the auditor to play the part of the Bride, to appropriate her utterance, as they follow the exegetical insight that the Bride is the *persona* of the soul (both communal and personal); the Song itself, written "in modum dramatis."

I have tried to show through the generic range of the works studied—alliterative dream vision, mystical autobiography, love lyric, and cycle drama—both the wide influence of the Song as a literary model and the intimate relationship between the ways the Song was interpreted and the way it was imitated. The works inspired by the *Canticum* clearly indicate that medieval readers saw the literal Song as inseparable from its gloss and felt the rhetorical appeal engendered by that two-in-oneness. The powerful fusion of letter and allegory in readers' experience of the Song from the twelfth through the fourteenth centuries provided the key definitional model for Christian poetics and rhetoric during that time, enabling poets and preachers alike to imitate the practice of the divine *Auctor* who used sensual imagery to convey "per dulcedinem" the quality of his love for humankind and to awaken the *affectus* of bridal love in return. As the *Glossa* says, "The end, the final cause, of the Song is the love of God" (PL 113, c1128: "Finis est dilectio Dei").

Bibliography

Primary Sources

Adam of St. Victor. *Sequentiae.* PL 196, c1423–534.
Alain de Lille. *Elucidatio in Cantica Canticorum.* PL 210, c51–110.
———. *Summa de Arte Praedicatoria.* PL 210, c111–98.
Aquinas, St. Thomas. *Basic Writings of St. Thomas Aquinas.* Ed. Anton C.
   Pegis. New York: Random House, 1945.
Augustine, St. *The Confessions of St. Augustine.* Trans. John K. Ryan.
   Garden City, N.Y.: Image Books, 1960.
———. *De Trinitate.* CCSL 50–50A. Ed. W. J. Mountain and Fr. Glorie.
   Turnhout: Brepols, 1968.
———. *On Christian Doctrine.* Trans. D. W. Robertson, Jr. Indianapolis, Ind.:
   Bobbs-Merrill, 1958.
Bede. *De Arte Metrica.* PL 90, c149–76. In *Opera Didascalia.* CCSL 123A,
   60–141. Ed. C. B. Kendall. Turnhout: Brepols, 1975.
———. *De Schematibus et Tropis.* PL 90, c175–86.
Bernard, St. *On the Song of Songs.* 4 vols. Trans. Kilian Walsh and Irene
   Edmonds. In *The Works of Bernard of Clairvaux.* Kalamazoo, Mich.:
   Cistercian Publications, 1971–80.
———. *Sermones super Cantica Canticorum.* 2 vols. Ed. J. Leclercq, C. H.
   Talbot, H. M. Rochais. In *Sancti Bernardi Opera.* Rome: Cistercian Edi-
   tions, 1957–58.
Brevis Commentatio. PL 184, c407–36.
Bruno of Segni, St. *De Muliere Forte.* PL 164, c1229–34.
———. *Expositio in Cantica Canticorum.* PL 164, c1233–88.
Chaucer, Geoffrey. "The Merchant's Tale." In *The Riverside Chaucer.* Ed.
   Larry D. Benson. 3d ed. Boston: Houghton Mifflin, 1987.

Damian, St. Peter. *Carmina Sacra et Preces*. PL 145, c917–86.

Glossa Ordinaria. PL 113.

Gregory the Great. *Expositio in Canticum Canticorum*. CCSL 144, 3–46. Ed. Patrick Verbraken. Turnhout: Brepols, 1963.

Guibert de Nogent. *Liber Quo Ordine Sermo Fieri Debeat*. PL 156, c21–32.

The Harley Lyrics. Ed. G. L. Brook. 2d ed. Manchester: Manchester University Press, 1956.

Honorius of Autun. *Expositio in Cantica Canticorum*. PL 172, c347–496.

——. *Sigillum Beatae Mariae*. PL 172, c495–518.

Hugh of St. Victor. *De Amore Sponsi ad Sponsam*. PL 176, c987–94.

——. *De Arca Noe Morali*. PL 176, c617–80.

——. *De Assumptione Beatae Mariae*. PL 177, c1209–22.

——. *De Sacramentis*. PL 176, c183–618.

——. *De Scripturis et Scriptoribus Sacris*. PL 175, c9–28.

——. *De Unione Corporis et Spiritus*. PL 177, c285–94.

——. *Didascalicon*. PL 176, c739–838. Trans. Jerome Taylor. New York: Columbia University Press, 1961, repr. 1968.

——. *In Salomonis Ecclesiasten*. PL 175, c113–256.

——. *Soliloquium de Arrha Animae*. PL 176, c951–70.

——. *Speculum de Mysteriis Ecclesiae*. PL 177, c335–80.

Innocent III, Pope. *De Quadripartita Specie Nuptiarum*. PL 217, c921–68.

Isaac of Stella. *Epistola de Anima*. PL 194, c1875–90.

Isidore of Seville. *Etymologiarum*. PL 82, c73–728.

Jerome, St. *Prologus in Hiezechielem*. CCSL 75. Ed. Francis Glorie. Turnhout: Brepols, 1964.

Middle English Lyrics. Ed. Maxwell S. Luria and Richard L. Hoffman. New York: W. W. Norton, 1974.

The Officium and Miraculum of Richard Rolle of Hampole. Ed. Reginald Maxwell Woolley. New York: Macmillan, 1919.

Origen. *De Principiis*. Trans. Rufinus. PG 11, c108–414. Trans. Rowan A. Greer. In *Origen*. Classics of Western Spirituality Series. New York: Paulist Press, 1979.

——. *In Canticum Canticorum*. Trans. Rufinus. PG 13, c62–198.

——. *Origenis in Canticum Canticorum*. Trans. St. Jerome. PL 23, c1117–44.

——. *The Song of Songs: Commentary and Homilies*. Trans. R. P. Lawson. Ancient Christian Writers Series 26. London: Longmans, Green, 1957.

Pearl. Ed. E. V. Gordon. Oxford: Clarendon Press, 1953, repr. 1963.

Pseudo-Richard of St. Victor. *Explicatio in Cantica Canticorum*. PL 196, c405–524.

"Quia Amore Langueo." In *Political, Religious, and Love Songs*. Ed. F. J. Furnivall, 180–89. EETS 15. London: Kegan Paul, 1866, reedited 1903, repr. 1965.

Rabanus Maurus. "De Poetis." In *De Universo* XV 2. PL 111, c419–20.

Religious Lyrics of the Fourteenth Century. Ed. Carleton Brown and G. V. Smithers. Rev. 2d ed. Oxford: Clarendon Press, 1952.
Richard of St. Victor. *Benjamin Major.* PL 196, c63–202.
———. *Benjamin Minor.* PL 196, c1–64.
———. *Benjamin Minor.* Trans. S. V. Yankowski. Gesamtherstellung: Wiedfeld and Mehl, Ansbach, 1960.
———. *De Quatuor Gradibus Violentae Charitatis.* PL 196, c1207–24.
———. *In Apocalypsim.* PL 196, c685–888.
———. *Selected Writings on Contemplation.* Ed. and trans. Clare Kirchberger. London: Faber and Faber, 1957.
Rolle, Richard. *Biblical Commentaries.* Ed. and trans. Robert Boenig. Salzburg: Institut für Anglistik und Amerikanistik, 1984.
———. *English Prose Treatises of Richard Rolle of Hampole.* Ed. George G. Perry. EETS 20. London: Oxford University Press, 1866, repr. 1921.
———. *English Writings of Richard Rolle.* Ed. Hope Emily Allen. Oxford: Clarendon Press, 1931.
———. *The Fire of Love.* Ed. and trans. Frances M. M. Comper. 2d ed. London: Methuen, 1920.
———. *Incendium Amoris.* Ed. Margaret Deanesly. London: Longmans, 1915.
———. *Melos Amoris.* Ed. E. J. F. Arnould. Oxford: Basil Blackwell, 1957.
Rupert of Deutz. *Commentaria in Cantica Canticorum.* PL 168, c837–962; CCCM 26. Ed. Rhaban Haacke. Turnhout: Brepols, 1974.
———. *Commentaria in Evangelium Sancti Johannis.* PL 169, c205–826; CCCM 9. Ed. Rhaban Haacke. Turnhout: Brepols, 1969.
Tertullian. *Adversus Marcionem.* PL 2, c239–524.
William of St. Thierry. *Commentaire sur le Cantique des Cantiques.* Ed. and trans. P. Robert Thomas, O.C.S.O. Collection Pain de Citeaux. Chambarand, 1961.
———. *De Natura Corporis et Animae.* PL 180, c695–726.
———. *Exposition on the Song of Songs.* Trans. Mother Columba Hart. Spencer, Mass.: Cistercian Publications, 1970.
———. *Vita Prima.* PL 185, c225–68.
The York Plays. Ed. Richard Beadle. London: Edward Arnold, 1982.

Secondary Sources

Alford, John. "Biblical *Imitatio* in the Writings of Richard Rolle." *ELH* 40 (1973): 1–23.
Allen, Hope Emily. *Writings Ascribed to Richard Rolle.* New York: Heath, 1927.
Allen, Judson Boyce. *The Ethical Poetic of the Late Middle Ages: A Decorum of Convenient Distinction.* Toronto: University of Toronto Press, 1982.

———. "The *Grand Chant Courtois* and the Wholeness of the Poem: The Medieval *Assimilatio* of Text, Audience, and Commentary." *L'Esprit Créateur* 18.3 (1978): 5–17.

Allen, Rosamund. "'Singuler Lufe': Richard Rolle and the Grammar of Spiritual Ascent." In *The Medieval Mystical Tradition in England: Papers Read at Dartington Hall, July 1984,* ed. Marion Glasscoe, 28–54. Cambridge: D. S. Brewer, 1984.

Astell, Ann W. "Holofernes' Head: *Tacen* and Teaching in the Old English *Judith.*" *ASE* 18 (1989): 117–33.

———. "*Sir Gawain and the Green Knight:* A Study in the Rhetoric of Romance." *JEGP* 84 (1985): 188–202.

Auerbach, Erich. "Figura." Trans. Ralph Manheim. In *Scenes from the Drama of European Literature: Six Essays,* 11–76. Gloucester, Mass.: Peter Smith, 1959, repr. 1973.

Baldwin, Charles Sears. *Medieval Rhetoric and Poetic to 1400.* New York: Macmillan, 1928.

Barraclough, Geoffrey. "The Investiture Contest and the German Constitution." In *The Origins of Modern Germany,* 101–34. 2d rev. ed. New York: Capricorn Books, 1946, repr. 1963.

Bogdanos, Theodore. *Pearl: Image of the Ineffable.* University Park: Pennsylvania State University Press, 1983.

Boucher, Holly Wallace. "Metonymy in Typology and Allegory, with a Consideration of Dante's *Comedy.*" In *Allegory, Myth, and Symbol,* ed. Morton W. Bloomfield, 129–45. Harvard English Series 9. Cambridge, Mass.: Harvard University Press, 1981.

Bynum, Caroline Walker. "The Female Body and Religious Practice in the Later Middle Ages." In *Zone 3: Fragments for a History of the Human Body,* vol. 1, ed. Michel Feher, Ramona Naddaff, and Nadia Tazi, 160–219. New York: Urzone, 1989.

———. *Jesus as Mother: Studies in the Spirituality of the High Middle Ages.* Berkeley: University of California Press, 1982.

Chambers, Raymond W. *On the Continuity of English Prose from Alfred to More and His School.* London: Oxford University Press, 1932, repr. 1957.

Charity, A. C. *Events and Their Afterlife: The Dialectics of Christian Typology in the Bible and Dante.* Cambridge: Cambridge University Press, 1966.

Chenu, M.-D. *Nature, Man, and Society in the Twelfth Century.* Ed. and trans. Jerome Taylor and Lester K. Little. Chicago: University of Chicago Press, 1968, repr. 1983.

Chydenius, Johan. "Medieval Institutions and the Old Testament." *Commentationes Humanarum Litterarum* 37.2 (1965): 1–140.

Colish, Marcia L. *The Mirror of Language: A Study in the Medieval Theory of Knowledge.* Rev. ed. Lincoln: University of Nebraska Press, 1983.

Collier, Richard J. *Poetry and Drama in the York Corpus Christi Play.* Hamden, Conn.: Archon Books, 1978.

Copeland, Rita. "Richard Rolle and the Rhetorical Theory of the Levels of Style." In *The Medieval Mystical Tradition in England: Papers Read at Dartington Hall, July 1984*, ed. Marion Glasscoe, 55–80. Cambridge: D. S. Brewer, 1984.

Daley, Brian E. "The 'Closed Garden' and 'Sealed Fountain': Song of Songs 4:12 in the Late Medieval Iconography of Mary." In *Medieval Gardens*, 254–78. Washington, D.C.: Dumbarton Oaks, 1986.

Davidson, Clifford. "The Digby *Mary Magdalene* and the Magdalene Cult of the Middle Ages." *Annuale Medievale* 13 (1972): 70–87.

Diehl, Patrick S. *The Medieval European Religious Lyric: An Ars Poetica.* Berkeley: University of California Press, 1985.

Dronke, Peter. *Medieval Latin and the Rise of European Love-Lyric.* 2 vols. Oxford: Clarendon Press, 1965–66.

———. *The Medieval Lyric.* London: Hutchinson University Library, 1968.

Eldredge, Laurence. "The State of *Pearl* Studies since 1933." *Viator* 6 (1975): 171–94.

Evans, G. R. *The Mind of St. Bernard of Clairvaux.* Oxford: Clarendon Press, 1983.

Fletcher, Jefferson B. "The Allegory of the *Pearl.*" *JEGP* 20 (1921): 1–21.

Flint, Valerie. "The Chronology of the Works of Honorius Augustodunensis." *RB* 82 (1972): 215–42.

———. "The Commentaries of Honorius Augustodunensis on the Song of Songs." *RB* 84 (1974): 196–211.

Fox, Michael V. *The Song of Songs and the Ancient Egyptian Love Songs.* Madison: University of Wisconsin Press, 1985.

Gallacher, Patrick J. "The Annunciation Pattern in Amorous Persuasion." In *Love, the Word, and Mercury: A Reading of John Gower's "Confessio Amantis,"* 26–43. Albuquerque: University of New Mexico Press, 1975.

Gardiner, Harold C., S. J. *Mysteries' End: An Investigation of the Last Days of the Medieval Religious Stage.* New Haven, Conn.: Yale University Press, 1946, repr. 1967.

Gillespie, Vincent. "Mystic's Foot: Rolle and Affectivity." In *The Medieval Mystical Tradition in England: Papers Read at Dartington Hall, July 1982*, ed. Marion Glasscoe. Exeter: University of Exeter, 1982.

Gilson, Etienne. *The Mystical Theology of St. Bernard.* Trans. A. H. C. Downes. London: Sheed and Ward, 1940, repr. 1955.

Gold, Penny Schine. *The Lady and the Virgin: Image, Attitude, and Experience in Twelfth-Century France.* Chicago: University of Chicago Press, 1985.

Gray, Douglas. *Themes and Images in the Medieval English Religious Lyric.* London: Routledge and Kegan Paul, 1972.

Greer, Rowan A. "Introduction." In *Origen.* Trans. Rowan A. Greer. Classics of Western Spirituality Series. New York: Paulist Press, 1979.

Hamilton, Marie P. "The Meaning of the Middle English *Pearl.*" *PMLA* 70 (1955): 805–24.

Heimmel, Jennifer P. *"God is our Mother": Julian of Norwich and the Medieval Image of Christian Feminine Divinity.* Salzburg: Institut für Anglistik und Amerikanistik, 1982.

Infusino, Mark. "The Virgin Mary and the Song of Songs in Medieval English Literature." Ph.D. diss., University of California–Los Angeles, 1988.

Iser, Wolfgang. *The Act of Reading: A Theory of Aesthetic Response.* Baltimore, M.D.: Johns Hopkins Press, 1978.

Jastrow, Morris, Jr. *The Song of Songs.* Philadelphia: J. B. Lippincott, 1921.

Jauss, Hans Robert. *Alterität und Modernität der mittelalterlichen Literatur: Gesammelte Aufsätze 1956–1976.* Munich: W. Frank, 1977.

———. "The Alterity and Modernity of Medieval Literature." *NLH* 10 (Winter 1979): 181–229.

Jung, Carl Gustav. *Aspects of the Feminine.* Trans. R. F. C. Hull. Bollingen Series. Princeton, N.J.: Princeton University Press, 1982.

Kantorowicz, Ernst H. *The King's Two Bodies: A Study in Medieval Political Theology.* Princeton, N.J.: Princeton University Press, 1957.

Kaske, R. E. "The *Canticum Canticorum* in the Miller's Tale." *SP* 59 (1962): 479–500.

Kean, Patricia M. *The Pearl: An Interpretation.* London: Routledge and Kegan Paul, 1967.

Knowles, David. *The English Mystical Tradition.* London: Burns and Oates, 1961.

Kolve, V. A. *The Play Called Corpus Christi.* Stanford, Calif.: Stanford University Press, 1966.

Kugel, James. *The Idea of Biblical Poetry: Parallelism and Its History.* New Haven, Conn.: Yale University Press, 1981.

Leclercq, Jean. *The Love of Learning and the Desire for God.* Trans. Catharine Misrahi. New York: Fordham University Press, 1962.

———. *Monks and Love in Twelfth-Century France.* Oxford: Clarendon Press, 1979.

Liegey, Gabriel M. "The 'Canticum Amoris' of Richard Rolle." *Traditio* 12 (1956): 369–91.

Littledale, Richard Frederick. *A Commentary on the Song of Songs from Ancient and Medieval Sources.* London: Joseph Masters, 1869.

Lloyd, G. E. R. *Polarity and Analogy: Two Types of Argumentation in Early Greek Thought.* Cambridge: Cambridge University Press, 1966.

Lynch, William F., S. J. *Christ and Apollo: The Dimensions of the Literary Imagination.* New York: Sheed and Ward, 1960.

McKeon, Richard P. "Poetry and Philosophy in the Twelfth Century: The Renaissance of Rhetoric." *MP* 43 (1945–46): 217–34.

Manning, Stephen Joseph. *Wisdom and Number: Toward a Critical Appraisal of the Middle English Religious Lyric.* Lincoln: University of Nebraska Press, 1962.

Marrou, Henri Irénée. *The Resurrection and St. Augustine's Theology of Human Values*. Trans. Mother Maria Consolata, S.H.C.J. St. Augustine Lecture Series. Villanova, Pa.: Villanova University, 1966.

Marshall, Mary Hatch. "Boethius' Definition of *Persona* and Mediaeval Understanding of the Roman Theater." *Speculum* 25 (1950): 471–79.

Matter, E. Ann. *"The Voice of My Beloved": The Song of Songs in Western Medieval Christianity*. Philadelphia: University of Pennsylvania Press, 1990.

Minnis, A. J. "Literary Theory in Discussions of *Formae Tractandi* by Medieval Theologians." *NLH* 11 (1979): 133–45.

———. *Medieval Theory of Authorship: Scholastic Literary Attitudes in the Later Middle Ages*. 2d ed. Philadelphia: University of Pennsylvania Press, 1988.

Moritz, Theresa Anne. "Married Love and Incarnational Imagery: Bernard of Clairvaux's *Sermones super Cantica Canticorum* within Medieval Spirituality as a Model for Love Allegory in Chaucer's *Canterbury Tales*." Ph.D. diss., University of Toronto, 1981.

Murrin, Michael. *The Allegorical Epic: Essays in Its Rise and Decline*. Chicago: University of Chicago Press, 1980.

———. *The Veil of Allegory: Some Notes toward a Theory of Allegorical Rhetoric in the English Renaissance*. Chicago: University of Chicago Press, 1969.

Nelson, Alan H. "Principles of Processional Staging: York Cycle." *MP* 67 (1970): 303–20.

———. "Some Configurations of Staging in Medieval English Drama." In *Medieval English Drama,* ed. Jerome Taylor and Alan H. Nelson, 116–47. Chicago: University of Chicago Press, 1972.

Nichols, Stephen G., Jr. *Romanesque Signs: Early Medieval Narrative and Iconography*. New Haven, Conn.: Yale University Press, 1983.

Ohly, Friedrich. *Hohelied-Studien: Grundzüge einer Geschichte der Hoheliedauslegung des Abendlandes bis um 1200*. Wiesbaden: Franz Steiner Verlag, 1958.

Ong, Walter F., S.J. "Wit and Mystery: A Revaluation in Medieval Latin Hymnody." *Speculum* 22 (1947): 310–41.

Owst, G. R. *Literature and Pulpit in Medieval England*. London: Basil Blackwell, 1952, repr. 1961.

Pasternack, Carol Braun. "Stylistic Disjunctions in *The Dream of the Rood*." *ASE* 13 (1984): 167–86.

Pearson, Lu Emily. "Isolable Lyrics of the Mystery Plays." *ELH* 3 (1936): 228–52.

Petroff, Elizabeth. "Landscape in *Pearl*: The Transformation of Nature." *Chaucer Review* 16 (1981): 181–93.

Pope, Marvin, ed. and trans. *The Song of Songs*. Anchor Bible Series. Garden City, N.Y.: Doubleday, 1977.

Quilligan, Maureen. *The Language of Allegory*. Ithaca: Cornell University Press, 1979.

Rabin, Chaim. "The Song of Songs and Tamil Poetry." *Studies in Religion* 3 (1973): 205–19.

Raby, F. J. E. *A History of Christian-Latin Poetry from the Beginnings to the Close of the Middle Ages.* 2d ed. Oxford: Clarendon Press, 1953.

Reiss, Edmund. *The Art of the Middle English Lyric.* Athens: University of Georgia Press, 1972.

Rollinson, Philip. *Classical Theories of Allegory and Christian Culture.* Pittsburgh, Pa.: Duquesne University Press, 1981.

Salmon, P. B. "The 'Three Voices' of Poetry in Mediaeval Literary Theory." *Medium Aevum* 30 (1961): 1–18.

Sanford, Eva Matthews. "Honorius, *Presbyter* and *Scholasticus.*" *Speculum* 23 (1948): 397–425.

Smalley, Beryl. *The Study of the Bible in the Middle Ages.* 2d ed. Oxford: Basil Blackwell, 1952.

Spearing, A. C. *The Gawain-Poet: A Critical Study.* Cambridge: Cambridge University Press, 1970.

Sticca, Sandro. *The Latin Passion Play: Its Origins and Development.* Albany: State University of New York Press. 1970.

Szövérffy, J. " '*Peccatrix Quondam Femina*': A Study of the Mary Magdalene Hymns." *Traditio* 19 (1963): 93–107.

Tate, J. "On the History of Allegorism." *Classical Quarterly* 28 (1934): 105–14.

Taylor, George C. "The English 'Planctus Mariae.' " *MP* 4 (1907): 605–37.

———. "The Relation of the English Corpus Christi Play to the Middle English Religious Lyric." *MP* 5 (1907): 1–38.

Trimpi, Wesley. "The Ancient Hypothesis of Fiction: An Essay on the Origins of Literary Theory." *Traditio* 27 (1971): 1–78.

Tuma, George Wood. *The Fourteenth-Century English Mystics.* 2 vols. Salzburg: Institut für Englische Sprache und Literatur, 1977.

Ulanov, Ann Belford. *The Feminine in Jungian Psychology and in Christian Theology.* Evanston, Ill.: Northwestern University Press, 1971.

Van Dyke, Carolynn. *The Fiction of Truth: Structures of Meaning in Narrative and Dramatic Allegory.* Ithaca: Cornell University Press, 1985.

Van Engen, John. *Rupert of Deutz.* Berkeley: University of California Press, 1983.

Watts, Ann Chalmers. "*Pearl,* Inexpressibility, and Poems of Human Loss." *PMLA* 99 (1984): 26–40.

Whitman, Jon. *Allegory: The Dynamics of an Ancient and Medieval Technique.* Oxford: Clarendon Press, 1987.

Wimsatt, J. I. "Chaucer and the Canticle of Canticles." In *Chaucer the Love Poet,* ed. Jerome Mitchell and William Provost. Athens: University of Georgia Press, 1973.

Wolff, Toni. *Structural Forms of the Feminine Psyche.* Trans. Paul Watzlawik. Private printing for the C. G. Jung Institute, Zurich, 1956.

Woolf, Rosemary. *The English Mystery Plays*. Berkeley: University of California Press, 1972.

——. *The English Religious Lyric in the Middle Ages*. Oxford: Clarendon Press, 1968.

Index

Library of Congress Cataloging-in-Publication Data

Astell, Ann W.
　The Song of Songs in the Middle Ages / Ann W. Astell.
　　p. cm.
Includes bibliographical references.
ISBN 0–8014–2347–3 (alk. paper)
　1. Bible. O.T. Song of Solomon—Criticism, interpretation, etc.—History—Middle
Ages, 600–1500.　2. Literature, Medieval—History and criticism.　3. Bible in litera-
ture. I. Title.
BS1485.2.H37　1989
223′.906—dc20　　　　　　　　　　　　　　　　　　89-70831